TEAM PSYCHOLOGY IN SPORTS

The ability to mould a group of talented individual athletes into an effective team takes effort and skill. *Team Psychology in Sports* examines the crucial factors in the development of an effective team, introducing important psychological and organizational concepts and offering evidence-based interventions for enhancing the performance of any sports team.

The book neatly bridges the gap between theory and practice, with real sporting case studies, examples, and practical tools included in each chapter. It covers the full range of issues in team sport, including:

- planning
- communication
- cohesion
- motivation
- emotions
- momentum
- leadership
- recovery.

No other book offers such an up-to-date, relevant, and applied guide to working with sports teams. It is essential reading for all students and practitioners working in sport psychology or sports coaching.

Stewart Cotterill is a Research and Teaching Fellow at the University of Winchester, UK. He is also a registered sport and exercise psychologist in the UK, running his own performance psychology consultancy business, Performance Mind. He has experience of working in professional soccer, rugby union, cricket and basketball, amongst other sports. His specif   ors impacting upon team performanc   ology.

TEAM PSYCHOLOGY IN SPORTS

THEORY AND PRACTICE

Stewart Cotterill

Routledge
Taylor & Francis Group

LONDON AND NEW YORK

First published 2013
by Routledge
2 Park Square, Milton Park, Abingdon, Oxon OX14 4RN

Simultaneously published in the USA and Canada
by Routledge
711 Third Avenue, New York, NY 10017

Routledge is an imprint of the Taylor & Francis Group, an informa business

British Library Cataloguing in Publication Data
A catalogue record for this book is available from the British Library

Library of Congress Cataloging in Publication Data
Cotterill, Stewart.
Team psychology in sports : theory and practice / by Stewart Cotterill.
p. cm.
1. Sports--Psychological aspects. 2. Sports teams--Psychological aspects.
3. Teamwork (Sports)--Psychological aspects. I. Title.
GV706.4.C688 2012
796.01--dc23
2011050414

ISBN: 978-0-415-67057-9 (hbk)
ISBN: 978-0-415-67058-6 (pbk)
ISBN: 978-0-203-13142-8 (ebk)

Typeset in Bembo
by Taylor & Francis Books

MIX
Paper from
responsible sources
FSC
www.fsc.org FSC® C004839

Printed and bound in Great Britain by
TJ International Ltd, Padstow, Cornwall

To my wife, Karen, and daughter, Isabelle, for always helping me to keep things in perspective and to remember just what is important in life

CONTENTS

FIGURES

TABLES

PREFACE

Psychology is a key determinant of performance in sport. The way the individual prepares for and deals with the sporting environment is crucial for success. In team sports this is further complicated by the presence of many individuals who are trying to combine to form an efficient and effective team. Understanding the interactions between these individuals and the pressures that impact upon them as a group is crucial to the success of the sporting team. This book seeks to explore a range of psychological factors that impact upon team performance, and understand their theoretical underpinning. Building on this solid base, the book then explores the applied techniques that can be utilized by the sport psychologist or coach to enhance performance and reduce the factors that can detract from effective performance.

Previous books investigating the psychology of sports teams have been narrow in their scope, focusing in the main on the 'group dynamics' aspects of the team, including such concepts as cohesion and role awareness. To help bridge this gap, *Team Psychology in Sports: Theory and practice* is the first book to integrate both theoretical and research-driven approaches as determinants of practical interventions. While this book explores the important factors related to group dynamics, it also expands its exploration to a much wider range of factors influencing team performance in sport: specifically communication, motivation, emotions, momentum, leadership, mental and emotional recovery, and the process through which to develop a supportive team environment.

This book is designed to benefit a diverse audience. It will appeal to sport and exercise students, at both undergraduate and postgraduate levels, who are interested in the dynamics of teams and how to make them more effective. This book will also be of use to coaches working with teams at all levels to enable them to better control the development and evolution of their teams. Sport psychology consultants will benefit from this book, as it will outline a wide range of potential interventions with teams that have a strong theoretical base, ensuring evidence-based practice. Finally, this book will also be of use to trainee sport psychologists outlining the types of interventions they could use and the evidence base underpinning them.

Each chapter in *Team Psychology in Sports* examines different psychological aspects influencing sports teams. Within each chapter the theoretical and empirical basis for each concept is explored, on the basis of the latest conceptual and scientific research in the area. This theoretical perspective is then used to underpin relevant practical applied strategies that can be used to enhance the relevant concept and maximize the effectiveness of the sports team.

The first chapter provides an overview of psychological factors determining team performance, presenting a rationale for why the factors discussed in subsequent chapters are important and how they are interrelated. This chapter also introduces the concept of team building and its application in sport.

The second chapter focuses on the importance of effective team planning. Often, coaches and managers do not spend time clearly framing their vision and how the team should operate. The development of an initial template is a crucial step in this process. Once this is achieved, the integration of both the vision and plan with the development of relevant targets is crucial to building the most effective base from which the team will operate.

Chapter 3 considers the importance of the environment in which the team operates. In particular, the importance of a positive, supportive environment is explored, and relevant interventions to develop and maintain this type of environment are presented.

In Chapter 4 the importance of the roles of the individuals within the team are highlighted: in particular, the importance of role clarity, role perceptions and role acceptance. The chapter will review the theoretical rationale for the importance of these areas, and consider strategies to enhance role acceptance, role clarity and role perceptions.

The fifth chapter focuses on the crucial concept of communication within teams. In most sports teams communication channels are incomplete and hinder the effective running of the team. Understanding the importance of clear and open communication is crucial to team effectiveness. Building upon this, knowledge strategies for enhancing team communication can be developed.

Chapter 6 explores the real evidence underpinning the concept of cohesion within teams, the potential link between cohesion and performance, and what strategies can be used to enhance the cohesive nature of a sports team.

Chapter 7 explores effective techniques for motivating the whole team, particularly focusing on the challenges of motivating a group that is composed of a range of individuals.

Chapter 8 examines the concept of emotion in sport, and in particular the existence of both group emotions and group moods. Intervention strategies in this chapter are considered both in terms of how to help individual performers to control their emotions and how to influence the overall group emotional climate.

Chapter 9 seeks to provide a greater understanding of the concept of momentum in competitive sport, questioning the existing empirical support for the concept and what steps can be taken by the team and the coach to influence perceptions of momentum.

Chapter 10 considers the challenges of effective leadership within the team, including both leaders within the team (the captain, for example) and the role of the coach/manager as a leader. The final chapter explores the often underconsidered issue of mental and emotional recovery for teams. While physical recovery is often planned for, often the requirements for mental and emotional recovery are overlooked. This chapter seeks to address this issue by exploring the impact of insufficient recovery on performance, and resulting conditions such as overtraining and burnout. Building on this, the chapter examines how to monitor recovery, and the strategies that can be used to ensure that this recovery takes place.

It is hoped that *Team Psychology in Sports: Theory and practice* will effectively bridge the gap between conceptual and scientific research into teams and the applied practice of making groups of individuals work and interact more effectively as a team: in essence, understanding the psychological factors that can make the team greater than the sum of its individual parts and able to perform when it counts.

ACKNOWLEDGEMENTS

I would like to thank Joshua Wells from Routledge for his support and prompting throughout the process of writing this book. I would also like to thank all my colleagues who volunteered to read and review various drafts of the chapters throughout the process. All comments and suggestions were gratefully received. I would also like to thank all the sports performers and coaches in the many sports teams with which I have worked, who provided the inspiration for this book. I also wish to acknowledge the love and support I have received from my parents, Tom and Jackie, and my two sisters, Charlotte and Nicola, over many years. Finally, thank you to my wife, Karen, for your unfailing love, support, and encouragement. It is because of your support and understanding that I have been able to follow my dreams.

1

INTRODUCTION

Introduction

Teams in sporting competition win or lose based on their ability to perform on the day, and the extent to which they defeat their opponent. There are many examples across multiple sports where the most talented teams have lost to the 'underdogs'. Games can change as a result of momentary slips in concentration, and teams can become paralysed by the pressure of the big occasion. Understanding the factors that can cause a team to fail underpins the development of effective strategies to make sure that this failure is not repeated in the future. Taking this one step further can ensure that well-planned and well-thought-through strategies can prevent these failures from happening at all. Indeed, most sports teams will not reach many finals or frequently be in a position to win a league or a title. In view of this, taking the opportunity to learn from its mistakes might already be too late for the team. It thus makes more sense to plan effectively from the start, in essence having all the bases covered, to allow the team to achieve its potential rather than to try and fix a problem after the event (closing the gate after the horse has bolted). Whilst the retrospective approach is obviously possible, and many examples exist of teams who return to be successful, many other teams don't get another opportunity. It therefore makes sense for the team to do all it can to plan and prepare effectively to achieve the greatest potential for success. Team planning and effective preparation for the main factors that impact upon performance underpin consistent performance when it matters in many successful teams. For sports teams these factors can be grouped into five main categories: technical, tactical, physical, psychological, and environmental factors. The team that considers each of these factors in turn will stand the greatest chance of living up to its potential and ultimately being successful and realizing its potential.

There is an increasing array of textbooks in sport psychology, but very few of these focus exclusively on the team/group performance of sports teams. Many of these sport psychology books offer a chapter or two on the topic (often only focusing on team cohesion), but fail to do more than a superficial job in discussing team-related psychology. This is coupled with a general lack of a specific focus on what applied practitioners do when working with teams. This book seeks to reconnect the theory and practice relating to sports teams. As a result, by understanding the psychological forces at play in any sports team, ranging from the recreational Sunday team right through to the professional sports club, we can develop effective, theoretically driven applied techniques. At the highest level sports teams are multimillion-pound businesses and, as such, performance outcomes matter. Even at a recreational level most players' sense of satisfaction is linked to the performance of their team. Understanding the factors that impact upon performance (whether technical, tactical, physical, psychological, or environmental) is important. Many sports commentators advocate that, at the higher levels where individual performers in the same environment can be at equal physical, tactical and technical levels, it is in their psychology that they differ. So why shouldn't this be the case for teams? Teams are always striving to be fitter, more skilful, and more tactically astute, but how many deliberately practise for the mental edge? The first step in this process of enhancing performance by developing the mental edge is to understand the psychological factors impacting upon performance, and then to build strategies and interventions to further enhance these factors based upon the relevant theory: essentially, evidence-based practice. Also, if the coaches, players or sport psychologists understand the range of psychological challenges that face the team, they can also then develop new and innovative strategies to meet these challenges and further raise the bar of performance for the team and the competition.

Sports teams have a strong social and cultural impact in many countries across the world, often with large proportions of the population involved either as participants or as spectators. At many levels the performance of professional clubs and national teams can have direct impacts on feelings of happiness, satisfaction, and well-being.

Whilst understanding the individual in the team is important, so too is appreciating how the interactions of many individuals guide the performance of the team, and other associated factors such as team communication, team psychological climate, and the team environment.

There is recognition in the sport psychology literature that a current limitation of much research is the predominant focus on the individual compared to specific groups of individuals such as teams (Woodman and Hardy, 2001). In one sense this is understandable, as focusing on the individual can provide the greatest clarity for the practitioner. It is also important to recognize the importance of the individual in the team, but this cannot be at the expense of the bigger picture. Understanding the impact that psychological factors can have on the whole team is crucial to performance. Even some very individual factors such as rest and recovery also need to be considered at a team level. It is fine for each individual player to plan their own recovery, but what they are able to do is constrained by the organization and operation of the team as a whole, the opportunities available, and the actions of others.

It is also important to recognize that a team of expert individual performers is not the same as an expertly performing team (Salas *et al.*, 1997). Often we see that groups of very talented individuals do not necessarily form the best teams. It is how well these individuals function as a whole that is most important. All good coaches and managers will consider the 'fit' of new team members to ensure optimal team functioning. Some coaches go one step further and will have a general template for the 'types' of players they want in their teams. It is also important to recognize that different challenges exist for the coaches in both professional and amateur teams. An amateur coach is often required to forge the best team they can out of the personnel who are existing members of that team. Professional coaches have greater flexibility (they can change personnel), but these coaches then have to consider the impact that changing the personnel will have on their existing team. Recognizing the importance of teams and group interactions in sport, this introductory chapter of the book will first, seek to clarify and define what sports teams are, and second, look to outline the main psychological factors that impact upon the effective performance of sports teams.

What are teams?

If you happen to read any of the existing group dynamics literature, sports teams are categorized as a subset of groups. It is therefore probably an appropriate starting point to consider what characteristics determine the existence of a group. Groups as a social structure exist across all levels of society and can include families, religious groups, workgroups, social groups, and sports teams amongst others.

Groups have specifically been defined by Brown (2000: p.3) as existing when 'two or more people define themselves as members of it and when its existence is recognized by at least one other'. This definition highlights the fact that groups must include a minimum of two people and also be recognized externally as being a group. An alternative definition of a group by Fiedler (1967: p.6) suggested that groups could be viewed as 'a set of individuals who share a common fate, that is, who are interdependent in the sense that an event which affects one member is likely to affect all'. This second definition further highlighted the idea that group members share a common fate.

McGrath (1984), in suggesting a conceptual framework of groups, highlighted four sets of factors that impact upon group functioning. These factors include: the group structure (the status of the individual and impact of others), the task or situation (training, attending a party, wedding), the group properties (age, personality, height, sex, weight, religion, ability), and the environment the group finds itself in (physical, socio-cultural and technological properties). McGrath (1984) suggested that all groups could be described and differentiated according to these four groups of factors.

As previously mentioned, sports teams are seen as a specialist subset under the umbrella term groups. Sports teams have specifically been defined as 'A collection of two or more individuals who possess a common identity, have common goals and objectives, share a common fate, exhibit structured patterns of interaction and modes of communication, hold common perceptions about group structure, are personally and instrumentally interdependent, reciprocate interpersonal attraction, and consider themselves to be a team' (Carron *et al.*, 2005: p.13). This definition clearly highlights a number of specific factors that characterize a sports team. Indeed, just by understanding this definition there is scope to enhance a team. Developing a common identity, developing clear goals, building good communication channels, and developing a coherent structure are all good places to start in enhancing the team.

Psychological factors influencing teams

Speak to coaches, players, or supporters in any sport involving teams and they will highlight a number of factors that impact upon team performance. Whilst physical, technical, and tactical aspects are cited as important, psychological characteristics are frequently quoted as crucial in impacting upon performance. These psychological characteristics range from more generic factors such as teamwork, to more specifically defined concepts such as momentum, motivation, and communication. Further still, there are a number of factors that exist at an individual level, but which cumulatively can combine to become characteristics at a team level, such as emotion, mood, and the underpinning psychological climate. There are many psychological factors that can impact upon team performance. Figure 1.1 provides a summary of these factors that have been highlighted in both sport- and business-focused literature as impacting upon sports performance. These factors include: group dynamics; emotions; momentum; preparation and planning; the team environment; leadership; and psychological recovery.

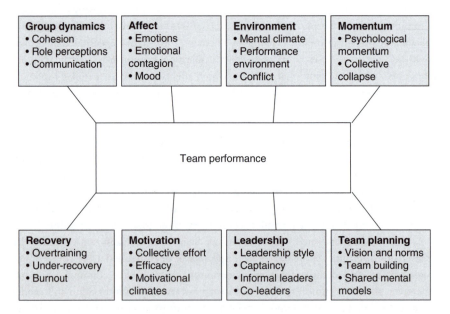

FIGURE 1.1 Psychological factors influencing performance in sports teams

Group dynamics at a descriptive level refers to the study of groups, and the energy, vitality, and activity that is characteristic of all groups (Carron *et al.*, 2005: p.14). As a field of study, group dynamics refers to knowledge about the nature of groups, the laws governing their evolution, and the interrelations with individuals and other groups (Cartwright and Zander, 1968). Affect is a general term in psychology that covers all feelings including both mood and emotions.

The environment refers to the structures and external factors that both determine and influence how the team operates. Understanding the impact that the environment can have on team performance is crucial. Momentum relates to the presence or perceptions of a force that is influencing performance, something that is perceived to be beyond the control of the team. Recovery explores the psychological and emotional costs of training (such as overtraining and burnout) and performing, and the steps required to fully 'recharge' the collective team batteries to maintain consistently high standards. Motivation, at a team level, refers to the collective will of the team to work towards set goals and to 'pull in the same direction' under adversity. Leadership highlights the importance of both formal and informal leaders at different levels within the team. Team planning focuses on the preparation and organization steps effective teams take to ensure that they give themselves the best possible chances to succeed.

Whilst some of these factors have been extensively researched in sports teams (group dynamics in particular), others have received far less attention. This has been, in part, down to the complexities in conducting research that has to consider both the characteristics of the individual and the characteristics of the team, as well as the interactions both between individuals and between the individual and the team.

The subsequent ten chapters of this book will explore these psychological factors in greater detail, outlining the relevant theory, but more importantly highlighting the practical interventions that can be used to further develop and enhance these characteristics in the team. The ultimate aim is to enable the team to achieve both higher and more consistent levels of performance.

Team building

Team building is the deliberate process of facilitating the development of an effective team (Stevens, 2002). Beer (1980) further clarified that team building is a process intervention (a series of ongoing interventions) designed to target and improve the functioning and performance of the team. In general terms, team building focuses on enhancing task-related performance, but this is not necessarily at the expense of relationships, which can also be an important contributory factor.

The aim of the team-building process is to build a more functional team that can execute greater levels of performance more consistently. In understanding the psychological factors that influence the operation and performance of the team, a coach, manager, or sport psychologist can help to build the team to higher levels of achievement and performance. Developing the team is one of the key themes that continues throughout this book.

Sports teams with continued success over time

While many sports teams achieve success, only a very few maintain this success over a significant period of time. In order to achieve this feat, these teams need to have talented individual players, but they also need something else that can maintain this success over time as the playing personnel come and go, and the challenges from other teams evolve. Examples of this continued success include Manchester United soccer team playing in the English Premier League, the Montreal Canadians in the National Hockey League (NHL), and the New England Patriots in the National Football League (NFL). Manchester United has been particularly dominant and successful in the English Premier League. Since its inception at the start of the 1992–93 season, Manchester United has won 12 out of the 19 available league titles (63%). Also, over the same period from 1992–2011 the team has won four Football Association (FA) cups, three league cups, and two European Champions League titles. The consistent thread throughout this period has been the club's manager, Sir Alex Ferguson, who in 2011 celebrated 25 years as the manager/head coach of the club. While many players have passed through the doors, Ferguson has been a constant presence. The New England Patriots enjoyed a run of success in the NFL in the 2000s, winning the Super Bowl in 2001, 2003, and 2004, and were losing finalists in 2007. Also, the Patriots were American Football Conference (AFC) champions in 2001, 2003, 2004, and 2007; and AFC east divisional champions in 2001, 2003, 2004, 2005, 2006, 2007, 2009, and 2010. Similar to Manchester United with Ferguson, the Patriots have had a consistent presence of Head Coach Bill Belichick throughout this period. Belichick has been able to maintain standards over a significant period of time, underpinning this constant success. The Montreal Canadians have historically been a very successful team in the NHL, and in particular in the Stanley Cup. The team has won a total of 24 cups in 34 appearances. It appeared in 12 cup finals between 1946 and 1960 (12 out of 15 finals), and then a further 11 cup finals between 1965 and 1979 (11 out of 15 finals). What is most interesting in this run is the impact that Head Coach Hector 'Toe' Blake had in the 1950s and 1960s. From 1946 through to 1955 the Canadians were coached by Dick Irvin who led the team to seven finals, but only managed to win two of them (29%). Blake took over in 1956 and proceeded to coach the Canadians to success in 1956, 1957, 1958, 1959, 1960, 1965, 1966, and 1968, winning an amazing eight out of the nine finals the team played in, and only losing in 1967 to the Toronto Maple Leafs, an amazing 89% success rate. He was known for his tough, but fair, coaching style; his players always knew he was on their side, and as a result Blake was able to get the best out of his players. For each of these three teams, the consistent factor in each team's success appears to be a long-serving, and very effective, Head Coach. As a result, the impact that the coach can have appears significant.

Summary

Understanding the psychological factors that influence sports teams and impact upon performance is crucial to any practitioner or consultant who is committed to enhancing team outcomes. There has to be a recognition that, while the characteristics of individual team members are important, so too is understanding the team at a group level. Understanding the effect of putting a certain group of players together is crucial for the aspiring coach, manager, or sport psychologist. A range of specific psychological factors has been highlighted as impacting upon sports performance. These include group dynamics, affect, the environment, momentum, recovery, motivation, leadership, and team planning. The next ten chapters will seek to explore each of these factors in greater detail, examine the relevant theoretical models, and crucially look at how this information can be used to develop practical interventions to enhance team performance.

2

TEAM PLANNING AND EFFECTIVENESS

Introduction

Efforts to build a team often start with the identification of team goals and the development of a clear team mission. The majority of sports teams that are successful are built on a clear vision and a subsequent plan of action to fulfil the vision of the team. Those teams that achieve continued success in sport are usually very well organized, not only in terms of the structures involved in the team, but also in terms of both what the team is trying to achieve and the planning of what steps are required to get there. However, in sport the approaches to planning are generally not as well structured and effectively executed as those in business environments. As a result, there is the opportunity for a team that plans well to gain a significant advantage over its rivals. Recent research on teams has characterized them to be dynamic, emergent, and adaptive entities embedded in a multilevel system (Kozlowski and Ilgen, 2006). Of particular interest here is the recognition that teams are dynamic and continually evolving. As a result, the process of planning should be an ongoing process.

This chapter seeks to understand the principles of good team planning and to explore examples of successful sports teams and the approaches they have adopted. Finally, this chapter will explore guidelines and strategies to plan effectively.

Team vision

Many successful teams begin with someone's vision for what that team aspires to be. These are often visions that are created by the coach, manager, owner, chairman, or director. As a result, the visions are often imposed on the team, and too infrequently originate with the team. Whether it is about winning trophies and championships, a philosophy of performance, or what benefit the team members take from playing the games, a vision is crucial to success. Successful coaches are able to create and develop a vision of what the team can achieve and strive for (Desjardins, 1996; Fisher and Thomas, 1996). Visions often involve perceptions of ability, personal characteristics, values, and motivations of the team's members. Good visions can unite the team around a task and also enhance emotional commitment (Stevens, 2002). One example of a vision is that outlined by Manchester United FC. The Club outlined the following vision for their business in 2004: 'our goal is through innovation to protect and develop the brand by sustaining the playing success on the field and growing the business to enhance the financial strength of the group'.

There is often some confusion around the use of the word vision. It is often a term that is used interchangeably with other terms, such as mission, objectives or targets. West and Unsworth (1998) conceptualized these terms using the example of a tree. The vision is the base of the tree, the mission statement (the observable statement of the team's purpose) is the trunk, the team's goals are the branches, and the action plans to achieve these goals are the leaves. West and Unsworth (1998) further identified five dimensions of a team's vision: clarity, motivating value, attainability, sharedness, and ability to develop.

- *Clarity* – in order for a team to be able to outline its goals and objectives it needs to have a clear vision that is understandable by all involved parties. Essentially, what does the team stand for and what does it want to achieve?
- *Motivating value* – the values of the team ultimately influence the effort and time invested by all the team members in pursuit of the team goals. Visions reflect the underlying values of the team, and as a result often motivate, enhance loyalty, increase effort, and foster greater commitment.
- *Attainability* – whilst the vision needs to be achievable, the time frame also needs to be realistic. If the vision is not realistic, it can have a demotivating effect on the team.
- *Sharedness* – the degree to which a vision is shared by the whole team has been identified as a predictor of team effectiveness (West and Unsworth, 1998). As a result, top-down planning can be less effective than bottom-up or integrated planning. The key message here is that, to be most effective, all members of the team need to be involved.
- *Ability to develop* – a good vision is able to evolve as the team and environment evolves. As a result, a team's vision should be regularly reviewed to ensure it is up to date and current, and reflects the team.

Stevens (2002) suggested a four-step strategy for developing a vision for a sports team. The four specific steps were: (i) plan an initial coaches meeting; (ii) run a subsequent team meeting; (iii) connect daily activities to the accomplishment of the vision; and (iv) evaluate progress towards the vision. Further details of each stage are presented in Table 2.1.

Team norms and rules

The most effective teams have, either formally, or through evolution, developed consistent team norms and rules of behaviour. In the most effective cases these rules and norms are agreed by all the team members (Bassin, 1988). These norms serve a

TABLE 2.1 A strategy for developing a shared vision for a sports team

1. Plan initial meeting with coaches – begin with the end

   - Ensure that the view of the future is clear, reasonable, and accepted by all members of the coaching staff. Accept input from all coaches to ensure their commitment to the future of the team.
   - Develop clear strategies for attaining the vision.

2. Run subsequent team meeting – develop ownership

   - Bring vision to all team members. Accept input.
   - Discuss how each member contributes to the team's future.
   - Discuss what will change under this direction for the future (e.g. what will be done differently, new competencies).

3. Connect daily activities to the accomplishment of the vision

   - There needs to be a clear link between the vision and daily tasks.
   - Always ask the question, 'How will this allow us to achieve our vision?'

4. Evaluate the progress towards the vision

   - How is the team progressing towards the vision?
   - How aligned are the different components of the team?
   - Is the vision still the right vision for the team?

Source: adapted from Stevens (2002)

number of specific purposes and reflect the core values of the team. But, in order to maximize the effectiveness of these norms, they need to be formalized. This is because by formalizing the norms each team member has a clear understanding of what is expected of them (Stevens, 2002).

Norms can be viewed as a way of thinking, feeling, or behaving that is deemed by the team to be appropriate (MacPherson and Howard, 2011). The most important norms in a team are those that define the team's basic values (Bar-Tal, 2000). These norms refer to values that the team seeks to uphold rather than clear-cut facts. The values or norms of the team are closely linked to the concept of social identity, which was defined by Stangor (2004: p.26) as 'the part of the self-concept that results from our membership of social groups'. Generally speaking, the groups that we are all members of (and the things they stand for) say something about who we are and who we aspire to be. There is another aspect to social identity that is referred to as task–orientated social identity. This is where the team acts as a vehicle for the individuals' personal aspirations and desires. So, whilst the team might not embody the individual in the way that it operates, it might embody the aspirations of the individual (Snyder et al., 1986). In this case the individual member is motivated to remain with the team until these ambitions and desires have been realized (MacPherson and Howard, 2011). The concept of group structure is closely related to team norms. Group structure can be defined as 'the rules that define group norms, roles and status' (Stangor, 2004: p.26). Group structure in this sense can be divided into formal and informal structures. Often, the informal structure is linked to the team members who have been part of the team for a long time, and who maintain and perpetuate the main norms and values for that team. This fact has particular implications for coaches and managers seeking to modify the norms and values of the team. If you want to change the norms and values of an established team, you either need to 'change' these long-serving individuals within the team, or replace them. To embed norms and values in a new team, it is the senior players who need to buy into the norms and then reinforce them throughout team interactions. The exception to this is where there are a significant number of new or young players joining the team. In such a case the new players can be used as the agents for change.

Stevens (2002) suggested a four-step process to develop team norms, highlighting the following four stages: (i) norm assessment; (ii) the education phase; (iii) the workshop stage; and (iv) reviewing team norms. In the norm assessment stage the aim is to identify the team's current norms. This is achieved through conversations with both coaching staff and team members. In the second, 'educational' stage the focus is on educating the team about the benefits of developing clearly defined norms, and also the types of norms that can be set. In the third stage a workshop is run to set the team norms. In this workshop stage the following steps are suggested: (i) individual team members construct a list of behaviours they would like the team to adopt; (ii) the team is then split into groups to discuss the suggested norms of each group member; and (iii) each group then reports its agreed list of norms back to the wider team to achieve some overall consensus. In the final stage the team's norms are reviewed after a period of time. This four-step approach is easy to apply in a wide range of team sports due to its simplicity and flexibility.

Team goal setting

In order to understand goal setting in teams it is first important to clarify what a goal is. One commonly accepted definition describes a goal as 'attaining a specific level of proficiency in a task, usually within a specified time limit' (Locke *et al.*, 1981). Importantly, there is evidence that goal setting can be highly effective in influencing behaviour, motivation and performance. Indeed, a number of meta-analyses in the sport psychology literature (Kyllo and Landers, 1995; Burton *et al.*, 2001) have consistently reported strong-to-moderate effects of goal setting on overall performance. Goal setting is particularly effective as it influences performance in four distinct ways. First, goals direct attention to important elements of the skills and tasks being performed. Second, goals prolong the efforts of the individual and team. Third, goals prolong player and team persistence. Finally, goals foster the development of new learning and problem-solving strategies (Weinberg and Gould, 2007). Thus, goals are important for all performers, but crucial for teams to both unify and clarify the collective direction of effort.

Types of goals

Within goal-setting literature in both sport and business there are generally two main classifications of goals. First, goals are classified as being outcome, performance or process focused. Second, goals are referred to as being short term or long term. Outcome goals focus on the ultimate outcomes linked to a positive performance and are, in the main, focused on winning. An example of an outcome goal for a basketball team might be winning the championship or winning the game. This type of goal has a very clear success or failure component. Unfortunately, achieving this type of goal is not necessarily within the team's or individuals' control as it also depends on environmental factors, officiating, and the performance of the opposition. Performance goals are linked to the explicit performance of the team or individual. At a team level performance goals in basketball might relate to the number of points scored, overall number of fouls, or team shooting percentages. An example of this for a specific player might be their foul count or shooting percentage. Process goals are usually focused on how a particular skill or set play is executed. This type of goal is equally useful in both training and competition. Process goals at the team level in basketball might relate to the way the team executes a fast-break strategy, or adopts a half-court press defence. There is evidence to suggest that using a combination of goal strategies (outcome, performance, and process goals) can produce significantly better results than just relying on one type of goal (Filby et al., 1999). As well as the three different types of goals outlined above, there is also a distinction drawn between short-term and long-term goals. Long-term goals are seen as ultimate goals. For Olympic athletes it could be winning a medal at the next Olympics in four years' time. For a team it could be building towards winning championships or titles over the same period. Short-term goals are more immediate and provide the stepping-stones for achieving the long-term goals. Burton (1992) made reference to a goal-setting 'staircase' with the short-term goals helping you to climb closer to the ultimate long-term goals. A successful team should set a mixture of both short-term and long-term goals to be most effective. Indeed, research has revealed that both short-term and long-term goals are needed to maintain motivation and performance in sport (Weinberg et al., 2001).

Research in sport and business has clearly demonstrated that just setting goals does not necessarily ensure improvements in performance or productivity. Instead, it is recognized that certain principles need to be followed to maximize the effectiveness of goals. Weinberg (2010) highlighted the following findings from a range of sport-related goal-setting research in seeking how to be most effective in using goal setting to enhance performance:

- Performance is enhanced when goals are moderately difficult and challenging, but also realistic.
- Goal setting can help to provide a focus for both teams and individual team members.
- Motivation and commitment are higher if the team accepts the set goals.
- Goals, and feedback relating to these goals, produce better performances than just setting goals.
- Barriers to goal achievement are usually categorized as physical, psychological, or external.
- Goals should be prioritized (either by order of importance or preference).

- Performance and process goals should be emphasized the most.
- A number of factors negatively affect goal achievement, including time pressure, stress, tiredness, and social relationships.
- Both short-term and long-term goals are important.

A number of sources within the sport psychology literature advocate the SMART approach to goal setting (Bull *et al.*, 1996), referring to effective goals as being specific (S), measurable (M), action related (A), realistic (R), and timetabled (T). Possibly the most important, and often overlooked, aspect of goal setting is the evaluation and re-evaluation of progress and achievement. This evaluation allows current progress to be monitored and changes to be made if required, thus maximizing the potential for the goal(s) to be realized.

Principles of goal setting

After reviewing the current goal-setting literature in sport Weinberg (2010) outlined the following seven principles for effective goal setting:

1 *Set specific measurable goals*
   This enables both individuals and the team as a whole to know what they are working towards, and ultimately how current behaviours can result in the achievement of these goals. Specific measurable goals also highlight criteria against which performance can be evaluated.
2 *Use short-term and long-term goals*
   Both types of goals are important. Long-term goals provide the ultimate aim and focus for the team, whilst short-term goals are especially important as they provide continuous feedback on progress towards the long-term goals. Thus, short-term goals can be used to either maintain or modify behaviour towards achieving the long-term goals.
3 *Write goals down*
   The norm in sport is not necessarily to formally record goals (Weinberg *et al.*, 2001), but recording and displaying goals in a prominent position (that players regularly come into contact with) has been suggested to have positive impacts upon performance (Weinberg, 2010). This approach keeps the goals active in the sense that all the team members involved are aware of them, but also makes others aware so that the team's/individuals' performance can then be evaluated.
4 *Use a combination of process, performance, and outcome goals*
   As highlighted in a previous section, setting a combination of goals is crucial to maximizing performance, motivation, and achievement.
5 *Use individual and team goals*
   Often in team sports there is an over-emphasis on the goals of the team. Whilst this is obviously very important, so are goals for individuals within the team. Often, team members fulfil quite specific roles within the team, which can be quantified and measured in their own right. Setting individual goals can help each

individual to perform their role optimally, resulting in an enhanced cumulative performance.

6 *Set practice goals*

   Often both individuals and teams have well-developed performance and outcome goals for competition, but in most cases they do not adopt the same approach for training. Better-defined practice goals can lead to enhanced performance outcomes in competition (Weinberg *et al.*, 2001). Also, more focused training goals can lead to greater performance increments, which can then increase the potential for success in competition.

7 *Develop plans to reach goals*

   Identifying the goals is an important step, but taking the next step and outlining a strategy to achieve these goals is also crucial. Without a systematic planned approach, achieving the goals might well become hit and miss, significantly lowering the potential for success.

Developing team goals

Widmeyer and Ducharme (1997) suggested six key principles for effective goal setting in sports teams:

- *Establish long-term goals first* – they will provide the focus for all subsequent planning, and also unify the individual team members.
- *Establish clear paths of short-term goals to aid the achievement of long-term goals* – for each long-term goal there should be an incremental programme of short-term goals working towards realization of the associated long-term goal(s). This allows for the development of more structured planning.
- *Involve all members of the team in establishing team goals* – in order to get player buy-in, team members need to be involved in the process to feel ownership of the goals.
- *Monitor progress towards the team goals* – it is important to continually evaluate and review progress to maximize performance and progress towards goal achievement.
- *Reward the progress made towards achieving the team goals* – this will further motivate the team to work towards the next goals. It will also place a greater emphasis on goal achievement.
- *Foster collective team confidence/collective efficacy relating to the team's goals* – as the team achieves its goals there should be further reinforcement of the ability of the team to perform. As a result, this should also enhance efficacy towards the next goal/task.

Team effectiveness

Effective teamwork is often seen as one of the key differences between success and failure in team competition (Voight and Callaghan, 2002). Effective teamwork has been conceptualized as taking advantage of the various abilities and backgrounds of the team members; interacting and working towards a shared goal; balancing the needs of the team with the needs of individual members; and structuring methods of communication (Carron *et al.*, 1997; Crace and Hardy, 1997). Williams (1997: p. 30) made reference to the concept of 'chemistry' in exploring team effectiveness in sport:

> Chemistry while harder to spot than talent, is even more important. What we call chemistry is really a combination of a lot of factors: ability and skill levels, drive, ambition, emotional makeup, values, communication, and people skills. Chemistry is not easy to assess until you actually put the team together under real world conditions. Often you have to experiment a few times, adding this, subtracting that in order to get just the right chemistry going.

To really understand how a team can be most effective we need to view teams as being embedded in a wider context within the task environment that drives the demands of the task. A dynamic and changing task environment produces corresponding team tasks that require solving through a coordinated process involving the cognitions, motivation, feelings, and behaviours of the team as a whole. The degree to which the team can align its processes with the environmental demands ultimately determines how effective the team is. The practical implications here are clear. In order to develop a team that is most able to cope with the relevant task demands you first need to clearly understand the task and environmental requirements. Also, truly effective teams are able to modify group processes as either environmental or task requirements change.

Team effectiveness has also been considered from the perspective of an input-process-output perspective (Kozlowski and Ilgen, 2006). In this approach, inputs refer to the composition of the team. Processes refer to the activities that the team engages in to combine resources to complete the task at hand. Essentially processes convert the inputs into an output. Outputs, generally speaking, have three components: (i) performance judged by others external to the team; (ii) the degree to which they meet the needs of the team members; and (iii) the willingness of team members to remain in the team (Hackman, 1987). As a result, team processes are seen as a way to capture and coordinate team member effort and the factors that influence it. Appropriately aligned team processes are critical to enhancing team effectiveness (Kozlowski *et al.*, 1999). As a result, the alignment of processes is an important consideration for the team.

Team building

In most teams the coach does not have unlimited resources or the pick of all the available talent. Indeed, for most coaches at both amateur and professional levels, factors such as geography, finances, level of competition (e.g. league level, or professional vs. amateur), and the attractiveness of the club or team, all appear to play a part. As a result, most coaches need to build an effective team rather than recruit one. Zander (1985) supported this notion by highlighting the fact that most teams that succeed do so not because of extraordinary individual talent (although it helps) but

TABLE 2.2 Purposes of team building

1. To set team goals and to ensure that what is required for their accomplishment is clear.
2. To ensure team members' roles are clearly understood.
3. To examine the way in which the team functions (e.g. norms, communication), and to plan effective structures and systems to enhance performance.
4. To examine the relationships among team members, and to foster greater interpersonal respect and understanding.
5. To ensure that team meetings and practices are efficient. Also, to always seek to enhance and improve team efficiency.
6. To diagnose potential weaknesses, minimize their influences, and develop enhanced performance strategies.
7. To ensure that leadership is coherent, visionary, and acceptable. Also, to seek to gain feedback on the impact of the current leadership approach.

Source: adapted from Stevens (2002); Yukelson (1997)

because of extraordinary teamwork. In this approach team building is the deliberate process of facilitating the development of an effective and close group (Stevens, 2002). Beer (1980) also conceptualized team building as a process intervention (that continues over time with a number of components).

Brawley and Paskevich (1997) specifically defined team building as 'a method of helping the group to: (i) increase effectiveness; (ii) satisfy the needs of its members; or (iii) improve work conditions' (p.13).

Team building seeks to help the team to both act on and understand its behaviours and relationships. Team building generally focuses on the following seven areas: setting team goals, ensuring role clarity, maximizing team functioning, developing relationships, ensuring efficiency, identifying potential weaknesses, and ensuring there is effective leadership (see Table 2.2 for further details). There is, in particular, significant support for the effectiveness of goal setting as a team-building strategy (Martin *et al.*, 2009).

Approaches to team building

Both direct and indirect approaches to team building have been suggested in working with sports teams. Indirect approaches involve the sport psychologist working with and through the coach to develop team-building strategies for the team. This approach has been shown to be particularly effective in developing cohesion (Stevens, 2002). Carron and Dennis (1998) suggested a four-stage process for conducting indirect team building:

- the introductory stage;
- the conceptual stage;
- the practical stage; and
- the intervention stage.

In the introductory stage the importance of effective group processes is introduced to the coach or leader. This is followed by the conceptual stage, which is used to facilitate communication about issues relating to team effectiveness, highlighting their impact and interrelated nature. In the third, 'practical' stage the coaches and leaders brainstorm to develop specific strategies that seek to address any issues impacting upon team effectiveness. In the final stage, the strategies developed in the previous stage are implemented and maintained by the coaches and leaders. While this process is relatively brief, it offers a good framework within which the team can be built indirectly.

In the direct approach to team building the focus is on the sport psychologist directly looking to improve and develop team processes. One particular model that outlines this process is the action research model (Beer, 1976; Woodcock and Francis, 1994). In this model there are nine specific steps:

- discussion between the sport psychologist and the coaching staff;
- education and contracting;
- data collection;
- data analysis;
- presentation of data to the coaching staff;
- presentation of data to team members;
- designing and implementing a step-by-step intervention;
- final action plan; and
- ongoing monitoring and support.

In this direct approach the sport psychologist needs to collect data in a short period of time in order to understand the team, its structure, its aims, and its personnel (steps one to four). Only once all this information has been collected, analysed, and interpreted correctly can the sport psychologist look to implement interventions and develop an action plan (steps five to nine).

The main differences between this direct approach and the indirect approach are that the sport psychologist is directly involved, and team members are also actively involved in the process.

Yukelson (1997) also suggested a direct team-building model that consisted of six specific stages:

- developing a shared vision;
- developing collaborative and synergistic teamwork;
- fostering individual–team accountability;
- developing team identity;
- adopting a positive team culture and cohesiveness; and
- fostering open and honest communication.

Each of the steps outlined by Yukelson is covered in greater detail elsewhere in this book.

A recent meta-analysis undertaken by Martin *et al.* (2009) provides support for using both direct and indirect approaches. In their study both types of intervention produced positive team-related effects. Martin *et al.* (2009) further highlighted the ineffectiveness of short-duration interventions (less than two weeks), with more effective interventions in sport lasting a minimum of a season (Brawley and Paskevich, 1997).

Shared mental models

In recent years both researchers and practitioners have been increasingly interested in the cognitive factors that enable a team of individuals to coordinate and collaborate effectively (DeChurch and Mesmer-Magnus, 2010). Shared mental models refer to an organized understanding of knowledge that is shared by a team. This sharing of knowledge is seen to enhance the accuracy of team member expectations of each other's needs (Banks and Millward, 2007). This leads to more efficient coordination as the members of the team can anticipate each other's requirements. Shared team mental models can be more specifically defined as:

> knowledge structures held by members of a team that enable them to form accurate explanations and expectations for the task, and in turn, to coordinate their actions and adapt their behaviour to demands of the task and other team members.
>
> *(Cannon-Bowers and Salas, 2001: p.228)*

In the area of 'learning sciences' this same concept is referred to as common ground or knowledge convergence, with organizational sciences referring to the same concept as shared mental models (Klimoski and Mohammed, 1994). Four primary content domains of team mental models were originally proposed (Cannon-Bowers *et al.*, 1993). These included: (i) knowledge about the equipment and tools used by the team (equipment model); (ii) understanding of the team task, including its goals, performance requirements, and problems (task mental model); (iii) awareness of team-member composition and resources, including representations of what individual members know and believe, and their skills, preferences, and habits (team-member model); and (iv) what team members know or believe about appropriate or effective processes (team-interaction model or teamwork schema). The assumption in the shared mental model literature is that team effectiveness will improve if team members have a shared understanding of the task, team, equipment, and situation (Kozlowski and Ilgen, 2006). So, building on this assumption, the greater the degree of shared understanding, the greater the potential benefits. One example of this was the approach adopted by the ex-England soccer manager Sven-Goran Erikkson and his sport psychologist Willi Railo. Erikkson and Railo targeted specific players within the team to act as 'cultural architects' through whom the shared mental model could be developed. The players selected had developed a good grasp of what was required and it was their understanding of the management's plans that was used to influence the understanding of their teammates.

A number of studies have demonstrated a positive relationship between shared mental models, team processes, and overall team performance (Crust and Lawrence, 2006). Cooke *et al.* (2000) suggested three different types of knowledge that can exist in mental models: declarative knowledge, procedural knowledge, and strategic knowledge. Declarative knowledge is seen as the facts, figures, rules, and concepts that exist relating to the task. An example of declarative knowledge could be the maximum number of players allowed to start for a team. Procedural knowledge refers to the steps, sequences, and actions that are needed to perform the task. In a sporting context this 'how' knowledge could relate to the process of scoring a goal in ice hockey. Finally, strategic knowledge is the overriding task strategies and knowledge of when to apply them. Relating back to the ice hockey example, this would refer to the different ways to achieve the scoring of a goal.

For teams to effectively develop a shared mental model of the key elements of the task environment, changes in the knowledge of the individual team members occur. The role of team learning is crucial in this developmental process (Mohammed and Dumville, 2001). This notion is supported by Van den Bossche et al. (2011) who cited evidence within team research literature demonstrating that interactions between team members are a primary cause of mental model agreement. The size of the group also appears to impact upon the degree of development of shared mental models (Jeong and Chi, 2007).

Team learning

Team learning refers to the acquisition of knowledge, skills, and performance capabilities of an interdependent set of individuals through interaction and experience. Team learning is based on independent learning, but is viewed as more than simply a pooling of individual knowledge and can be distinguished as a team-level property that captures the collective knowledge pool, potential synergies among team members, and unique individual contributions (Kozlowski and Ilgen, 2006) that exist in the team. Indeed, it is important that team learning is truly collaborative (Akkerman et al., 2007), as an individual approach fails to grasp the phenomenon of group work and group learning (Stahl, 2006). In order to develop effective shared mental models it is important to not only understand each member of the team's representation of the task and the environment (mutual understanding), but also to accept and incorporate other people's ways of seeing (mutual agreement) (Dillenbourg and Traum, 2006). To reach the points of mutual understanding and mutual agreement a number of stages are important. First, meaning needs to be constructed. This is achieved through the accumulation of the contributions from each individual. This process starts with one team member inserting meaning by describing the problem situation and suggesting a plan of how to deal with it. Other team members listen and try to understand what has been proposed. This information then evolves into collaborative construction that involves a mutual process of building meaning by refining and further developing the initial thoughts of the individual. Second, agreement needs to be reached about the proposed solutions. As this agreement emerges from different points of view, conflict has an important influence on the agreement process (De Dreu and Weingart, 2003a). As a result, shared mental models are developed when the team reaches agreement. Mutual understanding in itself is not sufficient. Conflict is often present in this second stage, and can be constructive as long as it is a difference in interpreting the problem or the solution. Conflict can be destructive if it is personal in its focus and built upon emotional rejection. The conflict in itself is not important, it is the fact that it can generate further communication in the group that is advantageous to the development of agreement. However, this agreement is only useful if it generates a deeper level of processing with the team (Holman *et al.*, 2007).

Planning for World Cup success

Sir Clive Woodward and his support team epitomized team planning in preparing the England rugby union team to win the rugby World Cup in 2003. When Woodward took over as England coach he had one simple aim, which was for England to be 'the best team in the world'. Woodward found his way into professional sport following a successful career as a businessman, and it was this professional, business like approach that he brought into the then recently professionalized game of rugby. Woodward challenged the traditional practices in the sport by introducing business practices into rugby. This approach specifically allowed him to set long-term goals; pay attention to the finer details of planning; and also develop the basic skills, tactics, and strategy of the players he worked with. Central to Woodward's approach in both sport and business environments was developing the individuals' ability to think clearly under pressure. Woodward had a clear view that enhancing the players' ability to think clearly under pressure (TCup) would be a key factor in developing a world-class team. Crucial to building the high-performance team that Woodward strived for was the development of a team environment that both emphasized and supported the development of this core skill of thinking clearly under pressure. Within this environment Woodward always strived to bring in the best experts in their respective fields to further enhance his team. This included the introduction of a vision-training specialist, a step that was previously unheard of in rugby or other team sports. Dr Sherylle Calder, a specialist in sports vision training, was employed to help enhance performance. Dr Calder's role was to enhance each player's all-round vision, ability to process information, and ability to react accordingly. This attention to detail enabled Woodward to build a very effective environment in which the team could develop. In utilizing Dr Calder and other specialists in their fields, Woodward was able to take the England rugby team to new heights, breaking many records along the way, and also elevating the team to number one in the world. This number one ranking was achieved ahead of traditionally much stronger southern hemisphere teams (including Australia, New Zealand, and South Africa). All this planning and attention to detail finally culminated in the England rugby union team being crowned world champions on 22 November 2003 in Australia, beating the hosts Australia 20–17 in a nail-biting final that went to extra time. England scored the winning points in a well-executed preplanned move that culminated in a drop goal from Jonny Wilkinson with just 26 seconds remaining on the clock: a play that epitomized the 'thinking clearly under pressure' approach.

Summary

Clear planning and preparation for a team is essential in ultimately determining how successful the team is. A crucial message from the information reviewed in this chapter is the dynamic nature of teams, and the resulting requirements for an active and dynamic planning process. The planning and evaluation of the team, its performance, and its ultimate direction should be an ongoing process. There should be a planning component in preparing for each season that builds upon the evaluation of the previous season and recognizes any changes to the environment in which the team performs.

Each team should also have a clearly articulated vision, and possibly a mission statement. The team goals that are then developed should operationalize the vision and then fuel the development of specific action plans and procedures to enable the team to achieve its goals and to realize its vision. In addition, good planning will evaluate the targets and goals of the team against the vision on an ongoing basis.

3

DEVELOPING A POSITIVE TEAM ENVIRONMENT

Introduction

Building a positive and supportive team environment is crucial to the successful development and performance of most teams, and in particular those that are successful over a longer period of time. Indeed, successful coaches often have their own way of fostering a positive and supportive environment that allows both the players, as individuals, and the team as a whole to fulfil their potential. However, whilst this ability appears to be an important aspect of team planning, there is very little attention paid to this concept in the sports team literature. Most of what is known about the team environment and the related concept of psychological climate has emerged from research that has explored the operation and planning of teams in business-related settings.

This chapter will seek to explore the relevant concepts of interest including psychological climate (both for the individuals in the team and the team itself), the performance environment (and its impact upon team performance), the development of team values (that often underpin the environment), and finally the closely related concepts of conflict, conflict management, and conflict resolution. As with other chapters in this book the current chapter will seek to explore the relevant theory and then to apply this theory to enhance the development of the team environment, and ultimately to explore practical interventions and guidelines to enhance the environment and overall team performance.

Psychological climate

Early research exploring teams and work groups suggested that the social climate, or the atmosphere in a group, could have significant consequences for that team. Team members' perceptions of their team influence the degree to which each team member is satisfied and performs to their potential. These two factors in turn are an indicator of the overall productivity of the team (Katz and Kahn, 1978). Building on this initial suggestion, the concept of psychological climate has grown and developed. In organizational psychology literature climate is often referred to as the individuals' perceptions of their environment (Rousseau, 1988). More specifically, climate has been defined as 'individual descriptions of organizational practices and procedures that relate to organizational influences on individual performance, satisfaction, and motivation' (Baltes, 2001: p.12356). Climate has also been highlighted as an abstract concept that often occurs at various levels including individual, group/team, and organization (Baltes *et al.*, 2009). More recently there has been a shift towards viewing psychological climates as multidimensional in nature, and thus seeking to recognize the increasing complexity in our understanding of this concept.

Psychological climate in essence relates to how team members perceive and make sense of team direction, policies, practices, and procedures in psychologically meaningful terms (Schneider and Rentsch, 1988). However, only when team members agree on their perceptions of the team and its environment can these individual perceptions be aggregated to represent a team climate (Klein *et al.*, 2000).

Team climate is seen as an emergent property of the team as it originates in the perceptions and cognitions of the individual team members and is then amplified through interactions and exchanges with other team members to result in a higher level collective phenomenon (Kozlowski and Klein, 2000). Research exploring factors that impact upon the development of a team climate highlights a number of specific factors. These include the size and structure of the team, along with the clarity and salience of team policies, practices, and procedures that can help to establish a common team reality and climate (Schulte *et al.*, 2006). Communication and repeated social interactions have also been highlighted as being important in the development of shared perceptions and meaning (Klein *et al.*, 2001).

In the psychological climate literature, distinctions are made between psychological climate and organizational climate. Individuals' own perceptions, generally speaking, constitute psychological climate (as analysed by the individual), whereas organizational climate has been proposed to be an organization- or team-level construct. An organizational climate is said to exist when the individuals within the group or team agree on their perceptions of the team (Joyce and Slocum, 1984). In essence, this organizational climate is the collective view from the players of the team or members of the organization.

A number of studies have demonstrated links between psychological climate and important individual-level outcomes such as satisfaction, commitment, performance, and stress (Schulte *et al.*, 2006). Further research has also demonstrated positive relationships between organizational climate and individual outcomes such as performance, satisfaction, commitment, involvement, and reduced performance errors (Ostroff *et al.*, 2003). These reported relationships suggest that the prevailing psychological climate can exert a significant influence over both the individual and the team.

A number of frameworks have been suggested that seek to outline the specific dimensions of psychological climates. One of the most popular and widely accepted is that proposed by James and colleagues (James and James, 1989). These authors clustered psychological climate variables within four factors: role stress and lack of harmony;

job challenge and autonomy; leadership support and facilitation; and work group cooperation, warmth, and friendliness.

- *Role stress and lack of harmony* – influenced by role ambiguity, role conflict, role overload, subunit conflict within the team, and management concern for individuals and awareness.
- *Job challenge and autonomy* – determined by the degree of job autonomy, job importance, job challenge, and job variety.
- *Leadership support and facilitation* – underpinned by the hierarchical and psychological influences of the leader, the levels of trust and support displayed by the leader, and the degree to which the leader has a goal emphasis for the team.
- *Work group cooperation, warmth, and friendliness* – influenced by the warmth and friendliness of the team, the team's responsibility for overall effectiveness, and team cooperation.

The above four factors were developed through exploratory factor analyses, the results of which suggested that individuals tend to separate emotional cognitions relating to jobs, leaders, teams, and individual/organizational interfaces into separate internal compartments. James and James (1989) suggested that each of these highlighted factors provides information regarding the efficacy of the environment. The stronger the feelings about the efficacy of the environment, the more positive the individual will feel towards it.

Developing a positive psychological climate

Understanding psychological climate and its constituent parts is crucial to effective planning, development, and manipulation of the psychological climate in any sports team.

First, it is important to recognize the factors that impact upon the development of psychological climate. These include the following three main factors highlighted by Schulte *et al.* (2006):

- *The organization of the team* – including the size and structure of the team and its processes.
- *Policies, practices, and procedures* – in particular how consistent, clear, and salient these are. These can then be used to establish a common reality that provides the basis for shared perceptions.
- *Communication and repeated social interactions* – these have a particular role in both influencing and shaping the views of the individual.

Each of the above factors has been highlighted as being important in the development of shared perceptions and meaning (Klein *et al.*, 2001) and, as a result, could impact upon the development of the psychological climate.

Second, understanding the components of psychological climate is also important to further aid the development of the climate in a sports team. If we refer back to the framework suggested by James and James (1989), understanding the following four components is crucial: role stress and lack of harmony; job challenge and autonomy; leadership support and facilitation; and work group cooperation, warmth, and friendliness. In particular, understanding the constituent parts of each of these factors and how each of them can potentially impact upon psychological climate must be central to the ability of the manager or coach to successfully understand and influence the psychological climate.

Understanding these factors and their constituent parts will go a long way to determine the required/possible interventions that can be applied to enhance the psychological climate. For example, role stress and lack of harmony is influenced by role ambiguity, role conflict, role overload, subunit conflict, and management concern and awareness. As a result, to enhance this aspect of psychological climate you need to enhance role clarity, reduce role conflict, limit role overload, manage conflict within the team effectively, and gain feedback from team members regarding management processes. Further suggestions are provided in Table 3.1.

The performance environment

In sport psychology, practitioners and researchers alike have increasingly taken a holistic approach in seeking to understand the performance sports environment (Fletcher and Hanton, 2003). However, until Gould *et al.* (1999) began studying Olympic athletes, there was very little explicit literature that focused on the performance environment in sport (Pain and Harwood, 2008).

Indeed, the only related works in sport have focused on the performance environment and the factors in that environment that impact upon performance (Pain and Harwood, 2008). In an attempt to understand the performance environment in greater detail for team sports, Pain and Harwood (2007) conducted a study commissioned by the Football Association (FA) in England to explore the factors influencing performance in youth soccer tournaments. This research highlighted eight dimensions

TABLE 3.1 Approaches to enhancing psychological climate

Factor	Approaches
Role stress and lack of harmony	Enhance role clarity, reduce role conflict, limit role overload, manage conflict within the team effectively, and gain feedback from team members regarding management processes.
Job challenge and autonomy	Enhance job autonomy, clarify job importance, maintain job challenge, and maintain job variety.
Leadership support and facilitation	Enhance the support and trust provided by the leaders in the team, and clarify the focus of the team and its goals.
Work group cooperation, warmth, and friendliness	Foster warmth and friendliness within the team. Enhance the responsibility placed on the team as a whole for effectiveness and cooperation.

Source: adapted from James and James (1989)

that emerged to describe the performance environment. These included: social factors, tactical factors, psychological factors, physical factors, planning and organization, development and performance philosophy, the physical environment, and coaching.

Each of these eight dimensions was further composed of a number of subfactors, as follows:

- *Social factors* – cohesion and the nature of players' free/down time.
- *Physical factors* – regeneration/recuperation strategy, the physical nature of the opposition, player preparedness, and physical fatigue.
- *Psychological factors* – motivation, tournament expectations, pre-game routines, anxiety and relaxation, use of goals, response to adversity, confidence, working with a sport psychologist.
- *Tactical factors* – the degree of tactical preparation, and the degree of tactical flexibility.
- *Planning and organization* – planning, consistent organization, differing priorities (club and country), and staff management.
- *Development and performance philosophy* – developing the individual, promoting diverse player experiences, and motivational climates for the team.
- *Physical environment* – specifically related to distractions, the playing environment, the training environment, accommodation, and travel.
- *Coaching* – aspects of squad rotation, teaching and learning, feedback and reflection, coach–player relationships, specifics of tournament coaching.

The factors that were deemed to have a positive impact on both team and individual performance included player understanding, strong team cohesion, managed free-time activities, and a detailed knowledge of the opposition. Factors that were deemed to have a negative impact on team and individual performance included over-coaching, player boredom, limited player free time, player anxiety, and physical fatigue. Based on this research Pain and Harwood (2008) went on to define the performance environment as 'the array of factors impacting individual and team performance in competitive situations. It includes only those factors that are temporally and organisationally related to the competitive situation' (p.1158). Other factors such as historical events and socio-economic influences in the external environment were deliberately excluded by the authors from consideration by this definition.

In a supplementary study of the performance environment in football, Pain and Harwood (2008) highlighted further factors exerting a positive influence in the performance environment. These included the presence of a positive team leader, strong team cohesion on the pitch, team commitment to the tournament, positive support from friends and family, an effective rest/recovery strategy, strong team–coach relationships, and personal feedback from the coach. Players also highlighted clear team goals as having a positive impact upon performance. The main negative factors highlighted included difficulties sleeping, the food options not satisfying player needs, players losing composure during a game, boredom, a lack of available activities in the hotel, too many meetings, disruption of normal pre-game routines, and poor training facilities as having an effect. Pain and Harwood (2008) concluded that, when preparing the environment for a team that is competing in a tournament, the coach needs to prioritize team and social factors, and where possible maximize team cohesion (both within the playing staff, but also across the whole team, including coaches and support staff). Understanding these factors that impact upon the performance environment can enable the team to prepare more effectively to remove, or reduce, the impact of negative factors, while supporting factors that can have a positive impact.

High performance environment

Historically the majority of interventions that have looked to enhance performance in sports teams have either opted to focus on the team, or alternatively focus on the individuals within that team. Few specific interventions have focused on the environment in which the team operates. There are a number of reasons why this has been the case. This has, at least in part, been down to a lack of specific and clear models through which these interventions could be applied. In an attempt to resolve this issue Jones *et al.* (2009) developed the High Performance Environment (HPE) model. The model itself was based upon extensive reviews of the literature in business, sport, and military domains in an attempt to understand the factors that determine the HPE and ultimately impact upon performance. Specifically, the model is composed of three traditional factors influencing performance (leadership, performance enablers, and people) and four factors that determine the team/organizational climate (innovation, well-being, achievement, and internal processes). Each of these factors is presented as part of the model in Figure 3.1.

Jones *et al.* (2009) highlighted that, from a leadership perspective, the role of the leader is ultimately to foster and develop the conditions in which both the team and its individual members can perform to their potential. Based on this assumption the authors of the model recommended that the goal of the leader in the HPE is to reduce, where possible, the constraints that exist and to maximize support for both the team and the individual team members. Jones *et al.* (2009) therefore recommended adopting a transformational approach to leadership (see Chapter 10 for further details). In the HPE model, performance enablers are presented as an amalgamation of a number of factors that include vision, support, and challenge, all of which are thought to be required to enhance both team and individual performance. These performance enablers were defined by Jones *et al.* (2009) as 'environmental supports required by people to operate effectively in any performance environment' (p.143). This category of performance enablers is further subdivided into the categories termed information, instruments, and incentives. In the HPE model, information refers to detail relating to the role, including the setting of clear goals, good role clarity, and clear detail of role performance evaluation. Instruments are composed of the physical, structural, or knowledge-based instruments required to complete the task. Incentives focus on the factors that motivate the individual to perform to the best of their abilities.

The people factor, as the name suggests, focuses on the characteristics of the individual team members. In particular, the model highlights the importance of individual attitudes, behaviours, and capacities.

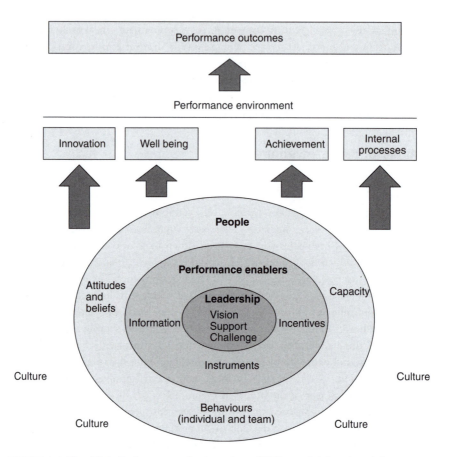

FIGURE 3.1 The High Performance Environment (HPE) model (reprinted from Jones *et al.*, 2009. Copyright Lane 4, 2009)

The organizational climate aspect of the model is composed of four factors highlighted by Quinn and Rohrbaugh (1983) in their Competing Values Theory. In the HPE model these factors have been labelled achievement, well-being, innovation, and internal processes. Jones *et al.* (2009) further described each of these factors as follows:

- *Achievement* – an emphasis on productivity and goal achievement.
- *Well-being* – an emphasis on the development of people within the organization.
- *Innovation* – an emphasis on creativity.
- *Internal processes* – an emphasis on formalization and internal control of systems and procedures.

In their Competing Values Theory Quinn and Rohrbaugh (1983) suggested that each of these four factors competes with the others to be the main focus. As a result, it is a challenge to try and balance these competing demands in the team climate. If a team overly focuses on one of these four factors (e.g. achievement) this would occur at the expense of some, and possibly all, of the other three. In order to achieve the optimal HPE each of these four factors needs to have a similar degree of focus within the team.

This HPE model has, since its development, been used to enhance the performance environments in a wide range of business and sports settings including management consulting, aviation, holiday and leisure companies, legal services, IT services, investment banking, engineering, and construction. It can thus be used as a helpful framework that the team management can employ to maximize the environment in which the team operates.

Team values

Most successful businesses, and increasingly successful sports teams, have clearly articulated and developed values. In many teams the specific values that underpin the team are not explicitly articulated or written down but, even so, they do fundamentally influence the behaviour of the team. Values are normally referred to as underlying guiding principles (Kouzes and Posner, 2007). It is these principles that guide the decision making and action within the team. It is then ultimately these actions that determine whether a team will achieve its goals. As a result, it is suggested that shared team values are the foundation of a successful team and are critical to building trust among players and coaches (Shoenfelt, 2010). Examples of common team values include achievement, accountability, challenge, communication, competition, cooperation, determination, fairness, honesty, integrity, pride, respect, responsibility, teamwork, and commitment (Shoenfelt, 2010). How important each of these different values is depends upon the team, its members, and the goals that the particular team has set for itself. One example of this is the value underpinning FC Barcelona soccer club in Spain. The club is driven by the key value of being '*més que un club*' (more than a club).

The development of shared values can have a number of positive impacts upon the team – not least that developing shared values helps to increase the perceived similarities within the team, and as a result increases the degree to which team members identify with the team (Kramer and Lewicki, 2010). The development of team values can be explicit and intentional, or alternatively team values can develop and evolve over time. There is a distinct advantage to the development of values being carried out in an explicit and intentional way. The process through which this is achieved clearly articulates what the values are, and as a result reduces the potential for ambiguity. Further details of this process are provided in the section on team building in Chapter 2. Values that evolve over time might be implicit in the way the team operates, but individual team members might not be able to articulate these values clearly. Shoenfelt (2010) suggested a five-step process for the identification of team values: (i) identify team goals; (ii) individual team members identify potential team values; (iii) the team discusses how values support the team's goals; (iv) gain consensus on the top five to seven team values; and (v) prioritize team values (see Figure 3.2).

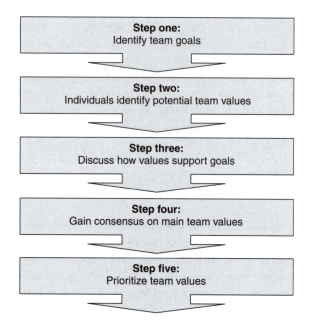

FIGURE 3.2 Five-step process to identify team values

The identification of team goals is suggested as the first step as there exists a range of empirical support for the effectiveness of goal setting in motivating both individuals and teams (see Chapter 2 for more details). In the second step each member of the team is encouraged to reflect on the values they think should help to guide the team to achieve the goals previously identified in step one. In step three, the team (as a whole) meets to share the team values highlighted by each individual.

The fourth step seeks to gain some consensus from the team about which of the values highlighted in step three are the most important (or universally accepted) for the team. In the fifth and final step the values are put into some kind of priority order. The agreed values should then guide and inform behaviour in the team, and as a result the team should also discuss what are the expected behaviours that are underpinned by the agreed values. Finally, there needs to be some form of agreement by the team that they accept the values and are willing to embrace them as a team. This process could be relatively informal (all those who agree put their hand up) or more formal (players sign an agreement, or sign a copy of the team's values). Getting the team members to make this commitment in front of each other increases the level of commitment and makes the agreement more public (Rousseau, 1995). These values can then be mounted somewhere visible (on the locker room wall), or alternatively personalized (each player having a copy for their wallet or bag). One associated benefit of developing team values is that there is then a need for fewer rules (Shoenfelt, 2010). Also, the development of a team motto can be used to further reinforce team values and to keep those values salient to team members. Examples of team mottoes include that for Everton FC soccer club in the UK, which has the following motto:

Nil Satis Nisi Optimum (Only the Best is Good Enough). This inspirational motto is also shared by Loughborough University in the UK, which has a specific focus on performance sport and sporting excellence. At a more global level, the motto for the International Olympic Committee is *Citius, Altius, Fortius* (Faster, Higher, Stronger). With professional sports clubs at least there appears to be a desire for mottoes to be presented in Latin.

Conflict

Conflict can be both a help and a hindrance to a team. On the one hand conflict can be dysfunctional, harm performance, and reduce cohesion, but on the other hand it can be beneficial in protecting the team from a tendency to move towards groupthink (DeChurch *et al.*, 2007). As groupthink develops, group members try to minimize conflict and reach a consensus decision without real critical evaluation of alternative options, ideas, or viewpoints. The main drawbacks of groupthink are the loss of individual creativity, reduced uniqueness, and limited independent thinking. As a result a team might not consider all available options, resulting in less than optimal decisions being taken, which can then have an adverse effect on the performance of the team. Deutsch (1973) referred to two different types of conflict which he termed constructive and destructive conflict. This distinction has led to suggestions that teams should look to encourage constructive conflict whilst reducing destructive conflict.

Conflict in teams usually begins with at least one team member perceiving a difference of opinion to exist regarding something they deem to be important (De Dreu and Weingart, 2003b). There is often a distinction made in the literature between a conflict of cognitive perceptions, and a conflict of behaviours. A conflict is usually highlighted as being a significant issue in which the present tension is rooted (De Dreu *et al.*, 1999). The main types of conflict highlighted in the literature are conflict regarding the task (task conflict) and conflict over relationships in the team (relationship conflict). Task conflict can be defined as 'disagreements among group members about the content of the tasks being performed, including differences in viewpoints, ideas and opinions' (Jehn, 1995: p.284). Relationship conflict is defined as 'interpersonal incompatibilities among group members, which typically includes tension, animosity, and annoyance among members within the group' (Jehn, 1995: p.284). In a number of research studies the existence of task-based conflict has been linked to positive outcomes including enhanced decision quality and acceptance, increased task performance, and a greater degree of innovation (DeChurch *et al.*, 2007). Relationship conflict has been shown to have clearly harmful effects on both task performance and affective outcomes like satisfaction (DeChurch *et al.*, 2007). Based on these distinctions task conflict is seen as being constructive whilst relationship conflict is destructive.

Conflict management

As highlighted in the previous section conflict can be both constructive and destructive. As a result, the aim of conflict management is to limit the destructive aspects of

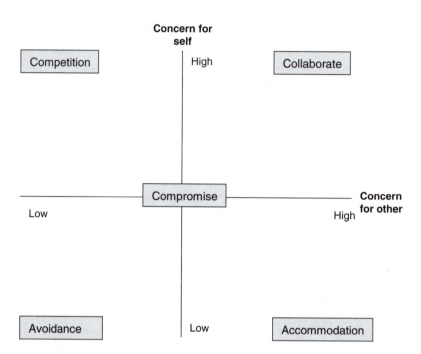

FIGURE 3.3 Styles of conflict handling according to dual concern theory

conflict and to increase the positive aspects. Conflict management can be defined as 'behaviour orientated toward the intensification, reduction, and resolution of the tension' (De Dreu *et al.*, 1999: p.371). Dual concern theory (Pruitt and Runbin, 1986) is often used to describe the different approaches that can be adopted when seeking to manage and resolve conflict. Dual concern theory suggests two underlying motives or dimensions for conflict: concern for relationships/people and concerns for tasks/productivity. Within this, concern for self refers to the extent to which conflict parties are concerned with their own needs, interests, values, and beliefs; concern for other refers to the extent to which conflict parties are concerned with their counterpart's needs, interests, values, and beliefs. These two dimensions have more recently been reinterpreted as attractiveness and agreeableness, and they encompass the five styles of conflict handling which are themselves characterized by being either high or low in each of the two dimensions (see Figure 3.3 for further details). Specifically, the five styles of conflict handling are collaborating, competing, accommodating, avoiding, and compromising.

- *Collaborating* – high agreeableness; high attractiveness.
- *Competing* – high attractiveness; low agreeableness.
- *Accommodating* – high agreeableness; low attractiveness.
- *Avoiding* – low on both dimensions.
- *Compromising* – moderate on both dimensions.

In adopting each of these conflict resolution techniques the individual would seek to achieve the following:

- *Collaborating* – you should state your views, listen to the other party's views, and then come to a negotiated solution. In this approach the solution should incorporate the views of both parties and be acceptable to both parties.
- *Competing* – the two parties have differing views regarding the situation and the relevant solutions that are either available or desirable. It is up to one party to convince the other party to accept their point of view, and ultimately their solution.
- *Accommodating* – whilst both parties have differing views regarding the issue and potential solutions, you deem there to be strategic reasons why accommodating the alternative view or solution is advantageous.
- *Avoiding* – the issue that forms the basis of the conflict is largely ignored, in the hope that with time the issue will resolve itself.
- *Compromising* – both parties have different viewpoints, but are willing to make concessions in order to resolve the issue.

In attempting to manage and resolve conflict situations within a team it is important to understand that certain responses can serve to escalate the situation. These escalatory responses can be both physical and verbal. The most common type of escalation involves retaliation aimed at punishing an annoying and offending other. The motivation for retaliation may be rooted in the desire to express anger, to deter further annoyance from the offender, to establish a tough impression, or to prop up social norms. Also, there may be an element of evening up the score. De Dreu (2010) highlighted a range of different forms of escalatory responses in conflict (see Tables 3.2 and 3.3).

The escalatory responses suggested by De Dreu (2010) can be categorized based on two criteria: the degree of activity and the directness of the response. Responses can either be active or inactive, direct or indirect. The same classifications are suggested for both verbal and physical responses. The degree of activity refers to whether the respondent engages in a particular action (active) or fails to respond (inactive). The response is either aimed at the responsible individual (direct) or designed to impact on the relevant person through other people (indirect).

TABLE 3.2 Physical responses that serve to escalate a conflict

	Physical	
	Direct	*Indirect*
Active	Murder, assault, displaying anger, obscene gestures, unfriendly, cold behaviour.	Theft, sabotage, defacing property, hiding needed resources.
Inactive	Going on strike and quitting.	Making target appear bad, failing to protect target's welfare.

Source: adapted from De Dreu (2010)

TABLE 3.3 Verbal responses that serve to escalate a conflict

	Verbal	
	Direct	*Indirect*
Active	Threats, yelling, being insulting, sarcasm, hostile comments.	Attacking associated individuals, whistle blowing and spreading damaging information.
Inactive	Failing to return calls, giving the silent treatment, refusing requests, damning with faint praise.	Failing to transmit information, failing to warn of impending situations, failing to defend target.

Source: adapted from De Dreu (2010)

Building an effective high performance environment

British (GB) cycling has built a very effective high performance environment in which talented cyclists have been able to develop, excel, and crucially win medals. Under the watchful eye of Performance Director Dave Brailsford, GB cycling has developed an effective performance hub housed at the Manchester velodrome. Over a 12-year period, from the 2000 Olympic Games in Sydney to the start of 2012, GB cycling has been exceptionally successful. This success culminated in a medal haul of 14 medals at the 2008 Olympic Games in Beijing. Of these medals, eight were gold, four were silver, and two were bronze. The success achieved by GB cycling on the world stage, though, has not been achieved by luck. GB Cycling has targeted success with ruthless efficiency, ambition, and attention to detail.

Every success along the way has been achieved through the development and continued evolution of an effective high performance environment. In this environment world-class coaches, cutting-edge bike technology, fantastic medical support, and innovative support staff selection has developed an environment in which the most talented cyclists can excel. Fundamental to the development of this environment has been the funding made available to the sport via the UK Lottery. While the funding is very important, it is the way that this funding has been maximized and targeted in its investment that has proven to be crucial. The GB cycling system is designed to support the most talented cyclists that emerge from the Olympic talent team programme. These cyclists then progress through the development and academy programmes up to the Olympic podium programme. Within this elite environment the best coaching, nutrition, psychiatry, mechanics, technical development, massage, and medical care is used to help maximize each cyclist's potential. Crucial to the success of this structure is what the team terms its 'cyclist-focused approach'. The support team knows its place and recognizes that the environment is designed to maximize the probability of success for riders in global competitions, including world championships and Olympic Games. This formula has proven to be very successful, and has been highlighted as an example of exceptional practice both within GB Olympic sport, and also across the global cycling community.

Summary

Understanding the impact that the environment has in both training and competition is important for all sports teams. Whilst much attention has focused on the individual and the team, little work in sport has really focused on the team/performance environment. Developing a greater understanding of the factors that impact upon this environment is crucial to unlocking the team's potential, with the logical next step being to focus on how to enhance this environment. Understanding the impact that the environment has on both the individual and the team can provide coaches and managers with a starting point to maximize the positive influence the environment can have on the team. Linked to this is the importance of conflict management skills for the coach and manager of a team, in particular understanding how to foster constructive conflict and reduce destructive conflict.

4

ROLE CLARITY AND ROLE ACCEPTANCE

Introduction

In successful sports teams each member of the team appears to 'just know' what their job is. The team as a whole understands what each player's responsibilities are, and how all these responsibilities fit together into a team performance. Each player knows what is expected of them and what they can expect of their teammates. In any team environment, each member of the team will have a specific role to play in the operation of the team. This understanding of individual role responsibilities has been identified as one of the most important team variables in sport (Carron, 2003). Roles in this context are described as a set of expectations about behaviours for a position in a particular social context (Eys *et al.*, 2006). As a result, these roles are a defining feature of groups and teams. Following extensive research in business settings, Belbin (1993) identified nine key roles including coordinator, implementer, specialist, resource investigator, and monitor evaluator. Belbin further contended that for a team to be successful a balance is required between these team roles. This approach suggests that team members should be carefully considered to ensure the right balance within the team. Within team environments evidence suggests that strategies to reduce role ambiguity and role conflict are essential to maintaining member morale and effective team functioning. It therefore appears crucial that developing clarity in the understanding and performance of roles is central to good team performance. This chapter will explore a range of factors that have a negative impact on role performance and consider a range of strategies that can be used to counter these highlighted factors.

Types of roles in sport

Two different approaches have been adopted in categorizing the types of roles that exist in teams. The first approach, by Bales and Slater (1955), suggested that the types of roles that exist in a team could be differentiated based upon the functions the roles serve.

Specifically, Bale and Slater make a distinction between task-related and social-related roles. Task-related roles are suggested to be directly orientated towards the instrumental objectives of the team. An example of this would be the leadership provided by the captain on the pitch. In contrast, social roles are related to the maintenance and the harmony of the team. These roles could be a social organizer, or joker, in the squad. These two different types of roles link well to the primary concerns of a team highlighted by Lewin (1935): locomotion (reaching the team's goals); and maintenance (ensuring the team is satisfying team members' needs).

Mabry and Barnes (1980) offered a slightly different categorization of team roles, specifically focusing on dividing roles into formal and informal categories. Formal roles are those that are directly prescribed to the individual within the team. A number of studies have sought to clarify the formal roles that exist in a range of sports. For example, Shoenfelt (2003) classified formal roles that exist in volleyball (e.g. setter), and Bray *et al.* (1998) highlighted offensive (e.g. offensive rebounding) and defensive roles (e.g. defensive position) in basketball. Informal roles evolve through association and interaction between teammates. Positive informal roles within sports teams that can contribute to success could include: social coordinator, clown, or an enthusiastic reserve/substitute (Eys *et al.*, 2006). Informal roles can also be task orientated, in that they focus on performing responsibilities related to the accomplishment of the group's objectives, or socio-emotional in orientation, whereby they promote harmony and integration within the group. In the sport-related literature the focus has been mainly on formal task-orientated roles. Two specific important functions of informal roles have been highlighted in the literature. First, that an informal structure within the team can arise to supplement the formal structure. This is particularly true if the formal structure is not meeting the needs of the group (Cope *et al.*, 2011). The second suggested function is to provide resistance to the formal structure that exists in the team. While there is the potential for this to have a negative impact on the team, it can also offer different perspectives and lead to better team outcomes (Cope *et al.*, 2011). While the dominant focus in the literature on formal roles is understandable in the context of formal team planning and performance, the importance of informal roles cannot be underestimated. Indeed, the informal roles such as clown and social organizer could significantly contribute to the development of a positive, supportive, and enjoyable team environment (see Chapter 3 for further details on developing a positive team environment and climate).

Cope *et al.* (2011) sought to gain greater clarity regarding the range and scope of informal roles in sport. In order to achieve this Cope and colleagues conducted a content analysis of articles in *Sports Illustrated* magazine. The results highlighted 12 specific informal roles that exist in sport: comedian; spark plug; cancer; distractor; enforcer; mentor; informal leader (non-verbal); informal leader (verbal); team player; star player; malingerer; and social convener. Cope and colleagues (2011: p.24) sought to further define each of these players' roles as follows:

- *Comedian* – entertains others through the use of comical situations, humorous dialogue, and practical jokes.

- *Spark plug* – ignites, inspires, or animates a group towards a common goal.
- *Cancer* – expresses negative emotions that can spread destructively through a team.
- *Distractor* – draws the attention of teammates away from the task in hand.
- *Enforcer* – is physically intimidating or willingly belligerent and is counted on to retaliate if the opposition look to intimidate or impose themselves.
- *Mentor* – acts as a confidant and sounding-board to other members of the team.
- *Informal leader (non-verbal)* – leads by example (by what they do).
- *Informal leader (verbal)* – leads through the encouragement and commands they give. Not the formal leader, but someone who can be inspirational.
- *Team player* – is committed to the team's cause and is willing to sacrifice themselves for the team.
- *Star player* – is distinguished and acknowledged for their contribution to the team.
- *Malingerer* – overprolongs injury (physical or mental) to gain some external rewards.
- *Social convener* – plans and organizes social events for the team.

Of these 12 roles Cope and colleagues highlighted that nine had a positive effect on the team (comedian, spark plug, enforcer, mentor, informal leader – non-verbal, informal leader – verbal, team player, star player, and social convener), whilst the other three roles had a detrimental effect on the team (cancer, distractor, and malingerer).

Eys *et al.* (2006) suggested a framework through which the different dimensions of roles could be considered. In this framework Eys and colleagues considered the critical elements of what they termed 'role involvement'. Within this framework Eys *et al.* (2006) considered the cognitive, affective, and behavioural elements of the individuals' role(s) within the team in respect of both formal and informal roles (see Figure 4.1 for further details).

For both formal and informal roles it was highlighted that either task or socio-emotional roles might exist for the individual. Relating to each of these roles there are then a

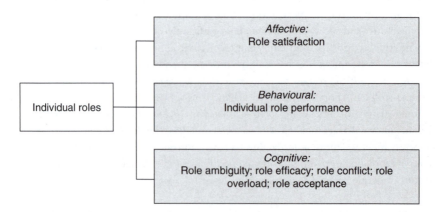

FIGURE 4.1 Critical elements of role involvement

range of cognitive, affective, and behavioural responses that might result from individual role involvement. From a cognitive perspective these relate to role ambiguity, role efficacy, role conflict, role overload, and role acceptance. From an affective perspective, these responses relate to role satisfaction. Finally, from a behavioural perspective, they relate to how the individual performs the role. Each of these highlighted cognitive, affective, and behavioural aspects of roles will be explored in further detail in subsequent sections of this chapter.

The emergence of roles

There is significant early research that has explored the emergence of roles in work groups (Carron and Hausenblas, 1998). Bales (1966) conducted research that focused on the observed behaviours associated with the appearance of different group roles within task-focused groups. The three general types of behaviours that Bale identified were activity, task ability, and likeability. Behaviour directed by the individual towards standing out from the crowd was referred to as activity. Task ability was characterized by behaviour that helps the group achieve its goals. Likeability was described as behaviour directed towards the development and maintenance of socially satisfying relationships. According to Bales (1966) the degree to which each individual exhibits these three behaviours has an influence on their roles within a group (see Table 4.1) with different roles being characterized by a different mix of these three types of behaviours.

Task specialists within the group are seen to be high in activity and task ability. Whereas a social specialist is high in activity and likeability but not necessarily high in task ability. In some contexts these two roles can be integrated, but this requires an individual high in activity, task ability, and likeability. Carron and Hausenblas (1998) also made reference to underactive deviants and overactive deviants within groups. Underactive deviants are seen to be low in all three behaviours, although Carron and Hausenblas noted that this type of individual is rare in sports team settings. Overactive deviants are referred to as chronic complainers; they exhibit high activity behaviour, but low task ability and likeability behaviours. This type of individual can act as a negative influence in the team, ultimately draining energy.

TABLE 4.1 Behaviours associated with role development in task-orientated, problem-solving groups

Group role	Activity	Task ability	Likeability
Task specialist	High	High	Low
Social specialist	High	Low	High
Leader	High	High	High
Underactive deviant	Low	Low	Low
Overactive deviant	High	Low	Low

Source: adapted from Bales (1966)

Communicating role expectations

One model that explores the process of communicating roles is the role episode model, which was originally proposed by Kahn *et al.* (1964) but then adapted specifically for sport by Eys *et al.* (2005). Key to this model is the interaction between two central actors. The first of these (referred to as the role sender) develops and communicates expectations to the second actor (the focal person). This model proposes that a number of factors influence the communication of information between the role sender and the focal person. These factors relate specifically to the communication ability of the role sender, the degree to which the focal person is paying attention, and the situation. Eys *et al.* (2006) highlighted a cycle of five events that take place during the communication, reception, and execution of a role. The first event involves the role sender (coach) developing some expectations for the focal person (player). The second event involves the role sender (coach) communicating to the focal person (player). The third event takes place when the focal person (player) experiences the associated pressures of the role expectation. Depending on the way the focal person (player) responds to this pressure, event four sees information communicated back to the role sender (coach). The final event, and culmination of this process, sees the original role sender (coach) interpreting the information they have received back from the focal person (player). The level of complexity of this model can be further developed by exploring the individual differences associated with the people occupying the role sender and focal person roles (e.g. the degree to which the focal person is paying attention). This cycle highlights a number of points at which there is potential for the requirements of the role to be miscommunicated or misinterpreted.

Role ambiguity

This refers to a lack of clear, consistent information associated with a particular role (Kahn *et al.*, 1964). In essence the player is unclear regarding what the role is, and what expectations might exist. Role ambiguity has been shown to be consistently associated with negative affect (Beauchamp *et al.*, 2002). It has also been considered to influence performance effectiveness (Carron and Hausenblas, 1998) and has been shown to be associated with the psychosocial well-being of the team members (Eys *et al.*, 2003). Eys and Carron (2001) operationalized role ambiguity as a multidimensional construct composed of ambiguity about the scope of responsibilities, the behaviours necessary to carry out those responsibilities, how role responsibilities are evaluated, and the consequences of not fulfilling role responsibilities.

There are a number of studies that have explored role ambiguity and its relationship with a range of other variables. Beauchamp and Bray (2001) explored role ambiguity and role conflict perceptions, reporting that participants who displayed greater levels of role ambiguity and role conflict had lower levels of efficacy. Eys and Carron (2001) explored the relationship between role ambiguity, task cohesion, and self-efficacy. The authors reported that individuals who were unclear of their roles perceived the team to be less integrated and reported lower levels of attraction to the team. Beauchamp and Bray (2001) highlighted two specific distinctions that should be made when considering role ambiguity. First, it should be determined whether it is subjective or objective ambiguity that is at issue. In this case subjective ambiguity refers to perceptions of ambiguity held by the individual, whereas objective ambiguity is something that exists in the environment. The second distinction highlighted by Beauchamp and Bray (2001) focuses on whether player perceptions relate to their formal or informal responsibilities in the team.

Beauchamp et al. (2002) developed a conceptual model of role ambiguity for interactive team sports. In this model ambiguity is assumed to be possible in both offensive and defensive contexts. In each context four dimensions of ambiguity were also highlighted: scope of responsibilities, behaviour required to fulfil role responsibilities, evaluation of role performance, and the consequences of not fulfilling role responsibilities. The scope of responsibilities dimension reflects a lack of clear information regarding the extent of a player's responsibilities. The behaviours required to fulfil the role responsibilities dimension relates to the potential for the player to be unclear about what behaviours are required. The degree of evaluation of the role performance dimension links to a lack of understanding by the player about how they are going to be assessed in the role. The consequences of not fulfilling the role responsibilities dimension reflects ambiguity regarding the consequences of not being successful in the assigned role.

Eys et al. (2005) sought to explore the reasons why role ambiguity might exist in sport, focusing specifically on soccer players. Responses were categorized under three main headings: the role sender, the focal person, and the situation. Results showed that the most prevalent categories were related to a lack of communication, unclear communication, and conflicting communication from the role sender (Eys et al., 2005). The clarity of communication from those sending role expectations was reported to be the most influential factor. A role sender, in this context (such as the coach), refers to the individual who develops and communicates (either formally or informally) a role expectation to the focal person (player).

Measuring role ambiguity

Beauchamp et al. (2002) developed a 40-item measure that assesses role ambiguity in both offensive and defensive scenarios. In each scenario four highlighted dimensions (scope of responsibilities, behaviours, evaluation, and consequences) are composed of five separate items. In this measure, the dimension of the scope of responsibilities refers to a lack of clear information about the range of the individual's responsibilities (e.g. relative to: 'I understand all my responsibilities'). The dimension of role behaviours refers to a lack of clear information about the behaviours associated with the individual's role (e.g. relative to: 'it is clear what behaviours I should perform to fulfil my role'). The dimension of role evaluation relates to a lack of clear information about how responsibilities are evaluated (e.g. relative to: 'the criteria by which my role is evaluated are clear to me'). Finally, the dimension of role consequences refers to a lack of detail regarding the specific consequences for not completing the role (e.g. relative to: 'I understand the consequences of my unsuccessful role performance'). This Role

Ambiguity Scale (RAS) requires participants to answer each question on a 9-point likert scale. This scale was anchored at the extremes by *strongly disagree* (1) and *strongly agree* (9). Higher scores on the scale are seen to reflect lower role ambiguity. The initial validation of this measure was undertaken with secondary school rugby players (mean age = 15) in the United Kingdom. Further support for this scale has also been provided by a range of other authors, including Eys *et al.* (2006) and Eys *et al.* (2007).

Role conflict

This refers to the presence of incongruent or conflicting expectations placed on an individual (Kahn *et al.*, 1964). From a theoretical perspective role conflict has been theorized to be multidimensional in nature (King and King, 1990). Kahn *et al.* (1964) further highlighted three different types of role conflict that might exist: intra-role, inter-sender, and person-role conflict. Intra-role conflict occurs when expectations from two or more contexts interfere with each other. An example of this could be the differences between what the coach says to a player individually, and the message that is communicated to the team. Inter-sender conflict occurs when two role senders apply incongruent expectations to the individual regarding the required role. An example of inter-sender conflict could be the coach and the manager expecting different things from the same player. Person-role conflict occurs when there is an incompatibility between the demands of the role and the needs or values of the individual player. This might relate to a player being asked to bend the rules when they have a very strong sense of fair play.

Although there are still discrepancies between potentially different types of role conflict that might exist in sport, some studies have explored the consequences for both the performer and team functioning. For example, Settles *et al.* (2002) explored aspects of role conflict experienced by students in relation to their athletic and academic identities. Beauchamp and Bray (2001) explored the relationships between intra-role conflict, role ambiguity, and role-related efficacy beliefs. Moore and Collins (1996) investigated the implications for both performer and team functioning when members of the management team are expected to perform incongruent role responsibilities. Collins *et al.* (1999) further extended this avenue of inquiry to include sports team support staff (including doctors, physiotherapists, strength and conditioning practitioners, sports scientists, sport psychologists, and nutritionists). Collins *et al.* (1999) suggested that one way to reduce the conflict that might occur between the team management and team support staff regarding the best interests of the player was the development of a player charter. This would then enable the development of effective and ethical support to the players with clear boundaries for professional practice. It is also important to consider the different manifestations of role conflict that arise. King and King (1990) highlighted that the nature of the conflict, and as a result the strategies required, will vary depending on the source of the conflict. In defining this further Eys *et al.* (2006) suggested that the conflict that exists for a player who receives conflicting instructions from two coaches will be different from the experience of a player who has differing expectations from the coach and his or her spouse.

Multiple roles and role overload

Related to role conflict is the associated concept of role overload. Role overload has been highlighted as an important factor impacting upon both psychological health and satisfaction (Pearson, 2008). Cooper *et al.* (2001) suggested that role overload is distinct from role conflict and refers to 'the number of different roles a person is expected to fulfil' (p.39). In outlining the potential impacts of role overload McBride (1990) highlighted a particular link between role overload and mental illness. A number of theories have been suggested that seek to understand the impact of multiple roles on the individual. Super (1990) suggested through the lifespan model that multiple roles could have a positive impact on happiness and satisfaction. This supported earlier work by Marks (1977) who highlighted that multiple roles can be energizing and provide greater opportunity for meaningful involvement. Conversely though, Goode (1960) suggested that when multiple roles result in role overload the limits of time and energy that the individual possesses become stretched and exhausted. This in turn can result in a number of negative outcomes including fatigue, decreased well-being, decreased satisfaction, reduced motivation, and a general decrease in mental health.

Eys *et al.* (2006) suggested a number of different types of role overload that might exist within sport. Specifically Eys and colleagues suggested that an individual player might be expected to perform a single role beyond their individual capabilities; an excessive number of roles; or a complex and demanding role that is difficult to further break down. Effective coaches and managers will be aware of the potential implications of multiple roles and manage workloads effectively to reduce the potential for role overload occurring.

Role acceptance and role efficacy

Historically role acceptance has sometimes been confused with compliance to expectations (Eys *et al.*, 2006). Compliance to expectations has been described as overt behavioural responses to role pressures (Biddle, 1979). By comparison, role acceptance has been defined by Eys *et al.* (2006) as 'a dynamic covert process that reflects the degree to which an athlete perceives his or her own expectations for role responsibilities as similar to, and agreeable with, the expectations for role responsibilities determined by his or her role senders' (p.245). Stevens (2002) further highlighted the development of role acceptance as being critical to effective team building, and as such it is an important consideration in both role and team performance.

Role efficacy is based on the more global construct of self-efficacy (see Chapter 7 for more details). Role efficacy was operationalized by Bandura (1997) as the team members' beliefs about their capabilities to successfully carry out interdependent formal role functions. Research to date exploring role efficacy has demonstrated correlations between role efficacy, mastery experiences, and performance. This further reinforces the idea that mastery experiences are one of the most important determinants of efficacy beliefs (Bandura, 1997; Eys *et al.*, 2006).

Role satisfaction

Role satisfaction can be described as the degree of fulfilment a role gives an individual (Eys *et al.*, 2007). Locke (1976) defined job satisfaction as 'a pleasurable emotional state resulting from the perception of one's job as fulfilling or allowing the fulfilment of one's important job values' (p.1342). Rail (1987) conducted research to explore the factors that lead to enjoyment and satisfaction relating to role completion. Rail highlighted that, no matter what level the individual works at, the same four principles are critical for satisfaction: the opportunity for the individual to use specialized skills or competencies; the extent to which the individual received feedback and recognition; how significant the individual viewed their role to be; and the level of autonomy that the individual was permitted in completing their role. Role satisfaction is seen as an important aspect of team functioning (Eys *et al.*, 2006). Specifically, satisfaction is suggested to be important for three reasons. First, because satisfaction and performance are inextricably linked. Second, satisfaction maintains individual involvement in team tasks and activities. Third, satisfaction is either an antecedent or a consequence of multiple other psychological constructs. Bray (1998) explored perceptions of role satisfaction in intercollegiate basketball players. Like role acceptance, role satisfaction was positively associated with task cohesion, role efficacy, and role importance and negatively related to role ambiguity.

Individual role performance

As the behavioural component of role perceptions, role performance is the aspect that is most easily assessable. As a result of this, role performance is the most readily assessable aspect of role completion. The way the individual player ultimately performs their role is related to the degree to which that player understands their role in the team, and how able the player feels to execute the role (Bray and Brawley, 2002). Thus, all the previously discussed elements of roles are likely to influence role performance. Role performance has specifically been linked to role ambiguity, with players who have a clearer understanding of their role performing better (Eys *et al.*, 2006). Eys and colleagues also explored mediating factors that impact upon the role ambiguity–role performance relationship, specifically highlighting role efficacy as being important. This notion built on research by Beauchamp *et al.* (2002) who demonstrated that, for both offensive and defensive situations, the player's beliefs about their ability to execute their role was influenced by how well the player understood their role. Role efficacy was also shown to subsequently predict how well the players performed their roles. Eys *et al.* (2006) highlighted two specific issues with how role performance is considered in sport. First, while role performance is predominantly seen as an outcome variable, it can also act as the trigger for other role dimensions. The second issue relates to how role performance is measured. Coaches can subjectively rate the performance of each player based on the coach's perception of the role the player should be fulfilling. The main limitation of this approach is the potential for the coach ratings to be subject to personal bias (Beauchamp *et al.*, 2002).

A second approach could be to ask the players directly how well they think they did. Again, this approach could be open to personal bias as well as the players trying to present a socially desirable impression of themselves. Based on this, Eys *et al.* (2006) highlighted the need for the development of an objective measure of role performance.

Enhancing role performance within sports teams

Enhancing role perceptions and role acceptance in sport

Communication appears to be crucial to this process (Eys *et al.*, 2007). It is important for the coach/manager to 'sell' the team vision to the team members and to reinforce all the roles in the team and the importance of each component part of the team in achieving success. The team and the individual also need to be clear regarding what is required for effective performance and how all the roles are as important as each other to ensure overall team success. Understanding how individual roles contribute to ultimate success and performance is important to create positive perceptions of the individual roles. Team members are far more likely to accept a role within the team if their perception (and more widely the team's perception) of the role is a positive one.

Reducing role ambiguity

Again, effective communication is central to this process. Ambiguity results from a lack of clarity. So, the messages regarding what is required need to be clearly articulated, and also the role sender needs to check for clarity of understanding by each individual and the team in general.

Reducing role conflict

Carron and Hausenblas (1998) suggested a number of ways to reduce role conflict. First, as role conflict is often a result of role overload, finding ways to reduce this overload is important. Role overload often leads to insufficient ability, time, motivation, or understanding on the part of the individual player. In this case a simple solution is to recruit other team members to fill any gaps. This can either be achieved through sharing responsibilities with existing team members, or alternatively recruiting extra members for the team. A second option is for the individual player to assume greater control over outcomes. This way the player can help to manage role expectations, and ensure that the behavioural and cognitive demands of the role are not beyond their capabilities.

Other techniques to reduce role conflict could include cognitive restructuring; essentially the way the player views the roles (Carron and Hausenblas, 1998). Henschen (1986) suggested scheduling time-outs, increasing participation in decision making, assuming control of outcomes, and planning mental practices as further techniques that can be applied to deal with role conflict.

Enhancing role performance

Carron and Hausenblas (1998) suggested a number of ways to enhance role performance. In particular, developing an effective goal-setting programme at both the team and the individual level. This approach is specifically designed to enhance role clarity and role acceptance. In this context goal setting is suggested to fulfil four important functions. First, goal setting directs the individual team member's attention and action towards appropriate behaviours. Second, the setting of goals motivates the individual team member to develop strategies to achieve these goals. Third, goal setting can contribute to increased interest in the required activity. Fourth, the setting of goals can also lead to prolonged effort on the part of the players (Locke *et al.*, 1981).

Difference that role clarity and understanding can make to a team

By the end of 2011 the Welsh national soccer team had completed a remarkable transformation. It had recovered from an all-time lowest world ranking position of 117th to climb 72 places to reach a new position of 45th in the world. All this was achieved in just a three-month period. Much of this success was attributed to the then Welsh manager, the late Gary Speed, who took over from the previous manager, John Toshack, on 8 February 2011. After taking charge Speed presided over two further defeats at the hands of Ireland and England, before embarking on a run of five wins in seven fixtures. In this run the Welsh also lost away 1–0 to England at Wembley in a game in which commentators universally acknowledged that the Welsh had been the better team. This run of form compared well with the final set of fixtures under the previous manager, where the team lost five out of six matches. One of the reasons highlighted for this transformation had been the understanding that the players in the team developed regarding their roles. Nathan Blake (a former Welsh international footballer), writing in the *South Wales Echo*, pinpointed the fact that the players were clear regarding the system they were playing and understood what was expected of them. Blake specifically highlighted this fact by stating that 'as a player, you want to know where you stand and what your job is going to be'. Part of the reason for this understanding was the approach adopted by Speed to not change the team too much from game to game, which enhanced each player's familiarity with their role and the roles that their teammates were being asked to fulfil. This contrasted with the previous regime under Toshack where there was far more continuous change in personnel that made this understanding difficult to achieve. The stability of the team was not helped by a number of senior players, including Ryan Giggs, Gary Speed, Robbie Savage, John Hartson, Mark Delaney, and Simon Davies quitting for various reasons. Toshack, awarded 43 caps in his time in charge, towards the end of his reign adopted an approach of fast-tracking talented young players into the team. In total Toshack won ten out of 29 qualifiers for major tournaments, but failed to beat a major footballing nation during his time in charge. In their final game under the direction of Gary Speed, before his untimely death, Wales beat Norway (ranked 24th in the World) 4–1 in Cardiff. But, after winning the game, in a typically understated way, Gary Speed simply stated that 'Wales are moving in the right direction'.

Summary

In any given sports team there are different roles and responsibilities that need to be fulfilled for the team to be successful. These roles can be formal regarding the leadership of the team, but can also be tactical. In all teams each individual player needs to understand what their role is, and how they should execute these roles. Just as important, though, is the understanding by other team members of what each of the other individual players' roles are and the behaviours associated with these roles.

The processes of communicating, clarifying, and executing given roles are crucial to ultimate performance. Any ambiguity, conflict, or overload could result in a significant decrease in team effectiveness and overall team performance.

5

DEVELOPING EFFECTIVE TEAM COMMUNICATION

Introduction

Communication is something we all engage in either consciously or subconsciously all the time. In teams this communication is fundamental to the effective operation of the team. Good communication is generally accepted as being crucial in all aspects of sports performance and preparation. The communication strategies adopted within any team underpin the effectiveness of that team to deliver its desired performance. Good-quality communication, and a structure that encourages both bottom–up and top–down communication, are both crucial to the development of optimal team processes. Yukelson (2006) highlighted the importance of effective communication for optimizing cohesion, team dynamics, and inter-group relationships within the team. Carron and Hausenblas (1998) went one step further to highlight the importance of intra-team communication for the development and maintenance of group structure, decision making, goal setting, cooperation, team building, and leadership, and to reduce within-group conflict. Effective communication has also been highlighted as being essential for the overall coordination and management of any team. The use of effective communication can have a positive impact on the development of good interpersonal relationships and trust, and creates a positive environment, which then facilitates the team's working towards achieving its goals (Athanasios, 2005). While communication is crucial in teams it is, at least in part, a skill. As such, it can be learnt and practised (Mullin, 2009). We communicate all the time, but are not necessarily aware of the messages we send. Understanding the nature of communication in teams can help the architects of that team to develop strategies to enhance team effectiveness through communication. The absence of good communication can result in a lack of cooperation and coordination, and confusion amongst team members. This chapter will explain the required mechanisms and approaches for enhancing communication channels, specifically exploring the different types of communication, communication networks, language use, and common communication errors, and strategies that can be used to enhance communication within the team.

What is communication?

Communication is a basic feature of social life. Good (2001) suggested that it is through communication with each other that personal relationships, communities, and societies are made and maintained, and it is through these networks and relationships that we become who we are. Fiske (1990) made the point that communication is one of those human activities that everyone recognizes but few people can actually define satisfactorily. Indeed, we often take our ability to communicate for granted and rarely stop to consider the processes and their effects. Fiske (1990), in attempting to define communication, suggested that it was 'social interaction through messages' (p.2). Communication actually seeks to transmit two distinct messages from the sender to the receiver. The first is the basic message; this conveys the words that the message is composed of. The second message is a metamessage that indicates how we want someone to interpret the basic message (Scollon and Scollon, 2001). In this context 'meta' refers to 'the interpretation of' the language, in this case words.

Shannon and Weaver (1949) suggested a basic 'process' model of communication when seeking to explain this process of communication. This model is composed of three separate parts (Figure 5.1). First, there is the transmitter (the person initiating the communication). Second, there is the receiver (the person being communicated with). In between these two elements is a third part, referred to as 'noise'. Noise refers to any factor or set of factors that can interfere with the communication of the message from the transmitter to the receiver. Specific examples of noise in sport could include emotions, distractions (such as the crowd, opposition, and officials), fatigue, and skill execution.

Communication is frequently divided into a number of different levels, including: interpersonal, group, organizational, inter-organizational, and mass communication (Baker, 2002). Other authors have used different terminology – micro, meso, and macro – to refer to levels of communication, with micro referring to interpersonal, meso referring to group/organizational, and macro referring to mass communication. Of particular interest to sports teams are interpersonal and group communication. Interpersonal communication at a basic level is simply the communication that takes place between two or more people. Group communication refers to the communication

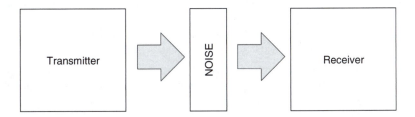

FIGURE 5.1 A basic model of communication

that takes place between a number of individuals who are members of the same group or team.

An important goal of interpersonal communication is to express oneself so that the other person (or people) is in a better position to understand you. At a general level, communication involves sending, receiving (encoding), and interpreting (decoding) messages through a sense of available modalities (Harris and Harris, 1984). Crucially, the way a message is expressed will impact upon how the message is received and interpreted (Yukelson, 2006). As a result, successful communication also requires that the transmitted message be appropriately decoded (Athanasios, 2005). Communication can also be influenced by a range of individual difference factors including the individual's personality, personal development, beliefs, styles of communication, past experiences, and situation-specific circumstances. A number of factors can further influence the communication of information including emotional episodes and experiences of stress (Yukelson, 2006). LaVoi (2007) highlighted three specific principles of interpersonal communication. First, that communication is inescapable. We are always communicating in one way or another (intentionally or unintentionally). Second, communication is irreversible. Once a message has been sent, it cannot be retrieved. Finally, communication is complex. It involves the interaction of the individual's perceptions of themselves, others and the relationship between the two.

In groups, communication is also required to coordinate the operation of that group. In sports teams this coordination is critical for team performance (Fiore *et al.*, 2001). Considerations of communication in sports teams have primarily been concerned with the impact of social constructs on communication (Eccles and Tenenbaum, 2004). Consistent with this approach, recommendations for enhancing team communication have included creating opportunities for team members to socialize together, promoting team member discussions, and modifying team member differences (Yukelson, 2006). Communication is, in essence, a dynamic process that involves both mutual sharing and mutual understanding (Martens, 1987).

Types of communication

There are a number of different types of communication that have been highlighted. Each of these types of communication offers a different benefit in terms of achieving the required outcome, and its own associated costs in terms of time (how quickly) and required cognitive resources (intensity) that are required (Eccles and Tenenbaum, 2004). The first categorization highlights that communication can be either intentional and unintentional, or verbal and non-verbal.

Intentional communication, as the name suggests, occurs when the sender intentionally sends a message to one or more recipients. Both verbal and non-verbal communication forms are common in groups, and sports teams in particular. Both forms of communication can be used to encrypt messages so that only the intended recipients can interpret the message. For example, in rugby union each team has its own team 'calls' which highlight which 'play' members are going to adopt in a specific situation, such as the line-out. In American football each team has a number that corresponds to a certain specific play. While effective, this form of communication is costly in terms of both time and cognitive resources. Depending on the situation, these resources may not be available without a corresponding decrease in performance. As a result, experienced teams will often avoid this type of communication in periods of high demand (Orasanu, 1993).

Unintentional communication occurs when individuals inadvertently send messages to recipients. Unintentional verbal and non-verbal communication can provide important information to a team member about the operations of other team members (Wittenbaum *et al.*, 1998). Unintentional verbal communication is quite rare, but unintentional non-verbal communication is always being transmitted to some degree. Unlike intentional communication, unintentional non-verbal communication has few time or cognitive costs to the sender, as these messages are incidental to their operations. It is also convenient for the receiver as it is readily available. In a sporting context, body language is a good example of unintentional non-verbal communication. In a game when performance is going against you, heads and shoulders can visibly drop, which in turn sends a clear message to the opposition that they have the advantage, and, as a result, they will seek to capitalize. However, unintentional non-verbal communication can often be more difficult to interpret correctly (MacMillan *et al.*, 2004). This is one of the reasons why players who have negative body language gestures can be misinterpreted as lacking desire, motivation, and interest by the coach and spectators.

Verbal communication

Verbal communication is quite simply communication through the use of verbalized sounds and spoken words. A central construct of verbal communication is language, its use, and the subtleties of its variation.

Language

Language is a major component of communication. In a very broad metaphorical sense 'language' can be used to refer to any system of communication. Human language specifically relates to the use of linguistic forms as the basis of interpersonal and social communication. Language in this sense refers to a system of units that, in combination, provide meaningful communication. These units might be words, sentences, or whole texts.

Speech

Speech is the vocalized form of human communication, specifically, the act of expressing or describing thoughts, feelings, or perceptions by the articulation of words. This form of communication is seen by many to be the main form of communication that they employ in their day-to-day interactions. The speech of any individual is governed by the lexicon (database) of words they have at their disposal.

Other important factors influencing speech include the pronunciation of the words and the dialect form of language being employed. While the words we use are reasonably clear (allowing for regional differences), the ways we modify our delivery to portray different messages is far subtler.

Paralanguage

This refers to the various elements that accompany and amend the spoken word. Paralanguage is important as it adds extra meaning to what is being said, or has the power to contradict or undermine the core meaning of the message. In sport a coach trying to give a rousing, inspirational speech during an interval might be completely undone by portraying negative body language and nervousness through their voice. Therefore, it is crucial for the delivery to match the content for effective communication. Paralanguage includes the following components (Thompson, 2003):

- *Speed* – fast speech can indicate a degree of excitement, while slow speech can indicate boredom or depression. In team talks the speed of speech can be used to calm down or psych up the players.
- *Tone* – pitch can be used in language to distinguish lexical or grammatical meaning, essentially distinguishing or inflecting words. Pitch is seen on a continuum of gentle tone at one end to harsh tone at the other. The harsher the tone, the more 'authority' and less flexibility is being added to the message.
- *Loudness* – changing the loudness of the speech is highly significant. Very loud speech can indicate specific emotions, such as aggression or anxiety, while quiet speech can indicate timidity, or be used to calm down others. Change in the loudness of the voice is the important factor. If you only occasionally raise your voice then it will have greater impact. Good public speakers will vary the loudness of their voice through their speech to emphasize specific points and to keep the delivery interesting.
- *Pitch and intonation* – pitch refers to how high or low a particular word is spoken. The pitch of the voice can be described as the rate of vibration of the vocal folds. The sound of the voice changes as the rate of vibration varies. As the number of vibrations per second increases, so does the pitch, meaning the voice would sound higher. Faster rates form higher voices, or higher pitches, while slower rates elicit deeper voices, or lower pitches. Intonation refers to the musicality, in essence the way the pitch rises and falls.

Language and emotion

The language used by players interacts with their emotion in three distinct ways (Thompson, 2003):

- *Language causes emotion* – often emotions result as a reaction to something that is said. Players engaged in sledging are attempting to use language to elicit a negative emotional response.

- *Language conveys emotion* – humans have developed subtle and effective ways to convey emotion through language. The use of paralanguage can add further meaning to a simple message (e.g. passion, or fear). This in turn modifies the way the message is received.
- *Language can be shaped by emotion* – The language forms that a person will use are often a result of the individual's emotional state. The response received is then also likely to be shaped by that same initial emotion. A player called a cheat by their coach will respond with words that display their emotional response to the accusation.

Non-verbal communication

Non-verbal communication is a generic umbrella term that includes a number of specific communication modalities. In particular, non-verbal communication includes facial expressions, gestures, body language and posture, proximity, eye contact, haptics, and appearance (see Figure 5.2).

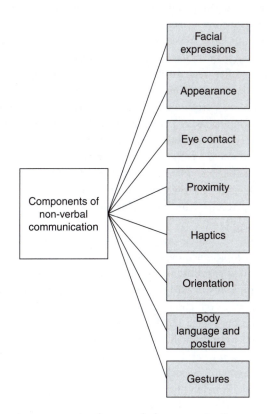

FIGURE 5.2 Different components of non-verbal communication

Facial expressions – facial expressions are responsible for a huge proportion of non-verbal communication. Consider how much information can be conveyed with a smile or a frown. While non-verbal communication and behaviour can vary dramatically between cultures, the facial expressions for happiness, sadness, anger, and fear are similar throughout the world. Ekman (2006) sought to establish the existence of these basic responses and to compare their similarities across cultures. Ekman (2006) concluded that there were consistent responses to specific emotions across cultures, but that differences in the interpretation of these might well exist between different cultures.

Gestures – deliberate movements and signals are an important way to communicate meaning without words. Common gestures include waving, pointing, and using fingers to indicate numerical amounts. Other gestures are arbitrary and related to culture. In sport, gestures are used at a general level (e.g. pointing) and to communicate specific information (e.g. in baseball, to the pitcher, for example).

Body language and posture – posture and movement can also convey a great deal of information. Research on body language has grown significantly since the 1970s, but popular media have focused on the overinterpretation of defensive postures, arm crossing, and leg crossing. While these non-verbal behaviours can indicate feelings and attitudes, research suggests that body language is far subtler and less definitive than previously believed. In tennis the body language and posture of a player is continually analysed subconsciously by the opponent. When messages suggest that a player is struggling, this has a facilitative impact upon the other player's mentality. It can also lead to a change in strategy or tactical approach.

Proximity – people often refer to their need for 'personal space', which is also an important type of non-verbal communication. The amount of distance we need and the amount of space we perceive as belonging to us varies and is influenced by a number of factors including social norms, situational factors, personality characteristics, and level of familiarity with the other people present. For example, the amount of personal space needed when having a casual conversation with another person usually varies between 18 inches and four feet. On the other hand, the personal distance needed when speaking to a crowd of people is around ten to 12 feet. A coach wishing to make a player feel uncomfortable can step into their personal space to achieve this effect.

Eye contact – looking, staring, and blinking can also be important non-verbal behaviours. When people encounter people or things that they like, the rate of blinking increases and pupils dilate. Looking at another person can indicate a range of emotions, including hostility, solidarity, concern, interest, attraction, and intimidation. When talking to the team the coach needs to continually make eye contact with the whole team. Fixation on a small number of players can be divisive.

Haptics – communicating through touch is another important non-verbal behaviour. The notion of 'putting your arm around someone' comes from this approach. Also, team members can congratulate each other or share positive emotions through touch (such as high fives, and touching fists).

Appearance – our choices of colour, clothing, hairstyles, and other factors affecting appearance are also considered a means of non-verbal communication. Research on colour psychology has demonstrated that different colours can invoke different moods. Appearance can also alter physiological reactions, judgement, and interpretations. Knowing this, the message that your appearance communicates to others (supporters, opposition) is very important. Individuals who attempt to communicate their individuality and difference from the group will often achieve this by individualizing their appearance.

Team communication

Hanin (1992) conceptualized team communication with a focus on task-orientated messages. In this conceptualization Hanin distinguished three different types of messages that occur within team settings: orientating messages, stimulating messages, and evaluating messages. Hanin defined these three different types of messages based on team performance. Orientating messages were seen as messages of encouragement that usually occurred prior to team performance. Stimulating messages were suggested to be motivating messages that were communicated during competition. Evaluating messages were characterized as strategic diagnoses that generally took place after team performance. Any messages that did not fit into these three types of messages were deemed to be task-irrelevant. Whilst this is intuitively appealing regarding the communication that takes place in teams, relevant research-driven theoretical models have not yet supported this categorization.

Communication networks and structures

Communication networks and structures seek to define and explain the ways in which we seek to, and are forced to, communicate with others. The basic structures could potentially be centralized or decentralized, formal or informal, and vertical or lateral.

In centralized networks, communication between individuals is supported by a centralized component. This centralized component is then accessible by all of the individuals. The central component guides and determines communication (see Figure 5.3). In a team this central facilitator might be the coach or manager.

Decentralized communication networks emphasize communication between individuals. There is no central component coordinating and 'managing' the communication (see Figure 5.3).

It has been reported in organizational psychology that groups with decentralized communication structures are usually better at solving complex problems. Simple problems can be solved quicker in centralized structures (Shaw *et al.*, 2005). However, centralized structures often result in lower group member satisfaction and enjoyment.

We can also differentiate between formal and informal communication. Formal communication, as the name suggests, takes place through formal communication channels within the team, generally along lines of authority. Informal communication, again as the name suggests, is less formal and refers to communication that takes place outside the formal structures in the team and which is often built around social relationships.

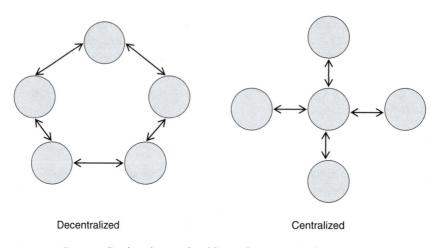

Decentralized   Centralized

FIGURE 5.3 Decentralized and centralized lines of communication

Differences have been reported in the level of effectiveness of both formal and informal communication channels. Johnson *et al.* (1994) in their exploration of communication channels concluded that informal channels of communication were far more effective than formal communication channels. Informal communication has been further shown to be important in ensuring effective performance outcomes in teams (Baker, 2002).

Finally, communication structures can be classified as being either vertical or lateral. Vertical communication occurs between hierarchically (above or below) positioned individuals and can involve both downward (top-down) and upward (bottom-up) communication flows (Baker, 2002). In groups and teams top-down communication is generally more prevalent than upward communication. Research suggests that the closer the individual is to the source of the message, the greater their overall satisfaction and performance level. Therefore, in sports teams the coach or manager communicating directly to the players is crucial. It is also important to ensure that a structure is in place to allow bottom-up communication. Lateral communication occurs between individuals at the same hierarchical level. In an organizational sense this could well occur between different departments. In a sporting context this would take place between players, or members of the support staff. Lateral communication is crucial to ensuring optimal task performance and integration of individual contributions.

Core communication skills

Harge (2006) highlighted eight core communication skills that are crucial to communicating effectively. These include: questioning, reinforcement, reflecting, explaining, listening, humour and laughter, and persuasion.

- *Questioning* – the basic function of a question is to elicit a response from those to whom the question is addressed (Hawkins and Power, 1999). Specifically, questions serve a range of functions including obtaining information, giving information, maintaining control in an encounter, arousing interest/curiosity, and initiating conversation (Harge and Dickson, 2004). There are a number of different types of questions which include open or closed questions, leading questions, recall/process questions, probing questions, and rhetorical questions.

- *Reinforcement* – this involves a stimulus (praise, rewards) that, when linked to a particular response, would most likely lead to that response being repeated. Reinforcement generally implies some changes and learning in a behavioural sense. Reinforcement might be verbal (offering praise) or non-verbal (raising of eyebrows, or clapping). A combination of these two approaches to reinforcement is particularly effective.
- *Reflecting* – in a communication sense, this is closely associated with active listening. The degree to which you can reflect the meaning of the communication (show empathy) highlights the degree to which you understand the message being transmitted. Central to this is to 'reflect' words or phrases that the other person is using. You can also reflect feelings and paraphrase the message that has been received.
- *Explaining* – the primary function of giving an explanation is to develop the understanding of others. By doing this you can also ensure learning takes place, clarify ambiguity, help others to learn procedures, reduce anxiety, change attitudes and behaviour, enhance personal autonomy, and improve your own understanding (Brown, 2006). There are three specific types of explaining: interpretative, descriptive, and reason giving. Interpretative explanations address the question, 'What?' These explanations seek to clarify an issue or specify the central meaning of a term or statement. Descriptive explanations address the question, 'How?' describing processes, structures, and procedures. Reason-giving explanations address the question, 'Why?' They involve reasons based on principles or generalizations, motives, obligations, or values.
- *Listening* – in a communication sense listening is the ability to perceive and process information presented orally. The listener must take care to attend to the speaker fully, and then repeat, in the listener's own words. A common error in conversations focuses on parties not listening fully. Instead, many people take the opportunity when they are not speaking to plan their next speech episode. In such cases important information can be missed.
- *Humour and laughter* – humour in one sense is a very complex phenomenon involving cognitive, emotional, physiological, and social aspects (Martin, 2004). Everyday conversation thrives on wordplay, sarcasm, anecdotes, and jokes (Norrick, 1993). These help to break the ice, fill uncomfortable pauses, negotiate requests for favours, and build group solidarity. Humour, above all else, is a shared experience. Indeed, in a group situation there are few more useful social skills than humour. In particular, humour might be used to achieve the following: searching for information, giving information, exerting interpersonal control, controlling a group, and managing anxiety. Laughter, while often linked to humour, is not necessarily linked explicitly. Indeed, different types of laughter serve different functions, including: humorous laughter, social laughter, ignorance laughter, evasion laughter, apologetic laughter, anxious laughter, derisory laughter, and joyous laughter (Foot and McGreaddie, 2006).

- *Persuasion* – skilled persuaders are experts in adapting their message to those groups that they seek to influence. This adaptation is achieved by, first, identifying current obstacles to agreement or compliance, these obstacles being in essence the basis for the individuals' resistance; and, second, constructing effective messages to remove or minimize those obstacles that are underpinning the individual's resistance.

Communication from the coach

The ability to communicate effectively is central to the role of the coach and the manager.

Communication in teams is strongly affected by the type of leader (coach or manager) who is in the position of authority (Athanasios, 2005). As a result, communication has been highlighted as the key vehicle for effective coaching (Vealey, 2005). The crucial foundation for effective communication for the coach is their credibility and the degree of trust and mutual respect that exists (Yukelson, 2006). The players' perceptions of the trustworthiness of what the coach says are crucial to his or her credibility. Trust is specifically linked to the related concepts of honesty, integrity, sincerity, and truthfulness. Research also suggests that players will be more motivated by a coach for whom they have a lot of respect (Lynch, 2001). Coaches who are good communicators are good at explaining, clarifying, and individualizing instructions to meet the needs of the individual player. Depree (1989) highlighted the importance of team synergy and/or team chemistry to the effectiveness/performance of the team. Depree suggested that team synergy emerged from the leaders (possibly coaches, managers, and captains) sharing their vision of what the team could be and could achieve. Yukelson (2006) suggested five communication principles to help this sharing process between the coach and the players and to achieve 'buy-in' from the team: impart, inspire, monitor, clarify, and reinforce.

- *Impart* – clarify the team's mission, rules, expectations, and goals. Also outline strategies and plans to achieve these outcomes (involving the team in the decision-making process). To be effective the coach needs to share information with the team.
- *Inspire* – instil a desire to be the best. Communicate with a sense of inspired enthusiasm. Be honest, direct, and sincere. Try and instil a sense of pride, passion, belief, and team spirit. It is important to make everyone feel valued and important.
- *Monitor* – specifically monitor progress, particularly related to the team goals and required actions. Give feedback to both the team as a whole and to individual athletes.
- *Clarify* – the current position. Talk openly about what is required to achieve the team's goals. Challenge all individuals to take responsibility for their own actions and continued effort and focus.
- *Reinforce* – in particular reinforce behaviours and attitudes that you want to be repeated. Provide a lot of support and encouragement and positive reinforcement.

Team member communication

Individual team members need to develop and maintain harmonious working relationships with their fellow teammates for the team to 'work' (Yukelson, 2006). Ideally this would involve genuine regard both within and outside the sporting context. However, it is also important to recognize that sports teams, through experiencing many shared events, become similar to families. In this respect there will be a degree of tension, frustration, and conflict. Team members learning how to communicate effectively is an important first step in the process of resolving these issues. Lausic *et al.* (2009) demonstrated a link between differences in communication and teams that ultimately either won or lost matches. In their study of doubles teams in tennis Lausic and colleagues reported that winning teams exchanged messages more frequently than losing teams. This supports the findings of both Orasanu (1990) and Mosier and Chidester (1991) in non-sports teams regarding the communication habits of effective teams.

Players communicate in a number of specific settings including training, before competition, in competition, after competition, and socially. However, communication during performance can become problematic due to the requirements of a number of concurrent task demands (Eccles and Tenenbaum, 2004). Planning for this performance environment is crucial. Sullivan (1993) summarized that effective communication is apparent when team members listen to one another and attempt to build on each other's contributions. Orlick (2000) and Yukelson (2006) suggested a number of strategies to enhance communication between team members.

1 Make sure everyone is pulling in the same direction (wants to achieve the same things). Make sure the team is aware of, and agrees with, the team's goals.
2 Openly discuss strategies to enhance team harmony, and for team members to support each other better both inside and outside the sporting environment. A good time to implement this is as part of the planning process in the pre-season period.
3 Listen to what other people have to say (they are then more likely to listen to you). Actually listen to, process, and discuss other options and views.
4 Learn how to give and receive feedback constructively. This is a skill that can be learnt and improved.
5 Learn how to tolerate each other better (accepting each individual for who they are). Players need the opportunity to resolve issues and differences.
6 Avoid backstabbing and gossiping about other teammates. This leads to a divided dressing room, confrontation, a negative environment, and a decrease in effort.
7 Keep confrontation private. Deal with issues directly with the other person. Once issues are public, individuals feel they need to 'act' a role as well as resolve the issue.
8 Recognize that not all conflicts can be resolved, but can be managed. You could have two players in the team who don't get on, but want to achieve the same thing, so in performance and training environments they put their differences aside.

Communication in teams can also be enhanced by developing each player's understanding of the two crucial components to team communication: good listening skills and good group communication skills. Stevens (2002) suggested that, to be effective listeners, athletes need to be able to maintain eye contact, ask clarifying questions, understand (not argue), check to make sure everyone has a chance to speak, paraphrase to ensure understanding, respect other speakers' views, maintain an open and relaxed posture, only offer advice if it is wanted, and use congruent verbal and non-verbal messages. Stevens (2002) also highlighted a number of crucial components to effective group communication. These include: respecting the thoughts, feelings, and experiences of others; using first-person singular pronouns ('I' or 'my'); not judging; not feeling you have to speak; not discounting others' thoughts; not monopolizing conversation; not trying to change someone's mind; and respecting silence.

Modes of communication

With the rapid advance in communication technologies in recent years there are now many different communication options available to coaches, players, and teams. However, it is important to recognize that optimal communication is generally face to face and verbal. This form of communication allows the greatest degree of clarity and reduces the potential for misunderstanding. Historically, the other main mode of communication was via written forms (such as letters). In order to try and make this mode of communication more effective a specific 'set of rules' were developed to punctuate the written word to enhance the clarity of the message. The use of the telephone and mobile phones is now widespread in society as an effective communication tool. The advantage of this mode of communication is that it is still verbal, and as such involves all the relevant speech and paralanguage. The downside is the lack of visual non-verbal communication to help the interpretation of the message. More recent electronic forms of communication such as e-mail and text (SMS) can also be problematic in communicating the full meaning of the messages. Trying to convey the relevant interpretation of the words is difficult in these forms of communication. As a result, messages can be misinterpreted. Texting (communicating via text) suffers the added pressure of having a limited number of characters (letters). As a result, messages have to be deliberately brief and to the point. For both of these forms of electronic communication there is the added dimension that original messages can be forwarded and viewed by third parties. This can significantly impact upon the breadth of impact of the messages (good or bad).

With both SMS texts and e-mail a range of symbols have been developed to further enhance the clarity of the message. In e-mails, smiley faces have evolved to be used to convey added meaning to the message. With SMS texts an innovative system of symbols using the standard keyboard has developed. This includes the use of a colon and bracket ':)' to represent a smiley face, and the use of a semi-colon and bracket to represent a smiley face winking ';)'. For SMS text messages, abbreviations have also developed to add further context to the message. Examples include LOL (laugh out loud), and IDK (I don't know).

Finally, the development of social networking modes of communication such as Facebook and Twitter can cause further communication problems for sports teams.

Status updates and tweets are instantly accessible to wide audiences. If the wrong message is communicated, it is very difficult to rectify. For example, Chris Johnson, the all-star running back for the Tennessee Titans, did not endear himself to the Titans fans when negotiating his contract in 2011. Some sections of the fans were critical of Johnson in holding out for more money and not practising with the team following the contract lockout. In response, Johnson tweeted: 'Can all these false Titans fans STFU on my timeline I don't have a regular job so don't compare me to you and I can care less if uthink I'm greedy.' Johnson followed this message up by tweeting: 'If you was a real fan my tweet would not bother you it only make the fake fans upset.' Neither of these tweets served to defuse the situation, and they further intensified the negative responses from the Titans fans towards Johnson.

Common communication errors

According to a number of researchers (Athanasios, 2005; Daft, 2000; Laios, 1999), the main errors that occur in the communication process between the coach and their team relate to time limits, language, perception, attitude, and external factors.

- *Time limits* – refers to the available time during performance that the coach has to communicate in such a way that the players understand the message. Half-time in a game of soccer is 15 minutes; by the time the players are in the changing room this is realistically a maximum of 10 minutes. Timeouts in basketball are one minute in duration, which further reduces the time available to the coach. As a result, messages need to be short and sharp to have impact and to be effectively delivered.
- *Language* – difficulties may arise because a team could be composed of multiple nationalities, or even athletes from different social and cultural groups who use a different language to communicate. Most professional teams are multinational; the communication language then needs to be basic to get the message across. Often teams will require new players to learn the relevant language for effective communication in the team.
- *Perception* – do the athletes interpret the message in the correct way? Do they extract from the message the meaning that the coach intended? You need to understand how to convey the right meaning to the message, and to ensure the players interpret the message correctly.
- *Attitude* – research by Olson and Zanna (1993) has reported that a player's attitude (degree of negativity) impacts upon their perception of the message. When a player is feeling down, criticism will tend to be interpreted more negatively. When a player is positive, it will be interpreted differently.
- *External factors* – these factors include the opposition, officials, spectators, and general noise levels. These external factors can work on two levels. First, the presence of these groups generates noise that can interfere with communication. Second, these external groups could well be trying to communicate to the team as well, sending competing, and often conflicting, messages.

Other common communication errors include not having a communication strategy, 'shooting from the hip', assigning blame, allowing rumours to exist, using the wrong communication tools, assuming everyone gets the message, thinking communication is a one-way process, and overcommunicating. All these factors have also been highlighted as recurring communication errors (Tharrett and Peterson, 2008).

If a coach, captain, or individual does not understand the individual members in the team, there is potential for any communication to go wrong. Understanding the team's language, preferred communication channels, and preferred formats is crucial.

Improving communication

Sullivan (1993) in her study of communication skills in interactive sports concluded that communication skills development programmes could be very effective in team sports. Mullin (2009) highlighted three approaches to improve a team's ability to communicate in a game. These were first to develop an agreed-upon language, understood by all the players. The second approach was to use the new language in practice. This would ensure maximum transfer to the competition environment. The final approach involved the development of a 'general' to relay a single coherent message to the team.

Mullin (2009) further highlighted the importance of developing drills in practice that integrate this communication approach into practice. Similar to other skills relating to performance, practice is crucial. Athanasios (2005) further suggested a number of specific strategies for the coach to enhance communication within the team. These included:

- communicating with clear, short messages during stressful or pressured periods;
- developing strategies for players to cope with external factors such as noise and the opposition;
- always projecting a positive attitude to players;
- providing detailed, relevant, and honest information to players when the situation allows;
- listening carefully to the players; and
- being aware of (and seeking to improve) non-verbal communication.

The first step in learning to communicate more effectively is increased self-awareness. Understanding how you communicate, how flexible your communication style is, and your ability to individualize communication according to both the individual and the situation is a crucial starting point.

It is also possible to seek to quantify communication in sports teams. Sullivan and Feltz (2003) developed the Scale for Effective Communication in Team Sports (SECTS). The SECTS was developed following the guidelines highlighted by Poole and McPhee (1985) for creating a communication measure for groups. This inventory is a theoretically driven and validated measure designed to assess within-team communication in sports teams. The measure is further underpinned by Foa and Foa's (1974) social exchange theory, where communication was described as the interpersonal exchange of information towards some valued outcome, e.g. team performance. The

SECTS measures four factors of effective communication: acceptance, distinctiveness, positive conflict, and negative conflict. Distinctiveness is measured in the scale by three items, while four items in the scale represent acceptance, positive conflict, and negative conflict. Each item is scored on a seven-point likert scale ranging from 1 (hardly ever) to 7 (very frequently).

Communicating plays in American football

When it comes to communication during a game, no sport has embraced technology quite as well as American football. As a sport, American football is very much coach driven, with the team on the field executing the discrete plays that the coaching team have opted for. In this context communication between the coaches, and between the coach and quarterback, is crucial. Communication regarding what the opposition is doing is also highly important to this process. To this end, American football has realized that a bird's-eye view from high in the stadium is a critical part of the jigsaw. In order to facilitate the communication of this information to the head coach on the sidelines the use of increasingly sophisticated technology has been adopted. In excess of ten members of the coaching team might be wearing headsets during a game, communicating via a number of lines of communication. These often include two lines for the offensive assistants and two for the defensive assistants. One offensive line is for a coach with a bird's-eye view in the box calling down the play to someone else on the sidelines, who then relays the call directly to the quarterback, who has a small radio receiver embedded in their helmet. One of the defensive lines is called 'coverages', which is relayed through hand signals. The other two lines are usually reserved for private communication relating to offense or defence. The head coach will have the ability to tune into any of the conversations that are taking place within the team.

The coaches in the coaching box (with a bird's-eye view) are given responsibility for tracking and relaying the opposition formations, fronts, and tendencies based on downs and distances. In the coach-quarterback system, the timing of the information is crucial. The coach calling the plays needs to be one step ahead and focusing on the next play. Being ready is critical as this system automatically switches off at the 15-second mark of the 40-second play clock.

With this system the coaches need to remain focused, and only speak when it is their turn to be heard. This system can, however, become stressful if the head coach has a short fuse. An example of this would be Jon Gruden, the head coach of the Tampa Bay Buccaneers from 2002 to 2009, who freely admits that he is tough on his coaching team over the radio. Gruden has openly admitted that he will call his coaches every name under the sun if he is not getting the right information delivered to him at the right time. In his open words, Gruden has described himself as 'brutal' and 'horrible', but it appears to have the desired effect in enhancing the quality and specificity of the information he receives from his coaching team.

Summary

Understanding that communication is central to effective team operation and can be enhanced is crucial for the coach. Through understanding the mechanisms involved in communication at both interpersonal and group levels communication within the team can be developed. In particular, understanding the factors that influence the interpretation of messages and the continuous nature of non-verbal communication is central to effective team functioning.

Interventions can be applied at individual, small group, or team level to further enhance the effectiveness and efficacy of communication approaches within the team. As a result, the team can achieve a double benefit. First, that communication within your team is far more effective and results in enhanced performance. Second, that the team is more coherent in its operation and the leader can also exert greater control over what information is communicated to external groups and, in particular, the opposition.

6

COHESION IN SPORT

Introduction

The relationships between the individuals in a team are crucial to the overall success of that team. Successful teams throughout history have been characterized by their ability to gel and perform as a group. Many coaches have an understanding of what that elusive quality is, but are less clear on how to enhance it. Cohesion refers to the set of factors that create a close-knit, well-performing team. Historically cohesion has been identified as the most important small-group variable (Loughead and Hardy, 2006). As a result, unlocking the secrets of cohesion can help to foster more effective and successful teams. A fundamental factor in the study of team cohesion is an understanding of group dynamics (Cox, 2002). Understanding both the group and the individual is crucial to understanding cohesion. It is also important to acknowledge the fact that players in the team come and go. This process in turn continually changes the make-up and quality of a team (Matheson *et al.*, 1997). As a result, this process of team building to enhance cohesion must be seen as a continuous process.

This chapter will seek to explore what cohesion is and how it can impact upon team functioning and team performance. The following sections will explore the evidence base for cohesion and the different factors that both influence and determine its development. Finally, this chapter will explore techniques and strategies that can be applied to enhance levels of cohesion and performance in a team setting.

What is cohesion?

Cartwright (1968) in his book chapter on group cohesion highlighted a number of factors that are usually present in normally functioning teams. These include: working harder, appearing happier, making sacrifices, and having higher levels of interaction. Cartwright described the presence of these characteristics as 'we-ness' because in these normally functioning teams individuals were far more likely to refer to 'we', rather than 'I', when referring to the team and their individual contribution to it. Other authors have coined the term cohesion to describe this phenomenon.

As with other areas of psychology, a number of differing definitions have been suggested for the concept of interest. One of the most readily adopted definitions for cohesion in sport is the one suggested by Carron *et al.* (1998). Carron and colleagues suggested that cohesion is 'a dynamic process that is reflected in the tendency of a group to stick together and remain united in the pursuit of its instrumental objectives and/or for the satisfaction of member affective needs' (p.213). This definition highlights four important characteristics of interest in understanding cohesion: the degree of multidimensionality, the dynamical nature, the instrumental nature, and the affective dimension. Cohesion is referred to as being multidimensional because there are many factors that can cause a group to stick together. It is also dynamic as it is continually changing over time. Teams become more or less cohesive as time goes by. All teams have a main reason or driver for forming. This is referred to as their instrumental reason for forming (either task related or socially related). The final dimension of cohesion highlighted by Carron *et al.* (1998) is its affective nature. As a group bonds, a number of positive feelings emerge, such as enjoyment and satisfaction (Baumeister and Leary, 1995).

Donnelly *et al.* (1978) emphasized the fundamental nature of cohesion in groups by suggesting that there could be no such thing as a non-cohesive group, highlighting that it is a contradiction of terms. If a group exists, then it must to some degree be cohesive. As a result it is not whether cohesion is present that is of interest but more to what degree it is present and how it is changing over time.

A number of research studies have shown that higher perceptions of group cohesion are associated with greater interpersonal interaction and communication among team members, along with more trust, self-disclosure, and acceptance (Jacob and Carron, 1998). Focusing on the group perspective, greater cohesion has also been associated with the enhanced stability of the group as a whole, greater overall group success, higher levels of collective efficacy, and more coordination and effectiveness in achieving group goals (Jacob and Carron, 1998).

Types of cohesion

Two specific forms of cohesion are highlighted in the literature and are characterized as either being task or socially focused. Task and social cohesion are seen as independent components of team cohesion (Cox, 2002). Task cohesion has been defined as 'the degree to which members of a team work together to achieve a specific and identifiable goal' (Cox, 2002: p.330), whereas social cohesion is defined as 'the degree to which the members of a team like each other and enjoy satisfaction from being members of the team' (Cox, 2002: p.330). Specific antecedents have been identified for social cohesion. These include the degree of social networks that exist among team members and the pattern, strength, and number of interpersonal ties that exist between team members (Friedkin, 2004). Individual-level indicators of social cohesion include two main factors: individual membership attitudes, and individual membership behaviours. Individual membership attitudes refer to the desire or intention of the individual to remain in the team, identification with or loyalty to the team, and other attitudes about the team, or its members. Individual membership behaviours refer to decisions to sever, weaken, maintain, or strengthen memberships or participation in the team, susceptibilities to interpersonal influence, and other behavioural indicators of commitment and attachment to the team.

A negative relationship exists between jealousy and cohesion. Jealousy has been shown to have a strong effect on the interpersonal relationships within a team (Kamphoff *et al.*, 2005). A specific reason for this was suggested by Bers and Rodin (1984), who highlighted that when others are jealous they might degrade the other person. This in turn could affect the team, and crucially, how well team members work together.

A framework of cohesion in sport

Carron, Brawley and Widmeyer (2002) developed a framework that attempted to demonstrate the nature of cohesion. In this framework Carron *et al.* (2002) distinguished between both individual and group-based perceptions of both task and social cohesion. These perceptions, in turn, could be further subdivided into either group integration, or individual attractions to the group, with either a task orientation or a social orientation. In this context group integration refers to the individual's perceptions about the closeness, similarity, and bonding within the group. Individual attractions to the group refer to individual perceptions about individual motivations acting to attract and to retain the individual in the group. Task orientation is a general orientation towards achieving the group's objectives. Social orientation is a general orientation towards developing and maintaining social relationships and activities. The identification of these two perceptions in turn led to the development of four dimensions to account for the majority of the variance in the cohesiveness of a team. These four dimensions are: individual attractions to the group – task, individual attractions to the group – social, group integration – task, and group integration – social (see Figure 6.1).

Four sets of factors have been highlighted that impact upon cohesion (Carron *et al.*, 1985). Specifically these include environmental factors, personal factors, leadership factors, and team factors (see Figure 6.2).

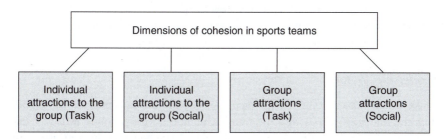

FIGURE 6.1 Dimensions of cohesion in sport (Carron *et al.*, 2002)

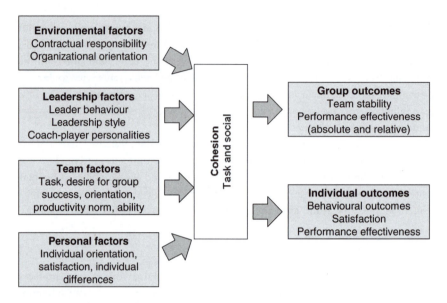

FIGURE 6.2 Predictors and outcomes of cohesion in team sports (adapted from Carron, 1985)

Environmental factors

A number of environmental factors have been reported to impact upon cohesion, including the size of the group (Carron and Spink, 1995) and the level of competition (Granito and Rainey, 1988).

It has been suggested that, as a group increases in size, it becomes far more difficult for the group to operate effectively and communicate effectively. Cohesion has also been shown to decrease as the level of competition increases (Gruber and Gray, 1982).

Personal factors

Personal factors refer to the characteristics of the individual team members. Carron and Hausenblas (1998) classified these personal factors into three specific categories: (i) demographic attributes, (ii) cognitions and motives, and (iii) behaviour. Carron and Dennis (2001) suggested that the most important personal factor regarding the development of both task and social cohesion in sports teams is individual satisfaction. Further supporting this, Widmeyer and Williams (1991) reported that member satisfaction was the best predictor of both social and task cohesion in golf.

Leadership factors

These include the leadership style adopted, the behaviours engaged in, and the relationships the leader establishes with the team. A number of research studies have highlighted the importance of the leader in influencing team cohesion. In particular, clear and unambiguous communication from coaches and captains regarding team goals, team tasks, and team members' roles has been shown to significantly influence cohesion (Brawley *et al.*, 1993). The compatibility between the leader and the team is also important. Ideally the leadership style adopted by the leader will be the same as the preferred leadership style for the team, and as that demanded by the situation (Chelladurai, 1990).

Team factors

These factors refer to group characteristics including team productivity norms, the desire for team success, team roles, team position, and team stability. Shared experiences are important in developing and maintaining cohesion. This is as a result of increased unity through developing greater common links with teammates. Collective efficacy has also been related to perceptions of team cohesion (Carron and Dennis, 2001).

Cohesion and different types of teams

Different sports require different levels of interaction or interdependence among players to be successful. The general concept of sports interdependence is divided into two categories: co-active or interactive (Murray, 2006). Sports that require little interaction among team members for success exemplify co-active teams. Sports that have a high need for interdependence are considered to be interactive in nature. Both of these distinctions exist along a continuum. Sports that require greater cooperation, such as basketball or rugby, will require greater task cohesion. Sports that are less interdependent, such as cricket or baseball, require less task cohesion for success. As a result, the amount of task cohesion should increase as the degree of interdependence increases. So, the more players rely on each other for success, the greater the task cohesion will need to be. The implications for the coach are important: the greater the degree of interactivity in the sport, the more attention should be paid to cohesion within that team.

Co-acting teams exhibit lower levels of cohesion than interacting teams (Carron and Chelladurai, 1981). One of the reasons for this is that intergroup rivalry and interteam competition exists in co-acting teams (Matheson *et al.*, 1997). In sports such as cricket and baseball there is a degree of competition between players on the team as well as between teams.

The link between cohesion and performance

One of the most interesting aspects of cohesion to the psychologist and sports coach alike is the link between levels of cohesion and performance. It has been suggested in multiple publications that this link exists, but does the empirical evidence back this up?

Mullen and Copper (1994) conducted a meta-analysis of 49 research studies from a range of sub-disciplines of psychology (business, sport, military, and social) and concluded that a relationship existed between performance and cohesion. Mullen and Copper also suggested that the relationship between cohesion and team success is positive. The authors also reported that real teams exhibited stronger effects than artificial teams, and sports teams exhibited even stronger effects than non-sport real groups. Finally, Mullen and Copper (1994) reported that the strongest relationship between cohesion and group success is present in sports teams, followed by military teams, and then finally non-military groups. Carron et al. (2002) provided further evidence of a strong relationship between cohesion and success in sports teams. One of the reasons Carron et al. (2002) suggested for the differences between their analysis and Mullen and Copper's (1994) findings could be the operational definitions of cohesion that were used. Carron et al. (2002) focused on task cohesion only, whereas Mullen and Copper used both task and social cohesion as the basis for their meta-analysis.

However, the issue of causality between cohesion and performance does not yet appear to be resolved. Does enhanced team cohesion lead to enhanced performance, or does enhanced performance lead to enhanced cohesion? Cox (2002), in answer to this dilemma, suggested that it was a degree of both. So, while enhanced cohesion does lead to greater levels of performance, there is a knock-on effect that the increased levels of performance also then lead to enhanced levels of cohesion. Turman (2003) further reinforced the notion that team performance and/or success can have a dramatic effect on the levels of cohesion. Results from the Group Environment Questionnaire suggest that the strongest relationship appears to exist between group estimates of task cohesion and group-related constructs such as team success (Carron et al., 2002). Indeed, Carron et al. (2002) supported Mullen and Copper's (1994: p.224) view that:

> The cohesiveness-performance effect does not seem to be a rare and delicate 'hothouse' variety phenomenon restricted to the controlled confines of the research laboratory. Rather, the cohesiveness-performance effect is even more robust in the real world among real groups.

Cohesion and mood

Baumeister and Leary (1995) suggested that at a fundamental level groups provide a forum for satisfying a fundamental human drive, the need to belong. The authors further clarified that this was not just the need for affiliation. Numerous or repetitive contacts with non-supportive or indifferent others do little for the individual's general well-being and fail to satisfy the need to belong. As a result, Baumeister and Leary (1995) identified that the degree to which the individual holds a perception of group cohesion is a good indicator of feelings of belonging. There is also support for the hypothesis that player perceptions of team cohesion are associated with positive affect. This was further supported by Courneya (1995), who reported that perceptions of group cohesion were associated with positive feelings towards structured exercise classes.

Terry et al. (2000) in their study exploring perceptions of group cohesion and mood in team sports reported that across different sport types (rugby, rowing, netball) the cohesion–mood relationship remained consistent. Higher levels of perceived cohesion were associated with higher vigour and lower depression, anger, and tension. Terry and colleagues' findings supported those of Prapavessis and Carron (1996) in reporting that players who perceived more deficits in task-related conditions were more likely to feel tense and angry.

Links have also been suggested between anxiety and cohesion. Cogan and Petrie (1995) reported that a programme designed to enhance social cohesion also had the knock-on effect of reducing somatic and cognitive anxiety in gymnasts. This was further supported by Prapavessis and Carron (1996) who reported that athletes possessing higher perceptions of task cohesiveness in the team they belonged to also reported lower levels of cognitive anxiety.

Measuring cohesion

A number of different tools have been developed in an attempt to measure cohesion. Five in particular have been developed and applied in a sporting context. These include the following:

- Sports Cohesiveness Questionnaire (SCQ; Martens and Peterson, 1971)
- Team Cohesion Questionnaire (TCQ; Gruber and Gray, 1982)
- Multidimensional Sport Cohesion Instrument (SCI; Yukelson et al., 1984)
- Group Environment Questionnaire (GEQ; Widmeyer et al., 1985)
- Team Psychology Questionnaire (TPQ; Partington and Shangi, 1992)

Of these five developed tools, the GEQ has been by far the most widely used and applied.

The Sports Cohesiveness Questionnaire developed by Martens and Peterson (1971) is a psychometrically undeveloped measure of cohesion (Carron et al., 2002), which had been used prior to the development of the GEQ by a number of authors (Carron and Ball, 1978; Landers et al., 1982; Williams and Hacker, 1982) to explore the relationship between composite team cohesion and team success. The SCQ contains seven items that measure group cohesion by assessing inter-individual relationships, individual influences, amusement or pleasure, teamwork, familiarity among team members, and team membership.

The Team Cohesion Questionnaire developed by Gruber and Gray (1981) consists of 13 items used often in research that focuses on cohesion. These 13 items relate to six factors called team-performance satisfaction, self-performance satisfaction, task cohesion, affiliation cohesion, desire for recognition, and value of membership. Responses to each item are scored on a nine-point likert scale. However, there is very little evidence of the psychometric underpinning of this inventory (Moran, 2004).

The Multidimensional Sport Cohesion Instrument suggested by Yukelson et al. (1984) also attempted to differentiate the specific components of team cohesion. The MSCI consists of 22 items, with participants scoring themselves on factors including attraction to the group, unity of purpose, quality of teamwork, and values roles. However, it was not based on a strong theoretical foundation, and was also not proven to be valid (Carron et al., 1998).

Carron *et al.* (1985) developed the Group Environment Questionnaire (GEQ) as an effective theoretically driven tool to measure cohesion in sport. The GEQ is an 18-item inventory that assesses four dimensions of cohesion; each item is measured on a nine-point likert scale that is anchored at the extremes by 1 (strongly disagree) and 9 (strongly agree). Out of the 18 items, 12 need to be reverse scored: the higher the score, the higher the perception of cohesiveness. As the GEQ is based on the conceptual framework for the study of cohesion in sport (Carron *et al.*, 1985), it scores items on the same four dimensions highlighted in the framework: individual attractions to the group – task (ATG-T), individual attractions to the group – social (ATG-S), group integration – task (GI-T), and group integration – social (GI-S).

A number of studies have explored the psychometric properties of the GEQ and have demonstrated good internal consistency, reliability, and validity (Loughead and Hardy, 2006). Slater and Sewell (1994) suggested that the GEQ holds great potential for further enhancing our understanding of team cohesion. A number of authors have also used the GEQ as an operational definition of cohesion (Carron *et al.*, 2002).

Finally, the Team Psychology Questionnaire devised by Partington and Shangi (1992) was developed to understand team effectiveness from a multidimensional perspective. The inventory is composed of 53 items that relate to seven specific dimensions: player ability and talent, coach-technical, coach-interpersonal, task integration, social cohesion, team identity, and style of team play. Each item is scored on a ten-point likert scale ranging from 0 (not at all like my team) to 10 (exactly like my team).

Coach impacts on cohesion

There is some evidence that team cohesion is related to coaching behaviour (Murray, 2006). A connection between coaching and cohesion has been described by a number of researchers (Gardner *et al.*, 1996; Spink and Carron, 1994; Westre and Weiss, 1991; Widmeyer *et al.*, 1993). As a result, Gardner *et al.* (1996) highlighted the importance of studying the relationship between leader behaviour, cohesion, and performance. Research by both Westre and Weiss (1991), and Pease and Kozub (1994) reported that the leader behaviours, training and instruction, democratic style, social support, and positive feedback, were all positively related to cohesion.

Interestingly, the point at which techniques or strategies are used to enhance cohesion appears to be important. Turman (2003), in exploring the impact of coaching techniques on team cohesion, reported some interesting findings. Sarcasm, teasing, embarrassment, ridicule, inequity, and bragging up other players were all described as being demotivating. However, later on in the same study, bragging, sarcasm, and teasing were also suggested by the same players as ways to enhance team cohesion. The crucial factor highlighted by Turman as moderating this effect was the importance of interpersonal relationships. The better the team members know each other, the more likely that sarcasm, teasing, and bragging would be seen as 'normal' team banter and as a result would not be isolating in their effect. Most recent attempts to connect cohesion with coaching/leadership have focused on one of the five leadership styles highlighted in the Multidimensional Model of Leadership (autocratic, social support, democratic, training and instruction, and positive feedback). Gardner *et al.* (1996) reported that coaches could promote higher levels of task cohesion for their players by using training and instruction, democratic behaviour, social support, and positive feedback styles and avoiding the use of autocratic coaching strategies.

Cultural differences in coaches' approach to enhancing cohesion

In their study exploring the development of team cohesion Ryska *et al.* (1999) compared the approaches adopted by coaches in both Australia and the United States of America. Ryska *et al.* (1999) concluded that Australian coaches made more frequent use of behaviours such as accepting individual differences among players and helping to satisfy individual players' needs within the team context, and as a result gained a greater understanding of each athlete as an individual. The US coaches in contrast placed greater emphasis on team ownership in each athlete, an increased awareness of each athlete's duties to the team, and developing cooperative team training. The US coaches appeared to make more frequent use of role development strategies that appear to target the task-related cohesion of the team, whereas the Australian coaches fostered the social cohesion of their teams through player integration strategies (Ryska *et al.*, 1999). However, across the different cultures the coaches did not significantly differ in their use of player integration when interactive sports were considered.

Enhancing cohesion

The process of developing or enhancing cohesion can be accomplished through the process known as team building. This process is often referred to as a method to 'promote an increased sense of unity and cohesiveness and enable the team to function together more smoothly and effectively' (Newman, 1984: p.27).

Widmeyer and Ducharme (1997) highlighted two specific processes as being at the core of team building: locomotion and maintenance. Locomotion is related to performance and/or productivity, whereas maintenance reflects a team's ability to stick together (be cohesive). Sports coaches naturally assume that a generic, positive approach to coaching maximizes team spirit, producing greater team success as a consequence (Kremer and Scully, 1994). A number of personal and situational factors have been shown to mediate how a coach influences his or her team.

Kremer and Scully further highlighted the following functions of team-building processes:

1 to increase the team's effectiveness;
2 to improve working conditions;
3 to satisfy the needs of the group members; and
4 to enhance cohesion.

In order to enhance team cohesion the four sets of factors highlighted as influencing cohesion (leadership, personal, environmental, and team) need to be considered.

In general, two types of team-building interventions have been distinguished in sports settings: direct and indirect (Carron and Hausenblas, 1998). In the direct approach the coach or psychologist works directly with the players in the team to foster a common sense of identity. In the indirect approach the psychologist instruct the coach in the skills of team building rather than working directly with the players (Moran, 2004). One specific difference between the two approaches is that the direct method actively includes team members in the team-building process, thus empowering the players, which then has the knock-on effect of developing ownership in the team-building programme. Carron and Spink (1993) developed a protocol and conceptual framework for an indirect approach to team building. This approach consists of four stages: introductory, conceptual, practice, and intervention.

1 *Introductory stage* – the rationale for the programme is outlined, and the potential benefits to enhanced cohesion are highlighted.
2 *Conceptual stage* – presents the coaches with a conceptual framework from which they can gain a greater understanding of the process of team building.
3 *Practice stage* – allows the coaches to brainstorm with the consultant to identify strategies that impact upon the highlighted team factors.
4 *Intervention stage* – the coach and their respective team implements the strategies/interventions that have been developed.

The main benefits to this approach are the reduced time demands/commitments of the consultant, reduction of geographical barriers, and delivery by someone who has acceptance from the team.

Yukelson (1997), in adopting a direct approach to team building, suggested four specific stages: assessment, education, brainstorming, and implementation. First, the assessment stage allows the consultant to develop an understanding of the teams' dynamics. Observation and discussion would form a strong part of this component. Second, in the education stage players are provided with information about how teams develop. Models of group development might be discussed as part of this stage. Third, brainstorming techniques are used to generate and prioritize current needs and then identify potential strategies. In the final (implementation) stage these needs are analysed to determine the goals of the team-building interventions. Yukelson further suggested a number of practical techniques for direct team building.

While both of these approaches appear to have merits if applied separately, for greatest success practitioners are encouraged to use elements of both approaches (Loughead and Hardy, 2006). Indeed Prapavessis *et al.* (1996) highlighted the absence of an assessment stage in the indirect approach to be a specific limitation. This notion is further supported by Yukelson (1997) who suggested that the assessment stage is 'the most important part of any good team building intervention' (p.86).

Pain and Harwood (2009) sought to develop team building through mutual sharing and open discussions focused on the way that the team that they were working with was functioning. The team, in this case, was a university soccer team in the UK. The intervention was a personal disclosure and mutual sharing approach that was first advocated by Yukelson (1997) and further supported by work by Holt and Dunn (2006). This personal disclosure and mutual sharing approach has been suggested to foster a greater appreciation of team members' values, beliefs, attitudes, and personal motives (Hirsch, 1993). This greater team member appreciation has also been shown to facilitate shared perceptions, shared meanings, shared constructs, and shared understanding (Ostroff et al., 2003). The self-disclosure approach has been demonstrated to be effective in enhancing empathy, developing social cohesion, and facilitating communication (Windsor et al., 2011). The approach adopted by Pain and Harwood (2009) had three main components: a systematic approach for all players and coaches to evaluate and be involved in the process; regular team meetings; and season-long involvement by the consultant. The study by Pain and Harwood highlighted improvements in cohesion, trust, confidence, and communication after the first meeting, and these were maintained throughout the intervention (the duration of the season). These outcomes further supported Yukelson's (1997) assertion that open and honest discussions are crucial to the team-building process. Holt and Dunn suggested a number of outcomes that could be used by sport psychologists to enhance the effectiveness of the intervention. First, that this approach is most effective with high performance adult teams. Second, that preparatory work should be undertaken with the team to become familiar with the team's culture. Third, that this personal disclosure and mutual sharing approach should be used prior to major or important performances (2006). Windsor et al. (2011), in concluding their study into personal disclosure and mutual sharing in professional soccer, highlighted the following recommendations for practice:

- The sport psychologist should seek to develop a rapport with team members, managers, and coaches.
- Ensure that both players and managers understand that anonymity in the process will be guaranteed.
- At all stages keep the manager informed and involved.
- Be selective in highlighting the right 'important match' before which the intervention will take place.
- Allow players the opportunity to think about the questions they will be asked beforehand.
- Allow all the players the opportunity to discuss and rehearse their input with the sport psychologist.
- Give the players the power to decide if coaches, managers, and support staff are present at the session.
- Be flexible regarding the timing and duration of the session.
- Expect some players to decline to participate, and others to be unable to participate.
- Deal with language and cultural issues sympathetically.
- Provide an opportunity for debriefing.

Developing closer ties in the team

In an attempt to enhance team cohesion in the England cricket team ahead of the biannual Ashes grudge match against Australia, the England management planned a team-building camp in Bavaria, Southern Germany. The five-day camp was organized by the team's security officer, Reg Dickason, and was based near Nuremburg. The camp involved the players participating in both physical and mental challenges that included boxing, hiking, and abseiling. The planning of the camp was a closely guarded secret beforehand, with players told to bring their passports and walking boots, and to leave their mobile phones at home. As well as performing a series of physical challenges, the team also learned more about making decisions under pressure, leadership, and the factors that contribute to team success. The camp also involved mutual sharing activities around the campfire, all of which sought to enhance team cohesion. This personal disclosure and mutual sharing approach has been adopted by a number of practitioners as a tool to enhance understanding and cohesion in teams. The trip was rounded off by a visit to the memorial site at Dachau, the first of the concentration camps where more than 40,000 people died during the 12 years of its existence from 1933–45. By developing such an intense shared experience the England management were able to further reinforce task cohesion (winning the Ashes) whilst also developing social cohesion (through relationship building). The England Captain Andrew Strauss was impressed with the experience, stating that 'it was a tough but rewarding five days and I know every player has gained greater insight into themselves, their own team environment and environments outside cricket'. At the time the media were less convinced, suggesting that it would have been more important for the players to rest ahead of the winter tour to Australia, particularly when it emerged that one of England's key bowlers, Jimmy Anderson, suffered a cracked rib after participating in the activities.

However, after a successful tour of Australia in which England comprehensively beat the Australians to regain the Ashes and win a series in Australia for the first time in 24 years, the England management, support staff, and players highlighted the camp in Germany to have been an important contributory factor, in particular due to the team bonding and relationship building that took place, making the team a closer unit ahead of the challenges that faced them all.

Summary

Understanding the factors that determine the degree of cohesion in a team is crucial to developing an effective team. Further understanding techniques to enhance levels of cohesion is also crucial for the coach/manager to enhance levels of cohesion or bring about changes in the team and its degree of 'togetherness'.

Understanding the reciprocal relationship that exists between levels of cohesion and performance in sport is also important for maximizing the positive impacts of good cohesion on performance and effective performance on cohesion. It is also important to reflect on the other side of this coin. If performance is suffering, it will potentially decrease levels of cohesion within the team and ultimately the overall effectiveness of the team.

7

MOTIVATING THE TEAM

Introduction

Understanding how to get the most out of the individual members of the team and the team as a whole is crucial to effective team performance. If you understand the factors that influence team motivation you can plan for and enhance the motivation of the team, and as a result indirectly influence performance. Successful teams are usually pretty clear in regards to what they want to achieve. Crucial to team success, though, is ensuring that the individual members of the team are driven to achieve the goals set for the team, and will strive for better performances. Most coaches understand that the greater the level of effort a team can be encouraged to give, the greater the potential for a successful performance and a successful outcome. Understanding the factors that influence motivation in a team, then, appears to be important in enhancing the potential for success.

This chapter will explore the concept of motivation and specifically how it relates to team sports. In particular the chapter will explore the main approaches to motivation in teams, including the concepts of collective effort, team proactive behaviour, collective efficacy, and motivational climates. As in other chapters of this book the focus towards the end of the chapter will be on practical interventions and techniques that can be used to enhance the motivation of the team.

Motivation

Motivation has been described in terms of energy and the direction of behaviour (Deci and Ryan, 1985). The energy component reflects the amount of effort that the individual chooses to devote to an activity or task. The direction of behaviour reflects the individual's unique level of personal interest in a specific task or activity. The direction of motivation is determined by the opportunities to which one is exposed and the outcomes of initial attempts at performance (Harter, 1978). Linked to the concept of motivation is the concept of amotivation. When individuals are in an amotivated state they cannot interact effectively or competently in their environment (Frederick-Recascino and Morris, 2004).

Contemporary theory on motivation in sport has embraced an interactionist approach that considers a combination of both social-environmental and individual difference factors to explain motivated behaviours (Weiss and Ferrer-Caja, 2002). One particular area of motivation that has been of keen interest within sport is the distinction between intrinsic and extrinsic motivation.

Intrinsic motivation is seen as the drive underpinning an individual wanting to do something for its own sake, because they find it pleasurable or rewarding. The pleasure gained from this type of motivation is inherent in the activity and so no tangible reward is required. In contrast, extrinsic motivation refers to the desire to do things for external rewards. There is always a reason for doing something, and the action becomes a means to an end.

Intrinsic and extrinsic motivations are both seen to exist on a continuum with intrinsic motivation at one end and extrinsic motivation at the other. With extrinsic rewards the motivation comes from external factors through positive and negative reinforcement. Individuals who are driven by intrinsic motivation are striving to be competent and self-determining and gain their own enjoyment from personal achievement. Both intrinsic and extrinsic motivation can be further divided into different subcomponents.

Intrinsic motivation

Specific subcomponents of intrinsic motivation include knowledge, accomplishment, and stimulation.

- *Knowledge* – the motivation comes from the pleasure and satisfaction experienced whilst learning and exploring something new.
- *Accomplishment* – pleasure and satisfaction are gained from feelings of accomplishment over the mastery of a new or difficult skill.
- *Stimulation* – the driver is to experience pleasant sensations such as excitement, fun, and aesthetic pleasure.

Extrinsic motivation

Specific subcomponents of extrinsic motivation include integrated regulation, identified regulation, and introjected regulation.

- *Integrated regulation* – the motivator here is the valued outcome, rather than a specific interest in the activity. One example could be a gold medal, or winner's bonus.
- *Identified regulation* – motivation results from a feeling that the required behaviours are highly valued among peers, resulting in prestige. In a sporting context this could relate to the wearing of a grey jacket following a major golf victory.

- *Introjected regulation* – the individual is motivated by internal drivers, but these are to achieve external recognition and reward. The performer is driven to practise to become the best, to achieve the associated sponsorship and financial rewards.

Collective effort

The collective effort model (CEM), which is largely a cognitive model of motivation, suggests that an individual will be willing to put effort into a collective task only if they feel that their efforts will be instrumental in achieving something that they deem to be important. If the outcomes, which are linked to the team, are not perceived to be important, meaningful, or intrinsically satisfying, individuals are unlikely to work hard within the team. This model is similar to the traditional expectancy-value models of effort (e.g. Vroom, 1964). In Vroom's original expectancy-value model the individual's motivation is determined by three factors: expectancy, instrumentality, and valence of the outcome.

- *Expectancy* – the degree to which high levels of effort are expected to lead to high levels of performance.
- *Instrumentality* – the degree to which high-quality performance is perceived as instrumental in obtaining an outcome.
- *Valence of the outcome* – the degree to which the outcome is viewed as desirable.

The CEM expands on this by specifying that the component of instrumentality is determined by three factors (Karau *et al.*, 2000):

- perceived relationship between individual performance and group performance;
- perceived relationship between group performance and group outcomes; and
- perceived relationship between group outcomes and individual outcomes.

Karau *et al.* (2000) suggested that a number of factors must be perceived by the individual as existing before that individual is willing to exert high levels of effort. Individual effort must relate to individual performance, which must also impact upon team performance. The group performance must then lead to a desired group outcome, that will also then relate to a desired individual outcome (see Figure 7.1). The individual will also not work so hard if the associated outcomes and rewards are not deemed to be of value. Relevant individual outcomes include objective outcomes (e.g. prize money or a trophy), self-evaluation information, and feelings of belonging to the team.

The CEM also expands on previous expectancy-value frameworks by highlighting which outcomes will be valued in different team settings. The valued outcomes can consist of either objective outcomes (such as money) or subjective outcomes (such as enjoyment and satisfaction). With objective outcomes it is the individual's evaluation of the outcome that is important, and not necessarily the outcome itself. With the model focusing on the group, there is a particular emphasis on team-level outcomes and the implications for the individual's self-evaluation.

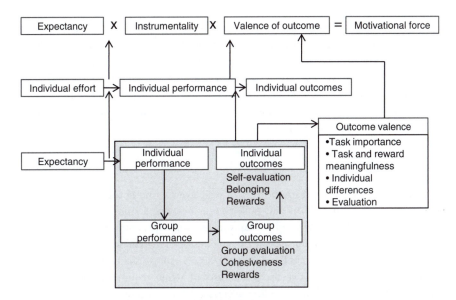

FIGURE 7.1 The collective effort model (adapted from 'Social loafing: A meta-analytic review and theoretical integration' by S. J. Karau and K. D. Williams, 1993, *Journal of Personality and Social Psychology*, p.685. Copyright 1993 by the American Psychological Association)

Karau *et al.* (2000) suggested that in adopting the CEM a number of steps could be taken which would ultimately enhance motivation and decrease social loafing within teams: (i) ensuring that individuals believe their collective performance can be evaluated; (ii) where possible, encouraging smaller group work; (iii) ensuring that individual contributions are seen as both unique and important; (iv) having professional standards for the team; (v) having team members working on things that are intrinsically interesting, important to the team, or high in personal involvement; (f) working with respected individuals or in situations that enhance the group's identity; (g) developing a dispositional tendency to view favourable collective outcomes as valuable and important; and (h) developing feelings of high self-efficacy and high collective efficacy.

Team proactive performance

Individual-level proactive behaviour refers to self-starting, future-focused action in which the individual aims to change the external situation, such as improving work methods, or to change some aspect of his/her self, such as improving one's performance by actively seeking feedback from a leader (Parker *et al.*, 2006). Individuals who are proactive are generally more active, change orientated, and future focused and thus are particularly useful in situations that lack predictability (Griffin *et al.*, 2007). Team proactive performance was proposed by Williams *et al.* (2010) to be a team-level concept that is similar to individual-level proactive performance and which as a result relates to the degree to which the team is self-starting, future focused and aims to change the external situation, or the team, or both. This team proactive performance is an emergent property of teams that reflects and shapes team interactions. The limited research in this area does suggest that proactive teams achieve positive outcomes (Williams *et al.*, 2010). Kirkman and Rosen (1999) highlighted team empowerment as a key determinant of team proactive performance, and empowerment in turn was predicted by a number of factors, including leadership, structure, communication, and support in the team.

Collective efficacy

The nature of competitive team sports involves players working together where there is a desire for both individual and collective achievement amongst team members (Chow and Feltz, 2008). As a result, teams make judgments about the functioning of the team as well as judgements about the abilities of individual team members. Collective efficacy was defined by Bandura (1997) as 'a group's shared belief in conjoint capabilities to organize and execute the courses of action required to produce given levels of attainment' (p.476). Bandura conceptualized collective efficacy as a state, rather than a trait. Zaccaro *et al.* (1995) offered a slightly different definition of collective efficacy, suggesting it could be viewed as 'a sense of collective competence shared among individuals when allocating, coordinating, and integrating their resources in a successful concerted response to specific situational demands' (p.309). Whilst the terminology differs between these two definitions, the general message is the same in that collective efficacy relates to the degree to which the team members think they will be successful. In sport, collective efficacy has also been referred to as team efficacy or team confidence. Collective beliefs are important because they influence what people choose to do as team members. These collective efficacy beliefs affect group behaviours such as the tasks the team selects to engage in, the level of effort that the team puts into an activity, and the extent to which the team will persist when faced with challenges. While these performance-orientated outcomes are the most salient factors associated with collective efficacy, beliefs regarding team functioning also contribute to group thought patterns. Collective efficacy beliefs are also thought to influence the use of available resources, persistence in the face of failure, and resistance to discouragement (Shearer *et al.*, 2009). According to Bandura (2001), the higher the perceived collective efficacy, the higher the team members' motivational investment in their undertakings, the stronger their staying power in the face of impediments and setbacks, and the greater their performance accomplishments. The nature of collective efficacy concerns the degree of interdependence that is necessary to achieve team performance goals.

The development of collective efficacy is closely linked to self-efficacy theory. Self-efficacy theory was first introduced by Bandura (1977) to explain and adapt human behaviour. Self-efficacy was defined by Bandura (1997: p.3) as 'beliefs in one's capabilities to organize and execute the course of action required to produce given attainments', reflecting the confidence the individual has in their ability to perform a specific task. Bandura suggested four specific antecedents of self-efficacy beliefs:

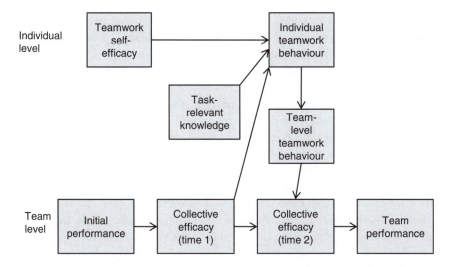

FIGURE 7.2 Longitudinal multilevel model linking efficacy beliefs, behaviour, and team performance (adapted from 'The development of collective efficacy in teams: A multilevel and longitudinal perspective' by K. Tasa, S. Taggar, and G. H. Seijts, 2007, *Journal of Applied Psychology*, p.18. Copyright 2007 by the American Psychological Association)

enactive mastery experiences, vicarious experience, verbal persuasion, and physiological/affective states. Collective efficacy is thought to share the same antecedents as self-efficacy, with the addition of leadership, cohesion, and group size (Carron and Hausenblas, 1998). However, a number of authors have also suggested that the factors that shape the evolution of collective efficacy may differ further from the antecedents of self-efficacy (Tasa *et al.*, 2007). Indeed, Gibson (1999) suggested that collective efficacy develops partly through exchanges of information and observed behaviours within the team. Based on this, Tasa *et al.* (2007) developed a model exploring the factors that influence teamwork behaviours at the individual level (see Figure 7.2). Tasa et al. (2007) sought to develop and test a longitudinal multilevel model of collective efficacy formation, the starting point of which was to explore the factors that influence teamwork behaviours at the individual level. The model also proposes cross-level effects where team-level constructs influence individual behaviour, which, in turn, influences team-level perceptions of performance. Specifically, the authors identified three individual-level factors (teamwork self-efficacy, individual teamwork behaviour, and task-relevant knowledge) and two team-level factors (team-level teamwork behaviour and initial performance).

Magyar *et al.* (2004) stated that, while Bandura (1997) proposed that individual perceptions of collective efficacy represent an emergent effect that emanates from the team rather than being the exclusive sum of the individual team members' efficacy, he also acknowledged that these collective perceptions of confidence are rooted within individual perceptions of self-efficacy. Specifically, self-efficacy and collective efficacy may be considered to be similar to yet distinct from one another.

According to Bandura (1997), in teams characterized by higher levels of system interdependence (e.g. soccer and basketball), collective efficacy should be more related to team outcomes than in teams with lower levels of interaction and coordination among members (e.g. track and field).

Ronglan (2007) suggested three specific dimensions to collective efficacy: production, activation, and evaluation. Production refers to the period prior to performance where the focus is on developing joint perceptions of capability in the team. This includes perceptions of being prepared, having sufficient ability, and being in a strong team. Activation refers to active display of collective efficacy by the team in a match situation. This includes demonstrating confidence by showing enthusiasm, willpower, persistence, and high team morale. Evaluation relates to the team's interpretations of shared experiences during games and in respect of overall outcomes and results.

Beliefs in team capabilities are also suggested to influence team goals, team affect, and group motivational processes (Chow and Feltz, 2008). It has also been reported that teams that have stronger judgements of collective efficacy tend to set high performance standards and select team goals that they can master (Bray, 2004). Teams with low confidence in the team's collective efficacy tend to opt for less difficult goals, especially following a team setback (Greenlees *et al.*, 2000). George and Feltz (1995) argued that a deeper understanding of the processes involved in the development, decline, and restoration of team efficacy is needed to comprehensively understand the impacts on team performance.

Sources of collective efficacy

According to Bandura (1997) the most salient factor contributing to one's beliefs about team functioning is mastery experiences or past performance accomplishments. Teams that experience success in a specific activity have an expectation that they will perform equally well in future tasks of a similar nature. If a team outperforms an opponent during the first meeting, they will have a high level of confidence that they can do the same in future contests against similar competition. Conversely, teams that suffer performance setbacks will lack confidence in their abilities to succeed in subsequent contests (Chow and Feltz, 2007). In support of this, Feltz and Lirgg (1998) found that ice hockey players' collective efficacy increased following a team win and decreased following a team loss.

Modelling, which Bandura (1997) referred to as vicarious experiences, can also provide information that affects collective efficacy beliefs. Watching a team that is similar in performance ability raises the observant team's level of confidence to succeed in comparable tasks. Similarly, seeing a team with similar attributes struggle undermines the observing team's level of collective efficacy (Chow and Feltz, 2007). This is supported by research undertaken by Chase *et al.* (2003) that reported that vicarious experiences were an essential factor that contributed to female basketball players' precompetitive perceptions of collective efficacy. The provision of feedback (verbal persuasion) is another way in which efficacy beliefs can be altered. Feedback that conveys information about the team's capabilities will be likely to have the most influence on collective efficacy beliefs (Chow and Feltz, 2007). A final identified type of social persuasion that may affect collective efficacy is spectator and media support (George and Feltz, 1995). George and Feltz suggested that team members who hear applause from fans may have more confidence in their team than those team members who are jeered.

Team emotions can also be affected by efficacy beliefs. These can include collective worry, shame, team pride, shared joy, and sadness. Teams high in collective efficacy should feel more in control and, as a result, have less reason to worry or falter under pressure (Ronglan, 2007). The motivational climate in terms of members' evaluations of the goal structures emphasized by coaches also has a bearing on informing collective efficacy beliefs.

Marks *et al.* (2001) suggested that emergent states such as collective efficacy are products of team experiences and become new inputs to subsequent processes and outcomes. As a result, this is a continual process where the previous experience impacts upon subsequent collective efficacy, but also one event can be the catalyst to future change. Tasa *et al.* (2007) suggested that this process begins at the individual level. If a player sees their teammates performing behaviours that are generally accepted and helpful with respect to team performance it should result in a sense of confidence about the team's capability. To this end Tasa *et al.* (2007) suggested that collective efficacy is, in part, shaped by individual behaviours. Stevens and Campion (1994) developed a typology of generic transferable knowledge, skills, and abilities necessary for teamwork that focused specifically on the individual team member. Stevens and Campion (1994) identified two broad categories of teamwork knowledge skills and abilities: interpersonal (conflict resolution, collaborative problem-solving, and communication) and self-management (goal setting and performance management; and planning and task coordination) skills. At least three factors have been identified that determine the extent to which an individual will engage in teamwork behaviour: task-relevant knowledge (how much does the individual know about what is required), self-efficacy for teamwork behaviour (how confident the individual is that they can do what is required), and initial collective efficacy (the degree to which they think the team is likely to be successful). Tasa *et al.* (2007) also reported in their study of student teams a significant relationship between teamwork behaviour and collective efficacy. There is significant evidence that suggests that collective efficacy has a positive effect on sports performance (Shearer *et al.*, 2009). Paskevich *et al.* (1999) reported strong correlations between task-related aspects of cohesiveness and members' shared beliefs about collective efficacy. A meta-analysis by Gully *et al.* (2002) also reported that the relationship between collective efficacy and team performance was both positive and significant.

Measuring collective efficacy

When seeking to measure self-efficacy, two main approaches have been adopted in the motivation literature. The first has seen the development of generic validated questionnaires such as the Collective Efficacy Questionnaire for Sports; the second, based on Bandura's (2006) guide, has advocated the development of sport- and situation-specific measures that may not necessarily be formally validated.

The recently developed Collective Efficacy Questionnaire for Sports (Short *et al.*, 2005) consists of five factors: ability, effort, persistence, preparation, and unity. The factors include items referring to behaviour visible to teammates and opponents, such as 'demonstrate a work ethic' (effort), 'show enthusiasm' (effort), 'be united' (unity), and 'keep a positive attitude' (unity).

Bandura (2006) outlined seven specific considerations for constructing instruments to measure efficacy in sports: domain specifications, gradations of challenge, content relevance, response skills, validity, phrasing, and minimizing social evaluative concerns. Domain specification refers to designing a tool specific to the particular sports and task demands. Gradations of challenge refers to the scale used to measure the extent of the task as perceived by the athlete responding to the question. Content relevance refers to the use of 'will do' instead of 'can do' statements in the inventory. Response skills relates to measurements of the degree of difficulty/complexity of the task. Validity refers to the validity of the measure used. Phrasing highlights the importance of the terminology used in the questions. Finally, minimizing social evaluative concerns relates to the conditions in which the participant completes the inventory.

Bandura (1997) recommended two approaches for deriving single estimates of a team's collective efficacy from individual team members. The first approach involves assessing each player's belief in their personal capability to perform within the group and then aggregating this self-efficacy to the team level. This estimate is referred to as *aggregated self-efficacy* (Myers *et al.*, 2004). The second approach involves assessing each player's belief in the team's capability as a whole and then aggregating these individual measures to a team level. This approach is referred to as *aggregated collective efficacy* (Myers *et al.*, 2004). Bandura (1997) suggested that, in group tasks that are highly inter-dependent, aggregated collective efficacy would be more predictive of team performance than aggregated self-efficacy. A meta-analysis of studies examining the relationship between collective efficacy and team performance found that task interdependence and level of analysis moderated this relationship (Gully *et al.*, 2002).

Collective efficacy, leadership, and cohesion

A number of other concepts have been suggested to impact upon collective efficacy in the team, in particular leadership and cohesion. Cohesion has been described as an antecedent of collective efficacy (Kozub and McDonnell, 2000) and as both an antecedent and a consequence of collective efficacy (Zaccaro *et al.*, 1995). As an antecedent, a number of positive changes associated with cohesion (greater acceptance of group norms, assigned roles, and performance standards; stronger resistance to disruption) should enhance the performance capabilities of the group and promote a higher level of collective efficacy (Bandura, 1997; Kozub and McDonnell, 2000; Zaccaro *et al.*, 1995). As a consequence, stronger perceptions of collective efficacy should increase the desirability of the group and, as a result, group cohesion (Zaccaro *et al.*, 1995).

Zaccaro *et al.* (1995) and Moritz and Watson (1998) further highlighted that leaders who display confidence might be more likely to enhance collective efficacy by modelling confidence and success. As a result, an important task for the coach is to make the key players aware of their potential and their responsibilities as role models in the team.

Leaders can directly influence collective efficacy through modelling, encouragement, persuasion, feedback, and enhancement of team functioning. Additionally, leaders who are confident in their problem-solving and decision-making capabilities as well as their ability to motivate and influence their team members can increase the sense of collective efficacy within a team (Vargas-Tonsing *et al.*, 2003).

Enhancing collective efficacy

Given that collective efficacy has a strong link to cohesion (Shearer *et al.*, 2009) it is likely that traditional team-building interventions often used to increase cohesion could work equally well for collective efficacy (see Chapter 6 for more details regarding team cohesion). Examples could include interventions focusing on personal disclosure and mutual sharing exercises that have been shown to enhance team dynamics (Dunn and Holt, 2004).

Collective efficacy perceptions are usually formed by perceiving what others feel. As a result, video footage of teammates, coaches, and significant others could be a useful way to catalogue team events that might positively influence an individual's collective efficacy perception. Examples could include footage of successful performances, inspirational team talks, and hard training sessions (Shearer *et al.*, 2009).

Chow and Feltz (2007) in their review of the literature highlighted a number of specific recommendations for enhancing collective efficacy. Specifically these include mastery experiences, team modelling, verbal persuasion, team-building interventions, and team goal setting. Of all the recommendations presented, mastery experiences were suggested to be the most powerful factor that determines a team's sense of efficacy.

It has also been suggested that transformational leaders can enhance collective efficacy by providing emotional and ideological explanations that can provide a link between team members' individual identities and the collective identity of the team (Kark and Shamir, 2002). Avolio *et al.* (2001) have further argued that the transformational leader can influence perceptions of team members' ability, integrity, and communication by highlighting the importance of cooperation in performing collective tasks. The leader can further emphasize the team's goals by stressing shared values and motives, and as a result connecting the team members' interests to those of the team. Transformational leaders can also build collective efficacy by raising the awareness in the team of individual member contributions and the value of self-sacrifice for the good of the team (Walumbwa *et al.*, 2004). Leadership has also been reported to be a good predictor of collective efficacy (Chen and Bliese, 2002).

Motivational climates

Central to understanding motivation in individual and team contexts is understanding the ways in which motivation can be enhanced. In particular, understanding motivation related to achievement has been of particular interest in sport. A number of cognitive theories have been developed to explain different achievement patterns and to understand ways in which this motivation could be enhanced. In particular, Achievement Goal Theory (Nicholls, 1989) has been of particular relevance.

Nicholls (1989) spent a number of years developing his theory of motivation because he was interested in understanding how all individuals' motivation levels could be optimized in achievement settings. He believed that the key to maximizing motivation was in helping individuals define success based on their own effort and improvement instead of based on normative comparisons with peers (Smith *et al.*, 2005).

Two qualitative achievement goal states have been identified that are regulated by individuals adopting one concept of ability over the other. These two goal states are referred to as task and ego involvement. Individuals are task involved when gains in personal mastery of a skill or task enrich them with a sense of competence. In this respect, self-referent improvement or learning on a task is sufficient to generate feelings of personal achievement (Chi, 2004). In contrast, individuals are ego involved when their sense of competence depends upon demonstrating superior performance to others', or via an equal performance to others' but with less effort exhibited (Harwood and Beauchamp, 2007). As a result, both achievement goals focus on different aspects of the self. When in a state of ego involvement, the perceived ability of the self and the demonstration of its adequacy compared to others are of primary concern. When in a state of task involvement, the main focus is on the development of the self irrespective of others (Harwood and Beauchamp, 2007).

Within contemporary achievement goal frameworks (Nicholls, 1989) there are three major constructs: namely perceived motivational climate, dispositional goal orientations, and goal involvement. Dispositional goal orientations refers to tendencies that predispose individuals to adopt either a task or ego involvement. Specifically, Nicholls (1989) described these as individual differences in proneness to the different types of involvement.

According to achievement goal theory the social situation created by significant others can vary in terms of the achievement goals emphasized. Ames (1992) introduced the term motivational climate to capture these overriding aspects of the social-psychological environment. Ames further proposed that the motivational climate is multidimensional and is comprised of different structures (e.g. the system of evaluation, the type of and basis for recognition, the nature of interactions within and between groups, and the source of authority (Duda and Balaguer, 2007)).

To date, perceptions of task-involving climates have been related to greater enjoyment; satisfaction and positive affect; the belief that effort is an important cause of success; self-ratings of performance and improvement; the use of adaptive coping strategies; perceptions that the coach provides positive feedback; perceived competence; higher ratings of team-task and social cohesion; positive peer relationships; positive morale and stronger sportsmanship; less self-handicapping (including the verbalization of excuses); and greater respect for rules and officials (Duda and Balaguer, 2007). An environment that has a perceived ego-involving climate corresponds to more maladaptive achievement patterns, negative cognitions, and associated negative emotional responses. This in turn has been related to higher anxiety and performance-related worry; the belief that ability is an important determinant of success; dropping out of sport; greater peer conflict; perceiving one's ability in terms of other-referenced criteria; perceiving the coach to provide less social support and more punishment; greater self-handicapping; less mature moral reasoning; and lower moral functioning (Duda and Balaguer, 2007).

Motivational climates then are specific constructs relating to the environment within which the team will train and operate. The perception of the motivational climate is the crucial factor in the effectiveness in any environment. The motivational climate is characterized by the key features that it emphasizes and supports the development of the right environment for both team development and functioning.

Enhancing motivational climates

Ames (1992) suggested the TARGET taxonomy as a tool to enhance the team's motivational climate. The acronym specifically relates to six dimensions of the motivational climate: task, authority, recognition, grouping, evaluation, and timing. Targets provide the player with a range of demanding tasks that focus on individual challenge and active involvement; help the team members to set self-referenced process and performance goals; and emphasize the demands of the task as a key focus of the environment.

- *Task* – specifically refers to what performers are asked to learn and the tasks they are given to complete.
- *Authority* – relates to the type and frequency of participation by the players in the decision-making process relating to training. It can be enhanced by involving the team members in the decision-making process; considering the views of the team; developing further opportunities for leadership (both formal and informal) within the team; and getting the team to take greater ownership by self-managing and self-monitoring.
- *Recognition* – relates to the approaches used within the team to motivate players and recognize achievement. It can be enhanced by making an effort to engage with each member of the team as an individual; recognizing the progress and development of each individual player; and ensuring equity in opportunity and rewards.
- *Grouping* – focuses on how performers are subdivided or combined within the training environment. It is most effective to be flexible in the allocation of players to groups, to continually refresh subgroups, and also to emphasize creativity and problem-solving approaches within these groups.
- *Evaluation* – relates to the specific standards that are set for the achievement and monitoring of players in the team. The process here is important. Ensure clarity of what the required standards are and how they will be assessed/evaluated.
- *Timing* – relates to the appropriateness of the time demands placed on the players. To enhance the effectiveness of the timing, develop assessment criteria based on

effort and team-related behaviour; look to involve individual players in self-evaluation and the team in evaluating the team's effectiveness and performance; be consistent regarding the points of reference for the team. Always remember to recognize that different members of the team will develop at different rates; as a result, provide sufficient time for learning to take place; also, try to be equitable in the time and effort given to different team members.

Impact of inspirational speeches

The coach can have a big impact on the team. Before the game the right speech, at the right time, can be used to motivate and inspire. One example of this is the speech given by Vince Lombardi, the then Head Coach of the Green Bay Packers, before Super Bowl II in 1968. Lombardi stated that 'winning is not a some time thing. It's an all time thing. You don't win once in a while. You don't do things right once in a while. You do them right all the time. Winning is a habit. Unfortunately, so is losing. There is no room for second place. There is only one place in my game, and that's first place. I have finished second twice in my time at Green Bay and I don't ever want to finish second again. There is a second-placed bowl game, but it is a game for losers played by losers. It is and always has been an American zeal to be first in anything we do, and to win, and to win, and to win, and to win.' After this speech the Packers went on to beat the Oakland Raiders 33–14 to win the Super Bowl for the second successive year.

Moments that inspire and motivate do not only take place before a game, and it is not always the coach that delivers the message. Tim Tebow, after a loss to Mississippi playing for the University of Florida in 2008 inspired the population of Gainesville when saying, 'to the fans and everybody in Gatornation, I'm sorry. I'm extremely sorry. We were hoping for an undefeated season. That was my goal, something Florida has never done here. I promise you one thing, a lot of good will come out of this. You will never see any player in the entire country play as hard as I will play the rest of the season. You will never see someone push the rest of the team as hard as I will push everybody the rest of the season. You will never see a team play harder than we will the rest of the season, God bless.' The speech inspired the team for the rest of the season, but has subsequently been engraved on a plaque outside the football training facility at the University, in the hope that it will motivate and inspire future generations of 'Gator' players.

There are a number of key components that need to interact to result in an effective motivational message. These include the language used, the emotions conveyed, the authenticity of the sender, and the receptive nature of the audience. The most inspiring individuals just appear to 'know' the right message at the right time, but usually it is just a result of practise, knowing your strengths, and knowing your audience.

Summary

The degree of effort and intensity that is shown by the team in both practise and game settings will have a significant impact on overall performance. As a result, understanding the factors that influence motivation is crucial to the coach. Understanding what makes individuals tick will enhance the coach's ability to motivate them by understanding what they hold to be important (values and goals). In the same way, being able to unify the team behind specific goals and targets will have the effect of motivating the team to work both harder and smarter in pursuit of those goals.

8

MANAGING EMOTIONS IN TEAM SPORTS

Introduction

Sport can be a very emotional experience. Winning can result in feelings of happiness and joy, whilst defeat can often result in disappointment, anger, and frustration. The emotional state of each player in the team can impact upon the outcome of team performance by influencing his or her personal effectiveness in both training and competition. Team performance, then, is an accumulation of these individual emotional responses. Both emotional awareness and emotional management have important consequences for team performance as they help individuals maintain effective relationships with other team members (Jordan and Troth, 2004). Emotions have also been shown to determine affect-driven behaviours such as impulsive acts, organization behaviours, and transient effort (Weiss and Cropanzano, 1996). This chapter will first explore what emotions are and how they impact upon the individual. The following sections will then explore the emotional characteristics of the group and the influences that the team can exert on the individual and the influence the individual has on the team. Finally, this chapter will explore strategies to enhance emotional control in the individual player and also how to influence and control group emotional responses and environments.

What are emotions?

Both emotions and mood are covered by the umbrella term affect, which refers to all types of feelings. Affect is often used at a general level to describe good and bad experiences (Vallerand and Blanchard, 2000). Lazarus (2000) specifically defined emotion as a 'phenomenon that is an organized psychophysiological reaction to on-going relationships with the environment, most often, but not always interpersonal or social' (p.230). A second definition is also worth considering at this point. Deci (1980) defined emotion as 'a reaction to a stimulus event (either actual or imagined). It involves changes in the viscera and musculature of the person, is experienced subjectively in characteristic ways, is expressed through such means as facial changes and action tendencies, and may mediate and energize subsequent behaviours' (p.85). This second definition offers greater details regarding the way emotions are experienced. In more general terms, Lazarus (1999) proposed that emotion is a response to the meaning we attach to our interactions with the environment. Different emotional experiences influence our interactions with the environment in different ways.

Types of emotions

One of the main approaches to understanding emotions suggests that there are a discrete number of basic emotions that underlie our emotional experiences. Reeve (2005), in reviewing work on emotions, highlighted between two and ten different types of emotions that were identified in the relevant emotion-focused literature. Lazarus (2000) in his cognitive-motivational-relational theory of emotion identified 15 discrete emotions and also provided an insight into their potential functions and possible effects (presented in Table 8.1). Eight primary emotions were highlighted

TABLE 8.1 Emotions and their core relational themes

Emotion	Theme
Anger	A demeaning offence against me and mine.
Anxiety	Facing uncertain, existential threat.
Fright	An immediate, concrete, and overwhelming physical danger.
Guilt	Having transgressed a moral imperative.
Shame	Failing to live up to an ego ideal.
Sadness	Having experienced an irrevocable loss.
Envy	Wanting what someone else has and feeling deprived of it, but justified in having it.
Jealousy	Resenting a third party for loss or threat to another's affection or favour.
Happiness	Making reasonable progress towards the realization of a goal.
Pride	Enhancement of one's ego identity by taking credit for a valued object or achievement: either one's own or that of someone, or of a group with whom one identifies.
Relief	A distressing goal-incongruent condition that has changed for the better or gone away.
Hope	Fearing the worst but yearning for better, and believing that improvement is possible.
Love	Desiring or participating in affection, usually but not necessarily reciprocated.
Gratitude	Appreciation for an altruistic gift that provides personal benefit.
Compassion	Moved by another's suffering and wanting to help.

Source: adapted from 'How emotions influence performance in competitive sports' by R. S. Lazarus (2000), *The Sport Psychologist*, Vol. 14, p.234. Copyright 2000 by Human Kinetics.

(anger, anxiety, shame, guilt, hope, relief, happiness, and pride). These primary emotions were very similar to the seven emotions identified by Vallerand's (1983) review of emotions in sport (happiness, surprise, fear, anger, sadness, disgust/contempt, and interest). Despite differing views regarding the number of basic emotions in the literature, there do appear to be five emotions that seem to represent a broad consensus among basic emotion researchers. These 'big five' emotions include anger, fear, sadness, disgust, and happiness. A range of cross-cultural studies conducted by Ekman (1999) appear to support the existence of these basic emotions within different countries and cultures. However, further work in this area suggests that varying languages and cultures do seem to differ in the number and categorization of their emotional terms. Also, the range of situations that trigger emotions vary across cultures. The fact that similar verbal labels are used across widely differing languages and cultures has been used as evidence to support the existence of a discrete set of basic emotions. Scherer and Wallbott (1994) compared verbal labels for emotions in 37 countries and were able to translate the English terms for the seven emotions studied (anger, fear, sadness, joy, disgust, shame, and guilt) into each of the other languages.

A second approach to understanding emotions has been referred to as the dimensional approach. This approach views emotions as existing within a few key dimensions. Within this tradition Larsen and Diener (1992) proposed the dimensions of pleasant–unpleasant and high–low activation. Other dimensional pairs have also been suggested, including Thayer's (1996) energy–tiredness and tension–calmness dimensions, and Russell's (1980) pleasure–misery and arousal–sleep dimensions. Usually these two dimensions are presented as a circumplex, with emotions arranged around the outside of a circle (see Figure 8.1). This dimensional approach offers an understanding of the relationship between different emotions and underlying states such as activation and pleasantness.

Some authors have suggested that a two-dimensional representation fails to capture important aspects of emotional experience, and might not represent some differences between emotions. For example, fear and anger are both negative–high–arousal emotions that are located in the same region of the circle, yet these emotions are quite different (Larsen and Diener, 1992). Also, different versions of the model sometimes suggest different locations for affective states (Watson *et al.*, 1999). However, despite these limitations, the model has achieved broad acceptance as a useful representation of emotion (Remington *et al.*, 2000).

There is a tendency when considering emotions to focus on negative emotion. Indeed, in sports settings negative emotions such as anxiety, anger, and depression appear to command the greatest attention. Positive psychology however points to the equal prevalence and importance of positive emotions. Fredrickson (2005) described positive emotions as markers of optimal functioning and argues that cultivating positive emotions is a way to foster psychological growth. Fredrickson further suggested that positive emotions broaden the individual's thought-action repertoire and build enduring resources. This is at odds with a focus on negative emotions that reduce choices to fight or flight. As a result, teams should actively seek to encourage and promote positive emotional experiences and not just focus on the reduction of negative experiences.

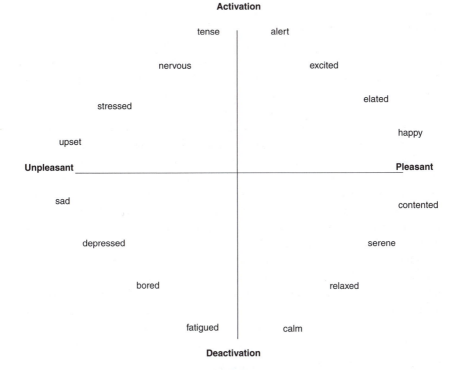

FIGURE 8.1 A circumplex model of emotion (adapted from 'Independence and bipolarity in the structure of current affect' by L. Feldman-Barrett and J. A. Russell, 1998, *Journal of Personality and Social Psychology*, Vol. 74, p.970. Copyright 1998 by the American Psychological Association)

The link between emotions and mood

Moods are low-intensity diffuse feeling states that usually do not have a clear ante-cedent (Forgas, 1992). They can be characterized as being relatively unstable short-term intra-individual changes (Tellegen, 1985). Lazarus (1991) specifically defined moods as a 'transient reaction to specific encounters with the environment, one that comes and goes depending on particular conditions' (p.47). Emotions and moods differ in a number of specific ways. First, the duration of both is highlighted as being different. Emotions are generally shorter (often lasting for seconds or minutes), whereas moods are longer (lasting in the region of hours or days). The onset of emotions is generally accepted to be much quicker and with a much greater intensity. The antecedents for emotions are more specific and result in distinctive facial signals and physiological responses. Moods are less specific and do not necessarily result in easily identifiable responses.

Mood is known to have an effect on a number of processes, including perception, reasoning, memory, and behaviour (Parkinson *et al.*, 1996). Emotions differ from moods in that they have a clear cause or object, are shorter in duration, and are more focused and intense (Kelly and Barsade, 2001). Positive mood in particular has been linked to a number of performance-related behaviours, including enhanced supportive behaviour, greater creativity, more effective decision making, greater cooperation, and the use of more effective negotiation strategies (Totterdell, 2000). A number of mechanisms have been suggested to explain how mood impacts upon performance. These mechanisms either involve a change in focus or the availability, allocation, or content of attentional resources. Matthews (1992) highlighted three types of mechanisms that seek to explain the impact that mood has on performance: interference, processing efficiency, and cognitive bias. In these mechanisms, mood diverts attentional resources when it interferes with processing; alters resource availability and resource allocation strategy when it affects processing efficiency; and selects particular cognitive processes when it biases processing. Totterdell (2000) suggested a simple model of mood and team performance. In this model the collective mood of the team influences the individual's performance through its influence on the individual's mood (see Figure 8.2).

Totterdell's (2000) model highlights the importance of both the individual's and the team's moods and their impact on performance. Focusing on the impact that the team has on the individual and the individual has on the team is crucial. In order to foster a positive environment both the team and the individual affective states need to be considered.

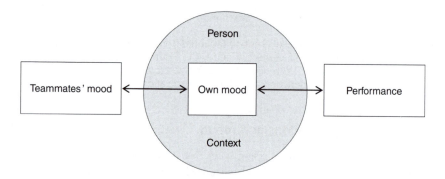

FIGURE 8.2 The influence of team mood on individual mood and performance (adapted from 'Catching moods and hitting runs: Mood linkage and subjective performance in professional sport teams' by P. Totterdell, 2000, *Journal of Applied Psychology*, Vol. 85, p.850. Copyright 2000 by the American Psychological Association)

Characteristics of the emotional response

Emotions are generally characterized by three specific responses:

- changes in behaviour;
- bodily responses (physiological); and
- subjective experiences (feelings).

The majority of behavioural changes that occur when an emotional episode is taking place are well known and easily identifiable. For example, when someone is happy they laugh, when they are angry they shout, and when they are sad they become quiet and withdrawn. Facial expressions in particular characterize individual responses to specific emotional episodes. Behaviour and facial expressions communicate emotional feelings well, and thus can be manipulated to convey certain desired emotional responses.

Bodily responses to emotions are relatively automatic and have developed as an evolutionary response. Examples of bodily/physiological reactions include sweating when anxious and heart-rate increases when excited. Many of the body's responses are controlled by the autonomic nervous system (ANS). This system is composed of a network of nerve fibres that transmit signals to various organs, muscles, and glands. The ANS can be further divided into two sections: the sympathetic and parasympathetic nervous systems. The sympathetic nervous system specifically produces effects associated with arousal. These include the secretion of the hormone adrenalin that initiates and enhances sympathetic activity leading to changes such as accelerating heart rate, vasoconstriction (a constriction of blood vessels), increased respiration rate and depth, and reduced gastro-intestinal activity. The parasympathetic system tends to be in control during rest and usually has the opposite effects on the body to the sympathetic nervous system.

Feelings, by definition, are subjective. In psychology the feeling component of emotion is linked to self-awareness and consciousness. It is at this point that an interpretation of a positive or negative response to a stimulus takes place. However, there is still debate regarding whether the feeling causes the physiological response or the physiological response causes the feeling. The individual's appraisal of the event, not the event itself, determines their emotional responses (Roseman et al., 1990). Individuals who are less prone to appraising a situation negatively are less likely to experience negative emotions. Similarly, individuals who are more skilled at managing their emotions following appraisal of an event should experience fewer harmful effects of negative emotions than individuals who are less skilled at managing emotions (Hartel et al., 2008).

Parkinson (1994) suggested a four-factor theory of emotional experience. In this model Parkinson suggested that emotional experience depends upon four separate factors: (i) appraisal of some external stimulus; (ii) reactions of the body; (iii) facial expressions; and (iv) action tendencies. Each of these factors was developed from earlier work on emotions including Lazarus (1991) for appraisal; James–Lange theory (Eysenck, 2004) for bodily reactions; Strack et al. (1988) for facial expressions; and Frijda et al. (1989) for action tendencies.

Vallerand and Blanchard (2000) observed that emotions can determine action tendencies by leading a player either towards, or away, from an object. They highlighted a link between the emotional episode and an overt behavioural response. For example, in soccer a player who loses the ball will either try harder to get the ball back, or will try to stay away from the ball to avoid making further errors. As a result, understanding how the individual reacts to an emotional episode is crucial to understanding the impacts that emotions will have on performance.

The emotional sports team environment

Howe (2004) highlighted a clear link between professional sports environments and emotional expression. Young *et al.* (1994) in their study of Canadian male athletes' reflections on their injury experiences reported that many coaches found the outward expression of pain to be disruptive and demoralizing to teammates. This supported the assertions made by Howe (2004) that the emotional expression of pain within the sporting environment is often viewed as a weakness. Highly competitive teams typically laud physical prowess, emphasize positivity, and admire risk-taking behaviour (Messner, 1992). Research exploring the players' view on the team environment found the player regularly felt pressure to conform to the team's values, or risk losing their status and respect within the team (Brewer *et al.*, 1993). As a result, players learn to distinguish between genuinely felt emotions and those emotions that are considered acceptable to express within the team environment (Howe, 2004; Tran, 1998). To cope with an emotionally inhibitive climate players often choose to adopt techniques that mask their genuine emotions and display socially desirable behaviours. Mankad *et al.* (2009) reported emotional acting and thought suppression as being the preferred methods of coping among players. However, the use of long-term acting, inhibition, and suppression has been shown to be linked to poor psychological and physical states. Pennebaker *et al.* (2001) specifically highlighted that the inhibition and suppression of emotions can lead to a greater susceptibility to psychosomatic disease and a further prolonging of the required coping process in recovery from injury.

Players engaged in emotional acting have been found to adopt two specific approaches. The first involves the cognitive control of outward emotions. In this approach, the player looks to modify their interpretation of the situation/event to focus on positive factors, looking to perceive the event optimistically and only display positive reactions. The second approach looks to deal with emotions at a more superficial level. The player looks to feign a desired emotion while suppressing the true emotional response. This then allows the player to interact with other team members in a positive way. Reasons given for this include acting to appear positive to younger teammates, and not knowing who in the team was genuine or trustworthy. Ashkanasy *et al.* (2002), when conducting research exploring the use of emotional acting, suggested that long-term acting can have detrimental performance outcomes, resulting in a decline in both physical and psychological well-being. One of the factors cited for causing this was the energy cost involved in suppressing emotions and 'acting' out other emotions.

One potential approach to help players cope with the non-verbal disclosure of emotions suggested by Mankad *et al.* (2009) is the use of private disclosures. This approach allows the player the benefits of a verbal emotional disclosure without the stigma in the sports environment of seeking help. Indeed, this is crucial as research on the psychology of traumatic experiences has found that disclosing one's thoughts and emotions relative to a trauma is associated with improvements in mental and physical health (King, 2001). The use of a narrative psychology framework can allow athletes to systematically construct a story related to their emotional experience, thus minimizing the confusion and disorder of their thoughts (Richert, 2006). Written disclosures have been shown to reduce stress and, consequently, susceptibility to illness and poor physical recovery (Booth *et al.*, 1997). Pennebaker (1989) further high-lighted that the process of disclosing emotions via a written format is effective because individuals are able to recognize inconsistencies and flaws within their own thoughts while writing narratives. This process is at the heart of Cognitive Processing Therapy (CPT; Resick and Schnicke, 1996). CPT uses writing as a key component to help individuals recognize inconsistencies in their emotional responses and highlights how their belief systems might change in response to a specific event. The primary focus of this therapy is to modify the athletes' beliefs about the meaning and implications of the event. CPT can also challenge and change distorted beliefs and self-blame. Strategies to reduce emotional acting can include both verbal disclosure and written disclosure.

Verbal disclosure

This can either be achieved through conversations with a member of the support staff (e.g. coach, physiotherapist, sport psychologist), or through conversations with trusted colleagues. The confidential nature of the disclosure here between parties is crucial. The aim of the process is to identify and challenge inconsistencies in situational perceptions and evaluations.

Written disclosure

If the verbal disclosure avenues are not available to the player(s), then a written disclosure through a diary or journal is another practical option. Ideally these written disclosures can then be discussed with the sport psychologist to further highlight faulting inconsistencies and flaws in the athlete's thought processes.

Team emotions

Kelly and Barsade (2001) developed a model exploring the effect of emotions on teams. In this model Kelly and Barsade proposed the existence of group emotion, a phenomenon that emerges from the individual group members' emotion traits and the context in which the group works. Group emotion has been defined by Kelly and Barsade (2001) as the 'group's affective state that arises from the combination of its 'bottom-up' components – *affective compositional effects* – and its 'top-down' components – *affective context* (p.100). Affective compositional effects refer to the group emotion that results from the individual-level affective factors that the group members possess. Affective context refers to the group- or contextual-level factors that define the shape of the affective experience of the group. This suggests that group emotions result from both individual affective factors and group- or contextual-level factors. Individual group members bring their own emotional experiences (dispositional affect, moods, emotions, emotional intelligence, and sentiments) with them to any group (Kelly and Barsade, 2001). Through a number of explicit and implicit processes these affective inputs are communicated to other group members and form the affective compositional group effects. Explicit processes include a range of socially induced affective states, including the deliberate creation or maintenance of emotional experience through affective influence, termed 'affective impression management'. Implicit processes can include automatic affective transfer processes, such as emotional contagion, feeling affect vicariously, and behavioural entrainment. Barsade and Gibson (1998) suggested that this spread and sharing of emotions formed the bottom-up process of affective team composition.

There is substantial evidence that people are sensitive to the emotional climate of a team and as a result they adjust their mood accordingly (Barsade, 2002). The ability to perceive other people's emotions is also important. Evidence from cricket (Totterdell, 2000) highlighted the importance of perceiving others' emotions for individual performance in the team environment. In this example players were asked to rate their own mood and their perception of the other team members' moods. The mood of the individual and the team correlated strongly. This player–team mood association has been described as mood linkage, which suggests that the player perceives the team's mood and modifies their own mood accordingly.

Many of the skills required for effective teamwork are influenced by emotion (Latimer et al., 2007). A number of authors have highlighted the link between emotions and decision making, planning, organizing thoughts, persistence, and problem solving in creative ways (Isen, 2001; Isen and Daubman, 1984; Isen et al., 1987; Mayer, 1986; Salovey and Birnbaum, 1989). As a result, the team that generates the right emotional climate is likely to experience greater success.

Totterdell (2000) suggested that the ability to manage emotions might have noticeable performance consequences: specifically, that a player's positive or negative emotions could easily influence the emotional tone of the entire team. Research into both teams and individual players has demonstrated much greater incidences of aggression in team sports compared to individual sports (Maxwell, 2004). The players' ability to regulate their emotions is vital to team success. The effects of negative emotions in a group setting could be amplified and sabotage the team's chances of success (Latimer et al., 2007).

Emotional contagency

An increasing body of research has highlighted the possibility for adjacent players to pick up on the emotions experienced by players in the team. The concept of contagion is derived from the theory of emotional contagion in which Hatfield et al. (1994) defined emotional contagion as:

> When people are in a certain mood, whether elation or depression, that mood is often communicated to others. Talking to a depressed person we may feel depressed, whereas when talking to someone who feels self-confident and buoyant we are likely to feel good about ourselves. This phenomenon, known as emotional contagion, is identified here, and compelling evidence for its

effect is offered from a variety of disciplines – social and developmental psychology, history, cross-cultural psychology, experimental psychology, and psychophysiology.

(p.i)

There is increasing evidence that we automatically mimic and synchronize with the manifestations of emotional behaviour in others.

Negative emotions can be caught more easily than positive emotions (Gump and Kulik, 1997; Tickle-Degnan and Puccinelli, 1999) and it has been suggested that interpersonal processes contribute to increased negative emotions among a player's peer group (O'Neill, 2008). This in part supports the view of coaches highlighted by Young *et al.* (1994) regarding the visibility of injured players in the 'normal' sporting environment.

A number of factors can influence the contagion process. Each individual differs in the degree to which they are good senders of emotion, and also the degree to which they are good receivers of information (Kelly and Barsade, 2001). The degree to which a good emotional sender occupies an important or central role might also influence this transfer process. Similarly, the degree to which the team is composed of good receivers would also have an effect (Hatfield *et al.*, 1994). Understanding the degree to which team members and staff are good receivers or senders of information will offer an insight into the potential for emotional contagency within the team environment.

Strategies to enhance individual emotional control

It is well known that understanding the causes and consequences of emotions can impact upon sports performance (Latimer *et al.*, 2007). Indeed one such approach suggested by Hanin (1999) requires athletes to recall a good performance and describe the emotions associated with this performance. The main aim of this process is to develop the athletes' understanding of the cause–effect relationship of emotions and performance. The next step is then to implement a strategy to elicit the required emotional state in competition. Golden and Dryden (1986), in a review of interventions used by practitioners to impact upon individuals' emotions, compiled a list of 11 strategies. These strategies were: self-statement modification, imagery, socratic dialogue, corrective experiences, vicarious learning, self-analysis, the didactic approach, story-telling and metaphors, reframing, the cognitive paradox, and teaching problem-solving skills.

- *Self-statement modification* – self-statements are suggested to influence emotions in two ways. First, replacing a maladaptive self-statement with a positive or neutral statement results in the removal of a stimulus that might result in an emotional state. Second, certain self-statements could be used to generate a specific emotional state or response.
- *Imagery* – according to bio-informational theory, when a player creates an image of a situation, they create a stimulus proposition. This describes the image and the

relevant contextual factors. In addition to this, a response proposition is also activated, which may include an emotional response to the situation. Martin *et al.* (1999) suggested that by modifying the response proposition a player could change any undesirable emotional responses. Imagery could also be used to alter athletes' appraisals. Martin *et al.* (1999) also suggest that motivational general-mastery (MG-M) imagery can result in a more positive interpretation of an up-coming event. This could then result in a positive emotional state. This MG-M imagery can be used to represent effective coping and mastery of challenge situations (Murphy *et al.*, 2008).

- *Socratic dialogue* – specific thought-provoking questions are asked of the player to challenge any self-defeating thoughts and ideas. This approach is designed to influence the primary appraisal of the stimulus. Jones (1993), in work with racquet sports players, successfully implemented this approach to challenge self-defeating thoughts. The approach was designed to challenge a player's view that arguing with the umpire would change the umpire's decision. Once the player was made aware of the futility of the course of action, she modified her response.
- *Corrective experiences* – the player makes the conscious decision to engage in the activity that is the source of the emotional response. This approach involves a preparatory period during which the player can 'try out' the actions before engaging in them for real. This approach seeks to modify the player's appraisal of the situation.
- *Vicarious learning* – the focus of this approach is to encourage the player to copy the behaviour of someone who exhibits the responses they wish to make. The technique is to make a behavioural rather than an emotional change, so that over time the change in the behaviour might modify the player's appraisal of the situation.
- *Self-analysis* – players may write down their feelings or experiences with a view to increasing their self-awareness of their emotional responses to situations and the potential triggers for these responses. Again, understanding the responses and the triggers can allow the player to modify the way that they respond and appraise the situation.
- *The didactic approach* – the player is educated regarding their problems in a similar approach to self-analysis. The focus is on increasing awareness regarding the response and the situations in which the response might arise. Peptitpas (2000) adopted this approach with an elite female athlete. Regarding the athlete's anxious response, she was informed that she was not the only one who experienced this. This resulted in a modification of the athlete's appraisal: 'feeling anxious is normal, therefore there is no need for me to focus too much on it'.
- *Story-telling and metaphors* – the coach or sport psychologist can use literary techniques to encourage the player to view the situation differently. Beswick (2001) explained how the use of a traffic-light metaphor helped a junior international soccer team when playing overseas. Green was seen as being in control, while red represented a loss of control. Specific emphasis was placed on the importance of 'staying in the green'. Players who felt they were in the amber zone were given strategies to regain control of their emotions.

- *Reframing* – while the behaviour remains the same, in this approach the meaning or frame of the behaviour is modified. This involves creating a different frame of reference on the world and using a behaviour that exists in a positive way instead of a negative way.
- *The cognitive paradox* – involves the sport psychologist or coach feeding back the 'irrational voice' of the player in a more exaggerated manner. This focus seems to get the player to re-evaluate his or her ideas. This seeks to force the player to replace maladaptive thoughts with more realistic and beneficial ones.
- *Teaching problem-solving skills* – enhancing a player's problem-solving abilities should give them greater coping resources. This enhancement of coping resources should then impact upon the primary appraisal of a situation and, as a result, influence the emotional response.

Strategies to enhance the team emotional climate

The ability to regulate emotion in both the self and other individuals is a critical factor for effective team functioning. The ability to regulate emotions to accept feedback, hold back from criticizing others' opinions, and try to maintain a relaxed atmosphere is an indicator of someone with good emotional control. This 'emotional management' is particularly important for creating positive interactions between team members. Totterdell and Leach (2001) reported in cricket that players who scored higher on a scale of perceived ability to regulate negative moods had better batting averages than those who did not. This relationship was present over the duration of the whole season. Koys and DeCotiis (1991) in a review of relevant literature summarized eight dimensions that determined the psychological climate of the group. These were: autonomy, trust, cohesion, pressure, support, recognition, fairness, and innovation.

- *Autonomy* – the perception of control over procedures, goals, and priorities. The greater the inclusion of the team in determining procedures, goals, and priorities, the more positive the general state of the team.
- *Trust* – this focuses on the perception of freedom to communicate openly with members at higher levels about sensitive or personal issues with the expectation that the integrity of such communications will not be violated. High levels of trust result in positive, supportive, and 'close' teams. A lack of trust will result in a negative emotional climate.
- *Cohesion* – the perception of togetherness or sharing within the team is also important. Here, strategies that can enhance both task and social cohesion will be beneficial.
- *Pressure* – the perception of demands with respect to task completion and performance standards is also important. The greater the perceived pressure on the team, the more likely a negative emotional climate becomes.
- *Support* – another important facet is the support provided to the team. This should focus on the perceptions of tolerance of team member behaviour by superiors, including the willingness to let team members learn from their mistakes without fear of reprisal.

- *Recognition* – acknowledgement of the contributions of each individual to the team is very important. All individuals want to be valued. As a result, recognition of both contribution and performance is important.
- *Fairness* – organizational practices must be equitable and non-arbitrary or changeable. Perceptions of inequality will lead to fragmentation in the team and the formation of antagonistic cliques.
- *Innovation* – the notion that change and creativity are encouraged, including risk taking into new areas or approaches where the member has little or no prior experience, is also important. To create a positive emotional team climate the team members need to feel free to express themselves.

Catching emotions in a penalty shoot-out

Emotions in team sports can be contagious. Particularly in emotional and tense situations the emotions that one player experiences can be transferred to other players. This is further heightened in very emotional events, such as a penalty shoot-out in soccer, the shoot-out in ice hockey, or the super over in twenty20 cricket. Research from the Netherlands by Moll *et al.* (2010) explored the transfer of emotions in penalty shoot-outs. Moll and colleagues studied a large number of penalty shoot-outs during important games, but only as long as the score in the shoot-out was still equal. After every shot at goal, each player was assessed on the degree to which they expressed happiness and pride after scoring. This revealed that the players who expressed this clearly (e.g. throwing their arms up into the air) usually belonged to the winning team. This enthusiastic and positive behaviour was seen to infect the team with a positive attitude. At the same time, the opposing team members were reported to feel a little bit more insecure. In the study this effect on the opposition was demonstrated by the finding that, when a player cheered with both arms in the air, it was more than twice as likely that the next opponent would miss their penalty.

Moll and colleagues also observed another interesting effect. Where the emotional behaviour was directed was also found to be important. If you want to transfer positive emotions to your teammates, you need to celebrate with them to get the greatest effect. If you go and celebrate in front of the supporters, they will react positively, but this does not enhance the transfer of positive emotions to a player's teammates.

As a result, once the penalty has been scored, the player needs to return to the rest of the team as quickly as possible to cause the greatest positive transfer of emotions to the remaining penalty takers.

Summary

Recognizing that sport is a very emotional experience is crucial to understanding the emotional responses of individual athletes. Further understanding how these individual responses contribute to and determine the team response is central to developing an effective team. An understanding of the team emotional climate and determining factors will allow the captain, coach, or manager to foster a desirable positive and supportive environment in which team performance can excel. Interventions are often required at both the individual and the team level to facilitate individuals experiencing positive emotions as a result of their involvement in sporting contexts. The influence of emotion on factors including decision making, planning, organizing thoughts, persistence, problem solving, and creativity has been linked to performance (Isen, 2001; Isen and Daubman, 1984; Isen et al., 1987; Mayer, 1986; Salovey and Birnbaum, 1989). Thus, the team that generates the right emotional climate is likely to achieve higher levels of performance and experience greater success.

9

MOMENTUM IN SPORT

Introduction

Both performers and observers often cite the phenomenon of momentum as a factor that impacts upon performance. It is typically conceived of as being both an unpredictable and supernatural force outside the control of individuals and teams, which often dictates the outcomes of competition (Taylor and Demick, 1994). This phenomenon of momentum is referred to at numerous levels for individual and team sports both within individual games and across multiple games (Vergin, 2000). Team sports invariably have an ebb and a flow, with often one team and then another in the ascendancy. The periods of good fortune, though, seem to differ in their duration and their frequency (Vergin, 2000). The gaining of momentum is usually thought of as a factor that can enhance performance, while the loss of momentum can be said to have the reverse effect (Perreault *et al.*, 1998). Although this phenomenon is well established in the minds of participants and spectators, research exploring momentum has been relatively inconclusive, with distinctions between momentum and psychological momentum being made. Understanding the influence that momentum can have on cognitions and subsequent performance could be beneficial to sports teams. Once the coach is aware of how changes in momentum impact upon the team's cognitions, then steps can be taken to enhance the potential benefits and reduce any negative impacts (Mack and Stephens, 2000). This chapter will explore the theoretical basis for momentum and seek to explore trigger events for momentum shifts. Finally, the chapter will explore intervention strategies for influencing momentum and momentum shifts in team sports.

What is momentum?

A number of definitions have been suggested to explain this phenomenon of momentum. Higham *et al.* (2005) suggested that momentum is:

The force that dictates the flow of a match: a hidden force because it is not always reflected in the score. It is invisible because it comes from the flow of energy between competitors that, in turn, affects their performance on the pitch. A player or spectator can feel things going for or against him or the team he is watching, sensing who holds the balance of power at key moments in the match.

(p.5)

This definition suggests that momentum is some external force that influences individuals and teams, but is not influenced by them.

Greater clarity is suggested in the research literature regarding the development of a specific definition of momentum. Adler (1981) defined momentum as 'a state of dynamic intensity marked by an elevated or depressed rate of motion, grace, and success' (p.29). Adler went on to suggest five interrelated components that are essential to momentum: (i) focusing on a specific goal; (ii) motivation to initiate the effort of goal attainment; (iii) emotional feelings attached to motivation towards the goal; (iv) increasing arousal associated with the activity; and (v) enhancing performance due to the other factors. These five components of momentum were combined by Adler (1981) to form a model of momentum. However, while descriptive, this model did not really explore cognition in relation to momentum.

Taylor and Demick (1994) in their definition of momentum sought to add greater clarity to Adler's definition by suggesting that momentum is 'a positive or negative change in cognition, affect, physiology, and behaviour caused by an event or series of events that will result in a commensurate shift in performance and competitive outcome' (p.54). This definition, building on Adler's (1981) approach, included cognitive aspects of the phenomenon.

Other conceptualizations of momentum include that of Iso-Ahola and Mobily (1980), who suggested that momentum is a gained psychological power, which may change interpersonal perceptions and influence physical and mental performance. Each of these definitions and conceptualizations of momentum suggests that a number of situational factors appear to form the basis of any momentum change, and that any change is as a result of the impact that these situational factors have upon cognition, affect, physiology, and behaviour. In support of this summary Mack and Stephens (2000) reported a significant interaction between momentum and cognitive states, specifically suggesting that changes in momentum lead to changes in self-efficacy and affect.

In looking to classify momentum further, Burke and Weinberg (as cited in Burke, 1993) suggested two different types of momentum: positive and negative. Positive momentum was described as a psychological state of mind affecting performance in a positive direction, when almost everything seems to go right, and, conversely, negative momentum was defined similarly but as affecting performance in a negative direction, when almost everything seems to go wrong. Higham (2000) suggested that, when a player experiences positive momentum: they feel in control; they are relaxed; their performance is smooth; they appear to have a lot of time; and there is a sense of inevitability about winning. When players experience negative momentum: they feel unsettled; nothing seems to be working; opponents are controlling the game; limbs feel heavy; their mind is unclear; and small things get on their nerves.

There are a number of other ways in which momentum can be considered. As well as the notion of momentum in a game, winning and losing streaks across a whole season have also been thought of in terms of momentum. When a team is in a prolonged slump, for example, explanations are often sought and changes demanded. Some changes are physical, but often it is a 'change in attitude' that is called for. Vergin (2000) cited a view reported in player statements that winning causes momentum, and then momentum causes more winning. This notion of winning and losing streaks is however complicated by the skill level of the teams competing, with better teams winning more often than inferior teams. As a result, the question remains: is it momentum that causes a team to continue to win or lose, or is it a difference in the skill level and ability of the team's players? Gilovich et al. (1985) suggested that belief in streaks could be due to memory bias. If long winning or losing sequences are more memorable than alternating sequences, observers are more likely to overestimate the correlation between successive wins.

Momentum can also be thought of in relation to individual performance. In basketball, for example, the notion of the 'hot hand' is considered to be important. This is where a player is more likely to make the next shot after making a shot, rather than after missing a shot (Vergin, 2000). The hot hand concept suggests that a player's performance is temporarily increased beyond their base rate following a string of successes (Koehler and Conley, 2003). There has been a great deal of debate in the literature regarding the nature of this phenomenon, with Koehler and Conley (2003) suggesting that it is best viewed as a historical commentary rather than as a predictor of future performance. Indeed Koehler and Conley (2003) suggested that beliefs regarding the impact of the hot hand rather than hotness itself should be the focus of future research into the topic. Bar-Eli and colleagues (2006) countered this by suggesting that saying that there is no hot hand contradicts spectator and player perceptions, as well as a body of research on the role of success and self-efficacy in the enhancement of athletic performance (Smith, 2003). When a player feels hot, their confidence in their ability increases, potentially leading to greater relaxation and a greater focus on successful task execution (Bar-Eli et al., 2006). The greatest support for the hot hand among empirical studies has been found in more individualistic sports (as opposed to team sports). Examples include both bowling (Dorsey-Palmateer and Smith, 2004) and tennis (Klaassen and Magnus, 2001). The concept of the hot hand may not exist as a separate phenomenon, but the perception of its existence by the athlete appears to have the potential to influence future performance in either a positive or negative direction.

Psychological momentum

In sport psychology the term 'psychological momentum' has been used to describe changes in performance based on success or failure in recent events that then change the performance, the beliefs, or the psychology of players. Adler (1981) suggested that psychological momentum is the tendency of an effect to be followed by a similar effect. This is seen as a bi-directional concept, with positive psychological momentum predicting an increased probability of success and negative psychological momentum predicting the opposite.

Three theoretical models have been suggested to date that seek to explain this concept of psychological momentum:

- antecedents–consequences psychological momentum model (Vallerand *et al.*, 1988);
- multidimensional model of momentum in sports (Taylor and Demick, 1994); and
- the projected performance model (Cornelius *et al.*, 1997).

Antecedents–consequences model of psychological momentum

In this model psychological momentum is conceptualized as a perception of moving towards a goal. This process involved changes in motivation, perceptions of control, optimism, energy, confidence, progression towards the goal, and synchronization. Vallerand *et al.* (1988) also acknowledged that both participants and spectators could perceive psychological momentum. The major difference between the perspectives of the participant and of the spectators is that, in addition to perceptions, players also experience related affect and motivations. So, the observer only perceives, while the player perceives and experiences the situation. In this antecedents–consequences model it was also acknowledged that psychological momentum could be further affected by both personal (i.e. skill level, motivation, anxiety levels) and situational variables (i.e. crowd behaviour, task difficulty). The psychological momentum perceptions in this model are produced by the interplay between these situational and personal (intra-individual) variables. The antecedents–consequences model also suggests that the crucial psychological variable that determines perceptions of momentum is the degree of potential perceived control inherent in the situation. It is also suggested that psychological momentum can have an important impact upon the individual's actual performance. The effects on performance, though, are moderated by both contextual and personal variables. Contextual factors refer to moderators such as the crowd and the game situation, and game importance. Personal factors relate to the individual's skill level and need/desire to achieve. The model further suggests that the belief that psychological momentum produces increased performance is important.

Vallerand *et al.* (1988) made two specific contributions to the understanding of psychological momentum. First, that psychological momentum referred to a perception that the individual is progressing towards their goals, so the perception of the situation is critical. Second, that, because psychological momentum is subjective, perceptions of momentum are influenced by intrapersonal factors (such as perceptions of control and experience) and situational factors (such as the score).

Multidimensional model of momentum

Taylor and Demick's (1994) model of momentum sought to develop a theory that clearly delineated causes, processes, and outcomes of psychological momentum.

Specifically in Taylor and Demick's multidimensional model, psychological momentum was developed through a series of changes consisting of: a precipitating event that could be either positive or negative; changes in cognition, affect, and physiology (again either positive or negative); changes in behaviour; changes in performance, opponent factors; and changes in the immediate outcome.

Components of the multidimensional model of momentum in sports are:

- *Precipitating event(s)* – the ability of an event to impact upon momentum is linked to its salience. Whether the event generates changes in the player's perceptions depends upon the individual player. Potential influencing factors include: competitive experience, self-efficacy, perceptions of control, cognitive schemas, and associated behavioural responses (Miller and Weinberg, 1991).
- *Change in cognition, physiology, and affect* – a number of potential cognitive changes might result from step (i) (precipitating events). These include perceptions of control, motivation, attentional focus, and self-efficacy. Physiological arousal changes include heart rate, respiration, and adrenaline levels. These first two factors (cognitive and physiological) result in a change in affective/emotional experiences. This change in affect will be the direction of the newly formed cognition.
- *Change in behaviour* – the changes in behaviour will depend on a number of factors, including the combination of psychological momentum and the current level of physiological arousal of the athlete. These changes could relate to activity level, pace of performance, posture and frequency of movement, and behaviour repetition.
- *Change in performance* – these changes should result in a shift in performance. Psychological momentum is not considered to be a force that is always present. The absence of psychological momentum is the normative condition during competition.
- *Opponent factors* – in order for a momentum change to produce enhanced performance for one individual/team, there might need to be a negative change for the opposition. This could include the experience and the ability of the opposition; changes in cognition, physiology, affect, and behaviour.
- *Immediate outcome* – the impact that all the other changes have on the outcomes in the subsequent passages of play.

Researchers including Kerick *et al.* (2000) considered the main advantage of this model to be the 'momentum chain', which lends itself to empirical testing of each component. Mack and Stephens (2000) provided some support for this model in their basketball-shooting task. In this study involving 125 male university basketball players, they found that changes in momentum led to corresponding changes in cognition. Further support for the multidimensional model was provided by Perreault *et al.* (1998), whose bike-race results suggested that precipitating events influenced perceptions of momentum. Indeed, Perreault *et al.* (1998) concluded that psychological momentum perceptions could be beneficial for tasks requiring a lot of effort. Taylor and Demick (1994) also suggested that, in head-to-head contests such as tennis or squash, the outcome was determined by one player experiencing positive psychological momentum while their opponent experienced negative psychological momentum.

Projected performance model

This model by Cornelius *et al.* (1997) proposes that both positive and negative momentum are labels used to evaluate performance, and that perceptions of psychological momentum have little influence on performance. In this model, positive and negative perceptions of psychological momentum are the result of an extremely good, or extremely poor, performance. As a result psychological momentum is considered a performance label. This model also suggests that perceptions of psychological momentum will be relatively short-lived because there are a number of factors that can influence performance, including positive inhibition and negative facilitation (see Figure 9.1). Positive inhibition reflects situations where teams may have caught up with opponents, but this momentum actually leads to negative changes in subsequent performances due to 'coasting'. Negative facilitation occurs when a team falls behind and this poor performance acts to motivate an increased effort (Crust and Nesti, 2006). These influencing factors further complicate the conceptualization and evaluation of psychological momentum. Competitors will often adjust to opponents' extremely

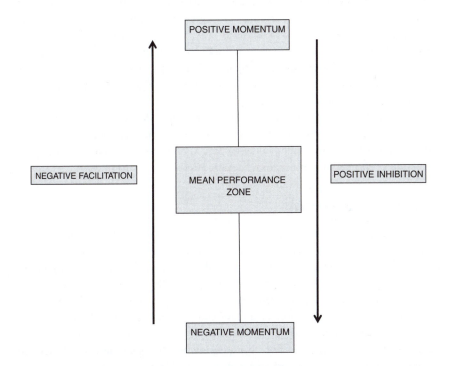

FIGURE 9.1 The relationship between negative momentum and positive momentum; and the impact of negative facilitation and positive inhibition on perceptions of momentum

good or poor performances. As a result, the competitors might seek to change tactics, increase concentration, or react to the opponents' performance.

In the projected performance model, if performance increases above the mean levels to an optimum level of performance shown in the upper left portion, the players are likely to report positive momentum. If performance is decreased below mean levels as shown in the lower right portion of the model, negative momentum will be reported. The right side of the model shows positive inhibition, with the left side reflecting negative facilitation. Cornelius et al. (1997) suggested that this model could account for many of the research findings concerning psychological momentum. It is also suggested that the model proposes a number of interventions with players, specifically that the goal of any intervention would be to maximize performance time in the optimal performance zone and decrease performance time in the suppressed performance zone.

Perceptions of psychological momentum

While there are three models of psychological momentum and a range of supporting research, there still remain questions regarding whether this phenomenon is actual or only perceived.

There is clear research evidence suggesting that the perceptions of psychological momentum do exist and that they shift in response to gaining or losing ground in competition (Eisler and Spink, 1998; Perreault et al., 1998; Shaw et al., 1992). Burke et al. (1997) in their study exploring tennis and basketball reported that good performance was often viewed as the precipitating event, with a combination of good play by the team and poor play by the opponent. It has also been suggested that perceptions of psychological momentum are likely to mediate performance via cognitive and affective processes as well as physiological factors. The cognitive and affective processes potentially include optimism, sense of control, motivation, self-efficacy, concentration, energy, and synchronization. As a result, understanding the events that could influence this perception of momentum either for or against a team appears to be key.

Momentum trigger events

Burke et al. (1999) reported that the three most recorded events in basketball that appeared to initiate and continue periods of momentum were directly related to defensive movements (e.g. defensive stops, steals, and turnovers). The next two most recorded events were reported to occur directly after the defensive events (e.g. three-point shot and a fast break). Crowd behaviour and a string of 'unanswered' points have been highlighted as being important in continuing momentum periods (Burke et al., 1999). The authors concluded that momentum in basketball occurs because of good game events by one team and poor game events by the opposing team. Jones and Harwood (2008), in their study of soccer players, highlighted a range of trigger events for momentum. Specific triggers included player confidence levels and opponent factors. High levels of confidence acted as a trigger and an outcome of positive psychological momentum and, conversely, low confidence was seen as a trigger and an outcome of negative psychological momentum. The actions of the opposition were also seen as triggers. Potential opposition triggers included body language, maintaining possession, and the opposition playing to their strengths. Burke *et al.* (2003), in a study of spectator perceptions of momentum, also highlighted that good performance by one team, or a combination of good play by one team and poor play by the opponent, was an initiating factor in relation to positive momentum.

Turning points in games were also highlighted by Higham (2000) as crucial in momentum shifts. Specifically, Higham suggested that these events relate to either:

- the actions of your opponent;
- your own actions; or
- external events that affect one or both teams.

Examples of potential turning points suggested by Higham *et al.* (2005) included: changes in the score; bad officiating decisions; substitutions/replacements; unsporting behaviour; significant individual performance; missed opportunities; injuries; poor communication; increased support; luck; changes in the conditions (e.g. weather); interruptions for treatment; and tactical changes.

A consistent theme through each of these studies highlighting momentum triggers is the importance of good performance by a team or opponent in positively or negatively influencing psychological momentum. Coupled to this, player confidence also appears to be crucial in moderating the impact of team or opponent events.

Collective collapse

Linked to the concept of momentum is that of collective collapse, which is characterized by a significant failing by multiple members of the team. Apitzsch (2006) suggested that collective collapse could also act as a specific momentum trigger event. Collective collapse has been defined as:

> The collapse that occurs when a majority of the players in a team sport suddenly perform below expected level in a match of great, often decisive, importance in spite of a normal or good start of the match or when a team underperforms right from the start of a match.
>
> *(Apitzsch, 2006: p.38)*

A number of possible mechanisms through which this collapse could occur have been highlighted, including groupthink, emotional contagion, and manifest behaviours (Apitzsch, 2006). Janis (1982) defined groupthink as 'a mode of thinking that people engage in when they are deeply involved in a cohesive in-group, when the members' striving for unanimity override their motivation to realistically appraise alternative courses of action' (p.8). Janis (1982) developed a theory about how groups may arrive at bad or completely wrong decisions. Within this theory Janis (1982) highlighted eight specific symptoms of groupthink. The first four relate to the development of a positive image of the relative strengths of the group in relation to its opponents. The final four relate to efforts by the group to reach a consensus. Five antecedents have also been highlighted which increase the likelihood of groupthink occurring: (i) high levels of cohesion; (ii) the isolated nature of the group; (iii) autocratic leadership; (iv) the homogeneity of the group; and (v) the task the group is involved in. Carron *et al.* (2005) suggested that groups involved in solving a crisis are more vulnerable to episodes of groupthink.

Emotional contagion relates to the communication of mood and emotion to other individuals (Hatfield *et al.*, 1994). A number of factors can influence this contagion process. These include the degree to which each individual is a good sender and receiver of information (Kelly and Barsade, 2001). The final mechanism suggested as causing collective collapse is manifest behaviour. This is displayed by individuals and is influenced by thoughts and moods. This behaviour is determined by underlying psychological mechanisms including information-processing structures in the brain and the relevant external and internal triggers.

Weick (1993) suggested four specific measures to help a group in a crisis deal with the situation in an effective way: (i) improvisation; (ii) a virtual role system; (iii) an attitude of wisdom; and (iv) respectful interaction.

- *Improvisation* – creativity is important, and the ability of the leader to improvise and for the team members to act upon new information is crucial.
- *A virtual role system* – individuals in the team need to be able to adopt a variety of roles in the group if a team member fails in their role or is unable to complete it.
- *An attitude of wisdom* – openness to new perspectives and being open-minded and curious regarding alternative solutions to the situation is key.
- *Respectful interaction* – this focuses on specific action to counter the vulnerability of the team. It is required if the role system fails to adapt to rapid changes and should be characterized by confidence, honesty, and self-respect.

The application of these four measures might help a team to deal with specific situational issues, which can help to remove the potential for collective collapse within the team.

Psychological momentum and performance

Research that has sought to test the relationship between psychological momentum and performance has failed to conclusively prove a stable relationship. A range of different approaches have been utilized in an attempt to explore this relationship. The first of these has used archival or observational data that has tested the notion of temporary performance increases being followed by a 'hot streak'. An example of this approach has examined statistical shooting data (Koehler and Conley, 2003; Vergin, 2000). The results of these types of analyses have failed to find evidence for greater outcomes than would be expected by chance (Gilovich *et al.*, 1985; Koehler and

Conley, 2003). Silva *et al.* (1988) suggested that focusing at the micro level (points and rallies) rather than the macro level (games and sets) might be more relevant for the study of psychological momentum and performance. In support of this Burke *et al.* (1999) reported that, during periods of perceived momentum, basketball teams significantly out-scored their opponents. The momentum team scored statistically significantly more points, but in real terms scored only five more than the opposing team. Experimental studies that have explored this relationship between psychological momentum and performance have tried to use false feedback and a range of scoring manipulations to create perceived momentum (Crust and Nesti, 2006). In both of these approaches the aim is to make participants feel that the score/game situation is different to reality. Results using these designs have also produced inconsistent findings. Perreault *et al.* (1998) highlighted a number of methodological weaknesses in this approach, suggesting that the conditions in these studies were not conducive to evaluating the psychological momentum–performance relationship. Crust and Nesti (2006) suggested that a qualitative approach should be adopted in the future to gain athlete perceptions of any possible link between momentum and performance. This approach was duly adopted by Jones and Harwood (2008) in their study of soccer players. Initial findings suggested that the participants clearly associated momentum with performance. While empirical studies have failed to prove this relationship between momentum and performance, this could in part be down to poor experimental representative design. Qualitative studies do at least point to the perception that performance is influenced by momentum, and in particular changes in momentum.

Momentum intervention strategies

Influencing the momentum of a game

In order to positively impact upon the game the coach needs to recognize the nature of momentum at the point in the game. Higham *et al.* (2005) suggested three specific phases of momentum:

1 When momentum is for a team or individual.
2 When momentum is in the balance.
3 When momentum is against a team.

Phase 1 – When momentum is for a team

When momentum is for a team, it feels like 'plain sailing'. Team members are confident and relaxed, feel in control, are more likely to step up a gear, and often their opponent will appear frustrated.

Phase 2 – When momentum is in the balance

In this phase the scales are balanced and teams are generally matched in their effort levels, energy, and standard of play.

Phase 3 – When momentum is against a team

This is often characterized by frustration. Heads can drop and conflict within the team can manifest itself. This is further compounded by the increased confidence and energy levels of the opposition.

Depending upon the phase of the game, the strategies adopted to influence momentum might be different.

Mace *et al.* (1992), in their study of college basketball, reported that calling timeouts or initiating other events that disrupted the flow of a game reduced the opponents' rate of reinforcement or behavioural momentum. Specific suggestions for influencing the momentum in a game include: the tempo, personnel changes, communication, refocusing, changing the flow of the game, practice, body language, investing extra effort, reading the opposition, sticking to your plan, and maintaining belief.

- *Tempo* – controlling the pace of the game to impose control can be effective, either by imposing the optimal tempo for the team or depriving the opposition of their preferred tempo.
- *Personnel changes* – changing the personnel alters the on-pitch dynamics of the team; also, introducing a fresh player can provide renewed energy to the team.
- *Communication* – clarity of communication is important. Often in the course of a contest communication levels slip. Conscious renewing of communication channels is a positive step. Greater communication enhances team functioning and the execution of plans and strategies.
- *Refocusing* – strategies to get the team members to refocus and double their efforts can enable the team to return stability to its performance.
- *Changing the flow of time/the game* – if the momentum is against you, disruptions to the flow of the game can be beneficial. Timeouts, personnel changes, and treatment breaks are all potential strategies.
- *Practising* – preparing for trigger events in particular can be beneficial. This can maximize positive momentum and reduce the impact of negative momentum. Working on 'what if' scenarios is a possible technique here.
- *Body language (non-verbal communication)* – the opposition pick up on body language. Negative body language encourages opponents, while positive body language can have the opposite effect and create pressure. Recognizing this fact and developing more positive team body language can have an effect.
- *Invest extra effort (be prepared to fight)* – the notion of raising your game is important, either to raise above or to meet the level of the opposition.
- *Read the opposition's tactics* – knowing what the opposition will do will enable greater planning and execution of strategies to counter these tactics. Enhanced preparatory work and research can lead to a greater ability to read the opposition in game situations.
- *Don't make changes for the sake of it* – always have a plan. Disrupting the flow of the game and the interpersonal interactions of players will potentially impact upon both teams.

- *Maintain belief* – confidence has been shown to mediate the impact of psychological momentum. Both self-efficacy and collective efficacy enhancement techniques can be implemented.

Higham and colleagues (2005) specifically highlighted possession in all types of ball games as a crucial factor in influencing momentum. They cited important factors including: who has the ball, where they have possession, what the circumstances are, and how they use the ball. Higham and colleagues also extended this point to suggest that possession can be used both positively and negatively. When being used positively, possession can be used to play for position, enact pre-planned moves or plays, draw opponents, and change the direction of play. Possession can also be used negatively to deny opponents possession, use up time, frustrate opponents, and prevent scoring opportunities.

Psychological intervention strategies

Jones and Harwood (2008) highlighted a specific weakness in previous work exploring momentum in sport. While the existence of conceptual models of momentum had developed the understanding of momentum as a theoretical concept, the hypothetical testing of models had limited applicability for research practitioners. Taylor and Demick (1994) alluded to the potential use of cognitive-behavioural strategies for players, but the findings in this particular model were developed based on data from spectators only, not from players. Due to a lack of research exploring the athletes' perspective, Jones and Harwood (2008) interviewed soccer players to explore their perspective regarding momentum, its triggers, and control strategies. Two specific types of triggers were highlighted: confidence and opponent behaviours. To support the development of confidence Jones and Harwood (2008) suggested that focusing on drawing out mastery experiences for players before the game as well as encouraging cumulative achievement of both within-match processes and performance goals would be useful strategies. To reduce positive perceptions of psychological momentum in opponents Jones and Harwood (2008) also suggested increasing awareness in the team of the effects of body language, and introducing strategies to increase positive body language.

Preparation is crucial in maximizing positive psychological momentum. Preparing the team physically, mentally, tactically, and technically is important to build confidence and to modify perceptions relating to personal and situational sources of confidence.

Adler (1981) suggested that perceptions of psychological momentum and team cohesion are linked. As a result, specific team-building activities might be of use. Higham *et al.* (2005) suggested that a series of exercises where team members in small groups individually discuss which triggers enhance or hinder their personal perceptions of individual and team momentum would be beneficial. This can then lead to an understanding of both the individual and team communication strategies, helping players to optimize perceptions of psychological momentum.

Jones and Harwood (2008) highlighted the importance of focusing on the individual player in any intervention, reinforcing the individual nature of the perceptual process. As a result, team interventions should also consider what the role of the individual is within these team activities or events.

Winning and losing streaks in sport

The concept of positive and negative momentum is also seen to underpin winning and losing streaks in sport. Often when teams are winning they will attribute success to internal factors such as effort or ability; this coupled with the magical ingredient of momentum can result in a team winning and winning and winning, until of course they eventually lose (and they always do). Losing streaks are a little more interesting to consider. Are continued losses just a function of negative momentum, an indication of the skill and ability level of the team, or only the function of learned helplessness in the team? The Cal-Tech Beavers basketball team who play in the NCAA Division III collegiate basketball league are a good example of a team with losing streaks. The California Institute of Technology (Cal-Tech) is home to 32 Nobel Prize winners among its alumni and faculty, but only boasts a student body of around 950. Cal-Tech is a world-renowned private research university known more for its accomplishments in science and engineering than in basketball. Before winning the game against Bard College on 6 January 2007 the Beavers had endured a 207-game (and 11-year) losing streak. Cal-Tech also has the dubious honour of holding the record for the longest losing streak in conference play. On 22 February 2011 the Beavers beat Occidental College 46–45 to finally end a 310-game losing streak stretching back 26 years. Coach Oliver Eslinger stated after beating Occidental that 'tonight's win is a testament to the hard work each member of this team, the alumni and the supporters have put into this program, I hope that everyone who has participated in Caltech men's basketball is able to celebrate a little tonight'.

At the other end of the spectrum there are instances of some quite extraordinary winning streaks in sport: for example, Pakistani squash player Jahangir Khan, who won an amazing 555 consecutive games between 1981 and 1986. In the English Premier league Arsenal won 14 consecutive games between 10 February 2002 and 18 August 2002. Arsenal also hold the record for the longest unbeaten run in the league, standing at 49 games, spanning six months. Finally, Mexican boxer Julio Cesar Chavez holds an amazing career record. He recorded 88 straight professional wins in the ring during a run that lasted several years. But the question remains, was this a function of momentum, or just the best team and player winning?

Summary

While momentum is an accepted aspect of sport, and team sports in particular, the research evidence to date has failed to conclusively prove that the phenomenon exists and that it directly influences performance. There is, however, a range of research evidence supporting the existence of psychological momentum. This appears to stem from responses to trigger situations and events. The way the individual responds to these triggers appears to be crucial. This perceived psychological momentum does have the power to influence performance by influencing individual player responses such as confidence, affect, and behaviour. Interventions should seek to focus on influencing these perceptions in the individual player: first, making sure that the players on the team can maximize their response to positive momentum trigger events and minimize their response to negative momentum trigger events. Finally, understanding how to minimize the impact that the opposition has on perceptions is as important as the ability to maximize the impact that events can have on the opposition's performance.

10

EFFECTIVE TEAM LEADERSHIP

Introduction

Sometimes in sport winning is not about having the best group of players, but about how well those players function as a team. A central aspect of this relates to the leadership of the team. Effective leadership can make all the difference in big games when the pressure is on.

Sports leadership research has a long tradition of borrowing models from industrial and organizational psychology (Rieke *et al.*, 2008). This is partly because sports teams are thought to possess many of the same characteristics as business and work teams. These characteristics include a specific group of personnel, a planned programme of activity, and a division of labour to achieve specific goals (Rieke *et al.*, 2008). Group leadership is probably the role most associated with group effectiveness (Carron *et al.*, 2005). In relation to sports teams and leadership, the majority of written sources focus on the roles and impact of both the coach and manager on the team. The role of the captain as a leader, while no less important, has received far less attention, as have the roles of 'informal' leaders within the team. There are many examples of great leaders in sport. But, interestingly, the factors that made them great appear to differ from case to case. Some great leaders are fantastic at leading by example, others have the capacity to inspire and motivate others, while others still are fantastically organized and manage the structure and environment effectively. Sir Clive Woodward is acknowledged as being a very good leader. He built a very effective structure that underpinned the England rugby union team winning the Rugby world cup for the first time in 2003. However, whilst effective in this environment, a subsequent change of sport to soccer with Southampton Football Club proved to be very unsuccessful, as did a return to rugby union with the British and Irish Lions and their tour to South Africa. As a result, understanding the situational factors that impact upon leadership appears to be as important as the personal characteristics of the leader.

This chapter will explore the main theoretical models that seek to explain the process of effective leadership in sport and the most effective approaches that can be adopted by leaders, whether by the manager, the coach, the captain, or other informal leaders.

What is leadership?

By the very nature of leadership and its application across multiple disciples, there are many differing definitions that exist. For example, Barrow (1977: p.232) defined leadership as ' the behavioural process of influencing individuals and groups toward set goals', whereas Gray (2004) adopted a slightly different approach, suggesting that leadership is 'knowing what should be done, and influencing others to cooperate in doing it' (p.76). This second definition in particular suggests the importance of the knowledge base of the coach as well as the demonstrated leadership behaviours. Yusof and Muraleedharan (2007) highlighted the complexity of leadership when suggesting that a good manager can be a good leader, but a good leader does not necessarily become a good manager. Looking at the differences between good leadership and good management, there is a slightly different focus for each. Management is seen as having a bottom–line focus: how we can best accomplish certain targets, in essence, doing the right things. Leadership looks at the top line: what are the things we want to accomplish, essentially choosing the right direction. Covey (2004) highlighted this by suggesting that 'management is efficiency in climbing the ladder of success; leadership determines whether the ladder is leaning against the right wall' (p.101). In order to become a good leader, you need the ability to be able to plan, organize, and control, as leadership is a concept that allows for both horizontal and vertical applications to human behaviour (Wildman, 2006). This suggests that leadership refers to inter-actions with your peers as well as your subordinates. Northouse (2001) highlighted a number of different components that are central to the concept of leadership: (i) leadership is a process; (ii) leadership involves influence; (iii) leadership occurs within a group context; and (iv) leadership involves goal attainment. Based on this Northouse (2001) went on to define leadership as 'a process whereby an individual influences a group of individuals to achieve a common goal' (p.3).

Glenn and Horn (1993) reported that perceptions of leadership vary depending on whose perspective is considered (self, teammate, or coach). As a result, there is no fully objective angle from which to view how effective a given leader is. Individuals rate themselves on leadership-identified instrumentality (psychological masculinity) and expressiveness (psychological femininity) as descriptors of effective leadership. Instrumentality in this context can be viewed as objectiveness and being instrumental. For ratings by teammates and coaches, skill level emerged as the primary characteristic, and perceived competence as a secondary factor associated with peer performance (Moran and Weiss, 2006).

Within a sports team there are two clear types of leadership role: formal and informal. Informal roles are those that emerge within the team as a result of interactions between teammates and the demands of the task. The team is influenced by the actions of individuals who are the most dominant, assertive, or competent (Carron et al., 2005). Formal leadership roles are those that are prescribed or awarded. Examples of these include coaches, managers, and captains. In general terms, formal leaders have two main responsibilities. First, to ensure that the demands of the organization/club are satisfied and that the team is effective in terms of the goals and objectives of the organization. The second responsibility of every leader is to ensure that the needs and aspirations of team members are fulfilled.

Theoretical models of leadership

In trying to understand leadership, researchers have explored the concept from a number of different perspectives. In order to bring some structure to this Behling and Schriesheim (1976) developed a typology to classify the different theoretical approaches. This was further modified by Carron et al. (2005).

Specifically, Carron et al. (2005) highlighted four main types of approach to the study of leadership: universal traits, situational traits, universal behaviour, and situational behaviour. In addition to these four main types of approach, Bass and Avolio (1994) suggested a full-range leadership model, which also explored transformational, transactional, and laissez-faire leadership approaches. Finally, Graen and Uhl-Bien (1995) suggested a leader–member exchange theory of leadership. Each of these approaches will be explored in the following sections.

The universal trait approach

This is the approach to understanding leadership with the longest history. The main focus of this set of approaches is to explore the personality traits of successful leaders. Numerous studies have sought to explore the relationship between traits and leadership. However, a major drawback of these studies has been the varying approaches to classifying traits. A meta-analysis on the subject by Lord et al. (1986) found two traits that have a statistically significant relationship with leadership emergence. These traits were dominance and masculinity-femininity. This trait approach to leadership was, in the main, abandoned by leadership theorists in favour of situational theories of leadership. However, a recent study by Judge et al. (2002) appears to provide some further support for this approach. In their study Judge and colleagues adopted the five-factor model of personality (neuroticism, extraversion, openness to experience, agreeableness, and conscientiousness) to determine relevant traits of successful and effective leaders. The authors reported a multiple correlation of 0.48 with leadership, which indicates strong support for the leader trait perspective when the five-factor model is used.

The situational trait approach

This approach focuses on both the traits of the person and the characteristics of the specific situation. This works on the assumption that some personality types will be more effective in some situations than others. One example of this is Fiedler's (1967)

Contingency Theory of Leadership. In this approach, leadership effectiveness depends equally upon the leader's style of interacting with the group and the favourableness of the situation. The style of interaction adopted by the leader is thought to vary along a continuum from task orientated at one end to person orientated at the other. Task-orientated leaders derive their greatest satisfaction from the group's performance, productivity, and successful task completion. Person-orientated individuals derive their greatest satisfaction from social contacts, affiliation, and successful interpersonal relationships.

Fiedler (1967) divided leaders into relationship motivated and task motivated by means of their relatively favourable or unfavourable description of the least preferred co-worker on a set of bipolar adjectives (Vroom and Jago, 2007). Fiedler then explored the effectiveness of these two types of leaders in eight different situational types that were created by the combination of three variables: leader–member relations, follower-task structure, and leader-position power.

Leader–member relations refers to the degree of mutual trust, respect, and confidence between the leader and the subordinates. Task structure relates to the extent to which group tasks are clear and structured. Leader-position power highlights the power inherent in the leader's position. Fiedler reported that the relationship-motivated leader was the best performer in four of the situations, but that the reverse was true in the other four situations.

The universal behavioural approach

The main focus in this approach is to understand the general behaviours of successful leaders. In essence, what is it that successful leaders do that makes them a success? Using this approach, different patterns of behaviour were grouped together and labelled as styles. One example of this is the Blake and Mouton Managerial Grid (1978). The four main styles that emerged under this approach were: concern for task, concern for people, directive leadership, and participative leadership.

- *Concern for task* – here, leaders emphasize the achievement of concrete objectives. They look for high levels of productivity and ways to organize people and activities in order to meet those objectives.
- *Concern for people* – in this style, leaders look upon their followers as people: with needs, interests, problems, development, and so on. They are not simply units of production or means to an end.
- *Directive leadership* – this style is characterized by leaders taking decisions for others, and expecting followers or subordinates to follow instructions.
- *Participative leadership* – here leaders try to share decision making with others.

The situational behaviour approach

Here the focus is on identifying behaviours that are successful in specific situations. One example of this is life cycle theory (Hersey and Blanchard, 1982). In this theory leader effectiveness is a product of the leader's behaviour and the level of maturity of subordinates.

According to the life cycle theory, a leader has to evaluate the maturity of his team before deciding on an appropriate leadership style. Maturity in this instance refers to an individual's desire for achievement, willingness to accept responsibility, and past team experience. Four specific phases of the life cycle are highlighted in this theory: high task – low relationship (phase one); high task – high relationship (phase two); low task – low relationship (phase three); low task – high relationship (phase four). In phase one the team needs direction and specific instructions, and also needs to become familiarized with the team's/organization's procedures and policies; as a result, a task-orientated approach is required from the leader. In phase two the leader becomes more familiar with the team members and puts more trust in their ability to perform. As a result, a people-orientated approach is adopted. In phase three team members display greater ability and enhanced performance, increasingly seeking greater responsibility. As a result, the leader should continue to be supportive and encourage greater ownership by the team. In phase four the team members have reached a point of self-directing, and gain greater confidence and experience in their ability to perform.

Multidimensional model of leadership

To date in sport the primary approach to understanding leadership has been through the multidimensional model of leadership. Chelladurai (1990) developed a framework through which the concept of leadership in sport could be better understood, called the multidimensional theory of leadership. This is a sport-specific model focusing on the congruence between three leadership behaviours – required, actual, and preferred behaviours – and their ability to influence team satisfaction and increase performance (Sherman *et al.*, 2000). This model is supported by previous studies on leadership (e.g. Gardner *et al.*, 1996; Ramzaninezhad *et al.*, 2009; Hoigaard *et al.*, 2008), which suggested that, when a coach's leadership style is not aligned with the player's preferred style, the performance of the player may develop but their level of satisfaction may decrease (Chelladurai, 1984).

The multidimensional model focuses on the suitability of, and the relationship between, the three leadership behaviours. Required behaviour refers to how leaders or coaches are required to behave based on the demands from the players and also based on the situation they are in (Frontiera, 2006). Actual behaviour is the behaviour demonstrated by the coach based on their final decision on how to proceed without taking into consideration the preference of the team (Cox, 2002). If the actual behaviour of coaches is congruent with what has been required and preferred by the members of the team, the latter's satisfaction and desired performance will be achieved. Actual behaviour is determined by the interactions of required behaviour, preferred behaviour, and the coach's abilities, experience, and personality (Chelladurai, 1990). Preferred behaviour refers to the behaviour desired by the group members. Normally, this type of behaviour is strongly dependent on the characteristics of the team or individuals.

This multidimensional model indicates that alignment between required, preferred, and actual leadership behaviour may increase the level of team members' satisfaction, thereby strengthening the leadership values among coaches (Cox, 2002). The multi-dimensional model of leadership proposes that the three aspects of leader behaviour need to be in congruence to achieve effective team performance and member satisfaction (Andrew, 2009). The required leader behaviour is influenced by situational char-acteristics such as organizational goals, formal structure, team task, social norms, government regulations, technology, and the nature of the team (Chelladurai, 2006). Team performance and team member satisfaction can be enhanced when the leadership behaviour required by the situation, the leadership behaviour preferred by the players, and the leadership behaviour perceived by the players are similar (Andrew, 2009).

Transactional/transformational leadership

This model of leadership is based on the notion that all leadership can be broken down into two contrasting approaches: transactional and transformational. The transactional leader works on the assumption that the goals and priorities currently in place are the right ones and what needs to be done is to put those properly into motion. The transformational leader works on the assumption that the status quo is no longer an option and a new vision is needed (Chen, 2010).

Transformational leadership

Yukl (1989) described transformational leadership as 'the process of influencing major changes in the attitudes and assumptions of organization members (organization culture) and building commitment for major changes in the organization's objectives and strate-gies' (p.174). Transformational leadership describes four leader behaviours that have been shown to influence team members' values, needs, awareness, and performance (Bass and Riggio, 2006). These four specific behaviours are idealized influence, inspirational motivation, intellectual stimulation, and individualized consideration (Hoption *et al.*, 2007). Idealized influence seeks to instil pride in the players, setting a good example and earning the respect of the team. Bass and Steidlmeier (1999) highlighted the importance of the leader's morals and values in influencing this process. Inspirational motivation refers to leaders who convey optimism and enthusiasm to the players, and in doing so enhance the players' self-efficacy. This inspirational motivation also includes the development of a collective purpose and a shared vision, which contributes to team spirit, morale, and psychological climate. Intellectual stimulation encourages players to be creative, solve problems in innovative ways, and question established assumptions (Bass and Riggio, 2006). Individualized consideration seeks to address the unique needs and capabilities of each member of the team through advising, listening, compassion, and empathy (Hoption *et al.*, 2007).

Transactional leadership

In transactional leadership the leader clearly outlines tasks and how the tasks should be performed. Team members agree to complete the assignments in exchange for either pay or psychological compensation (e.g. recognition or awards). Three specific leader behaviours have been identified for the transactional approach: contingent reward, active management-by-exception, and passive management-by-exception. Contingent reward is a leadership behaviour where the leader is focused on clearly articulated tasks, while also providing followers with rewards for the completion of these tasks. Active management-by-exception behaviours see the leader watching and actively searching for deviations from rules and standards in order to avoid these deviations. Management-by-exception passive interventions only occur once errors have been detected and standards have not been met (Rowold, 2006).

Leaders can be both transformational and transactional. However, transformational leadership is associated with significantly greater leader effectiveness when compared to transactional leadership (Lowe *et al.*, 1996). Bass (1990) also suggested that transformational leadership is particularly effective in crises or in situations undergoing change. In a study of South African cricket association members, Ristow *et al.* (1999) found that the relationship between transformational leadership factors and organization effectiveness was significant, and that the relationship between transactional leadership and organizational effectiveness was not significant. It has been demonstrated that it is not an either/or situation, however; in order for a leader to act in both of these ways they need themselves to be transformational (Chen, 2010).

Leader–member exchange theory

The leader–member exchange theory is based on the assumption that the type of relationship that exists between leaders and followers can provide results more predictive of how an organization or team is doing than can trait or behaviour studies. This theory examines relationships rather than individual leaders and followers, and looks at the linkages among people rather than simply the leader themself (Chen, 2010). In this way this theory seeks to understand the leadership environment rather than just the leader, recognizing that leader effectiveness is based on the interaction between the leader, the team members, the environment, and the situation.

The role of the captain in the team

Captaincy, like coaching, varies significantly depending on the sport and the level of competition. Some sports do not identify a formal on-field 'leader' or captain, but do have informal leaders in the team; whilst, in the sports that do have formal captaincy roles, the scope of the position can vary greatly. For example, in soccer the captain is a formal leader on the pitch and a role model off it, but the way the team plays and major tactical decisions during the game are determined by the head coach. In cricket, on the other hand, the team is very much run by the captains. The captain makes all the decisions on the pitch and is part of the formal leadership structure off the pitch. Whilst the role of the captain can change from sport to sport there is a consensus that an effective captain is invaluable to the team and its performance outcomes.

A number of researchers have highlighted the importance of the captain as a source of leadership within a team (Kozub and Pease, 2001: Loughead and Hardy, 2005). In spite of this highlighted importance, leadership literature in sport has mainly focused upon the role of coaches as leaders and their impact on the individuals and teams they lead. According to Glenn and Horn (1993) a coach or manager will have one or two players on a team whose role includes providing motivation and direction to their teammates. As a captain, these individuals are sometimes clearly marked for the purpose (wearing the letter C in ice hockey, or an armband in soccer). Often captains are selected based upon their level of performance (Yukelson et al., 1983) and the position they play (Lee and Partridge, 1983). Mosher (1979) suggested that team captains have three main responsibilities. First, the captain acts as a liaison between the coaching staff and the team. Second, the captain acts as a leader during all team activities. Third, the captain represents the team at events, meetings, and press conferences. In addition to this, Mosher also highlighted specific duties that the captain might perform. These included: ensuring a constant flow of information between the coach and team; to lead by example; to help the coach in the planning stages for the team; and to conduct themselves in a professional manner before, during, and after the game with respect to teammates, opponents, and officials. Dupuis et al. (2006) reported a number of similarities between ice hockey captains from different teams. These included being effective communicators, remaining positive, controlling emotions, and remaining respectful to coaches. The tactical position in the team also appears to be an important consideration in the selection of a captain for a team. Melnick and Loy (1996), exploring the recruitment of captains in New Zealand provincial rugby teams, found that 35% of captains played in the two most central positions (no. eight and half-back). The three most peripheral spatial positions (centre, wing, and full-back) yielded no captains.

Brearley (2001) highlighted the sacrifices that the captain makes within the team. While the role often rewards them with influence and standing in relation to the task, there is often a social cost. Brearley specifically highlighted the difficulty in being 'one of the boys' and engaging in normal banter and gossip like the rest of the team.

The use of the vice-captain role also differs from sport to sport and team to team. Indeed, some sports do not formally award vice-captain roles, whilst others do in a relatively haphazard way. Also, linked to the notion of the vice-captain is the role that these individuals actually fulfil in the team. Is the role of the vice-captain to be the 'next in line' just in case something happens to the captain? Or, is the role of the vice-captain to be someone with a different skill set who can complement the captain's approach whilst still subscribing to the same vision for the team? The majority of teams adopt the former approach (with the vice-captain the next in line). But, it can be argued that adopting the latter (with the vice-captain fulfilling a supportive and complementary role) might be more beneficial to team functioning and, ultimately, team performance.

Co-leaders

Co-leadership typically describes situations where two or more individuals are designated as leaders of a group (Rilling and Jordan, 2007), and it is generally accepted to be a positive practice for team leadership. Co-leadership approaches have been associated with positive outcomes for both team members and leaders (Gladding, 2003). These positive benefits have specifically been linked to co-leaders modelling relationships, providing more diverse feedback, providing mutual support, broadening transference reactions, developing enhanced group interaction assessments, and sharing specialized knowledge (Okech and Kline, 2005). Co-leadership has also been highlighted as a popular method for training and developing novice leaders (Posthuma, 2002). While co-leadership is generally seen as positive, it is important to highlight potential disadvantages. The main disadvantages emerge from issues in the co-leaders' relationships. These problems include a failure to coordinate efforts, excessive leader interactions, collusion, and co-leader competition (Kline, 2003). These issues usually emerge from different theoretical backgrounds, disagreements about leadership style, incompatibility, and different views on strategy (Okech and Kline, 2005).

Dugo and Beck (1997) developed a model of co-leadership development that highlighted nine specific phases:

1 *Creating a contract* – the co-leaders agree on norms and expectations for the group.
2 *Forming an identity* – this builds on the development of an understanding of both the similarities and differences between the co-leaders.
3 *Building a team* – setting up the structure and organization of the team and how it will operate.
4 *Developing closeness* – co-leaders adjust to a greater understanding of each other.
5 *Defining strengths and limitations* – understanding the issues that might cause conflict either with the team or between leaders.
6 *Exploring possibilities* – this is essentially a revisiting of the contracting stage.
7 *Supporting self-confrontation* – developing the ability to be critical of the self and the other leader.
8 *Integrating and implementing changes* – this is based on the new understanding that develops from the previous stage.
9 Closing – this involves a termination and review of the relationship and process.

This model was developed based on group dynamics literature and presents a comprehensive overview of the development of co-leader relationships. Whilst this is a comprehensive model, it is not the only one. A number of simpler models have been suggested, including the one developed by Gallogly and Levine (1979). In this model there are five stages: parallel phase, authority crisis and inclusion phase, intimacy crisis phase, mutuality phase, and the separation/crisis/termination phase. The stages highlighted in Gallogly and Levine's (1979) model are similar in general content to those suggested by Dugo and Beck (1997). Gallogly and Levine also highlighted the potential for regression into the previous stage within this model.

Enhancing leadership

Zacharatos *et al.* (2000) suggested several factors that distinguish effective leaders:

- leaders have to be effective in meeting the organizational requirements of the role;
- leaders have to ensure a high degree of team member satisfaction; and
- leaders need to continually help team members to develop their physical and mental abilities to improve their performance.

Leaders can also seek to increase their influence or power within the team by paying attention to their appearance, demonstrating self-confidence and expertise, appropriately allocating rewards and sanctions, and being an example to try to emulate (Murray and Mann, 2006).

- *Appearance* – the relevance of the appearance to the situation is important. The 'accepted' dress code differs from sport to sport. How clean and professional the leader looks is also of importance in setting the tone for the team.
- *Demonstrating self-confidence and expertise* – the team members are more likely to follow someone who has expertise and prior experience relating to the task in hand. Also, the individual needs to have confidence in his or her own ability and be confident (and also be seen to be confident) in the choices that they make.
- *Allocation of rewards and sanctions* – the degree to which the leader can apply rewards and sanctions has a direct impact on their power. If this ability is compromised, the leader's power will be reduced in the team.
- *Being an example to try to emulate* – leading by example is also important for a leader. Team members are far more likely to follow someone who leads from the front or has the relevant experience than someone who does not.

Laios *et al.* (2003) suggested that effective leaders should engage in the following behaviours:

- *Continue to develop interpersonal skills* – interacting with other people is crucial to the role of the leader in sport. In particular, verbal and non-verbal skills are central to this (see Chapter 5 for more details).
- *Work towards building a cohesive team* – the cohesiveness of the team is a key determinant of performance outcomes and team effectiveness. Thus, the leader should be looking to enhance cohesion where possible (see Chapter 6 for more details).
- *Listen well* – this is linked to the first point and effective interpersonal skills. Listening is crucial to building good relationships, and relationships are central to leader effectiveness. As a result, learning to understand people in greater detail is crucial.
- *Make strong decisions and be willing to be accountable for those decisions* – in order to be most effective leaders need to have a plan. They need both the determination to do it their way and be willing to accept the responsibility for the ultimate success or failure of the plan.

- *Be an active and direct problem solver* – active problem solving requires a pragmatic approach focusing on the direct issues that need resolving. Dealing with issues when they arise reduces stress in the long term, as issues do not drag on unresolved.
- *Create standards for performance* – effective goal setting and quantifying performance is also important. Developing minimum standards of behaviour and performance is a key component of an effective team. Crucially, linked to this is the need for the team to buy into these performance standards and to not necessarily see them as being imposed.
- *Recognize and reward generously* – reward and praise are important tools for the leader to use. The consistency and equality of these is also important. Consistent approaches give clear messages and guidelines to the team; as a result, the consistent meaning of the rewards and praise is enhanced.
- *Convey enthusiasm* – a key role of the leader is to motivate and empower the team. So the leader needs to adopt a positive outlook on situations. The leader's outlook and demeanour will be transmitted to the rest of the team. As a result, the leader's enthusiasm and positivity will be transmitted to the team. If the leader is defeatist and downbeat this will also be transmitted to the team.
- *Teach relevant skills* – often the leader also needs to act as a coach to 'up-skill' members of the team to be able to fulfil their role and to cope with the demands placed upon them. Sharing knowledge and skills is important to empower individuals within the team, but also creates a closer bond between individuals.
- *Use punishment as a last resort, but make punishments clear at the start* – the development of rules and boundaries is important. Crucially these should be developed and communicated at the start. This way the team is aware of the punishment associated with relevant behaviours. This prior development of punishment also removes the emotion from the decision making at the moment when team members have broken team rules for behaviour.

Being a more effective captain

Dupuis *et al.* (2006) highlighted the importance of the captain in mentoring younger players, and in particular the importance of providing information, support, and guidance. The team captain makes an effort to set the right example, and in return the younger players will follow in the captain's footsteps. Captains in most sports are the on-the-pitch leaders as well as off-field representatives for the team and also potential role models. As such, captains need to adhere to a standard of behaviour both on and off the pitch that is reflective of the values of the team and/or organization. The captain also needs to lead by example in game situations, in relation to the style of play, response to environmental factors, and response to officials within the sport. The captain will also act as a source of inspiration and motivation to the rest of the team. Therefore, developing each of these areas is important to be effective.

It is important to remember that a successful team is built upon a series of successful individual performances. Due to this fact an effective captain needs to value the performance and input of all team members during the game/performance. The ability to influence all of the team in slightly different ways either before or during a game is a key characteristic of truly effective captains. Also, as with other forms of leadership, the ability to empower others is crucial to ultimate success.

Effective co-leadership in elite cricket

At the end of 2008 the England cricket team was in disarray. The then team captain Kevin Peterson and head coach Peter Moores were publicly battling for control of the team. This struggle ultimately resulted in the removal of both men from their leadership positions in the team. Appointed into the leadership void that resulted were Andrew Strauss and Andy Flower. Andrew Strauss had fought his way back into the team following being dropped due to poor form a couple of years earlier. Under the previous leadership regime Andy Flower had been assistant coach to Peter Moores, before assuming the role of England Team Director. The first game with the new leadership in charge was a disaster. The team were bowled out for 51 by the West Indies to lose the first test by an innings. At this point Strauss and Flower formulated a plan for the team, its regeneration, and an effective approach to co-leadership that culminated two-and-a-half years later in the summer of 2011 with the England cricket team becoming ranked number one in the world. This remarkable transformation has been attributed, at least in part, to the leadership and working relationship that Strauss and Flower embody. The England and Wales Cricket Board managing director, Hugh Morris, highlighted the importance of the clear shared direction and vision presented to players and management alike. The pair developed into a very effective leadership team who have a clear approach and whose differing interpersonal styles further complement each other. The challenge for the leadership team, though, will change, having become number one in the world. Andrew Strauss highlighted this fact by stating that 'we won't prepare any differently but obviously we're the hunted rather than the hunters. There is a different mindset now, but we have to make sure we approach the games the same way we always have.' Flower highlighted the importance of resetting the team's goals: 'we used the goal to be No 1 as a motivational tool, but what Strauss and I don't want is just to hang on to No 1 status. We've always had a goal of constant self-improvement and that doesn't change just because our ranking points change.' Central to the success of the England team has been the environment created by Strauss and Flower. The team environment is now a very honest and open environment where all the players can have their say. There has also been an increase in personal responsibility for players who are more responsible and accountable for their actions and performance. All of this has led to the rise to number one in the world. The question, though, is how long can the team stay there?

Summary

As this chapter demonstrates, the leadership that a team receives is fundamental to the team's success or failure. This is true for managers, coaches, captains, and informal leaders. Effective leaders influence, inspire, and motivate both individuals and the team. Mike Brearley (2001), in his book titled *The Art of Captaincy*, suggested that fundamental to the role of captain is the desire to understand what makes people tick. Whilst understanding the characteristics of the individual and the situation are important, the interaction between the two appears to be critical to success. The more the coach is aware of the situational demands, the more likely they are to be successful in a variety of environments. As a result, the self-awareness of the leader and in particular their style, strengths, and weaknesses appear to be important.

11

MENTAL AND EMOTIONAL RECOVERY

Introduction

Performing and training can take a significant physical and psychological toll on sports performers. Indeed, whilst the volume of physical training is an important factor in how hard a team is working, other important factors need to be considered, including the team environment, the interactions between team members, and the logistics associated with being a competitive team. While many teams plan for physical recovery, the planning for mental and emotional recovery is less well defined. This issue is of particular concern due to the psychological and emotional costs of performing and continually interacting in a team environment. The effective planning of team recovery is further complicated by the degree of personal preferences and individual differences that exist regarding what is considered to constitute effective recovery. A particular challenge for the management and coaching staff of a team is how to ensure all team members have the opportunity to recover effectively between training sessions and matches/competitions.

This issue is easier to manage when training and performing in the 'normal' home environment. But, when travelling to away fixtures and performing in tournaments, the provision of opportunity, time, and space to recover effectively is more difficult. Without sufficient recovery both the team and its individual members are at risk of a number of negative outcomes including overreaching, overtraining, staleness, and burnout.

Overtraining often develops because specific indicators of fatigue have not been detected or monitored over a period of time, or the player or the coach is not aware of the symptoms – both factors that relate to underrecovery, with research specifically highlighting underrecovery as a precursor of overtraining (Kellmann, 2002a). As a result, an active and proactive recovery programme is an important factor in preventing overtraining. Four specific levels within the training process have been identified that include undertraining, optimal training, overreaching and overtraining (Foster and Lehmann, 1997). Understanding the factors that moderate the shift from optimal training to overtraining is crucial.

The aim of this chapter is to explore in greater depth the role and types of recovery relating to team sports. The chapter will also explore the impact that underrecovery has and the symptoms and outcomes relating to overtraining and burnout. Finally, the chapter will explore techniques to monitor the symptoms of overtraining and burnout, explore strategies to enhance the quality of recovery, and consider team-related factors that can impact upon the recovery process.

Recovery

Recovery from training, travel, and competition is seen as a key aspect of effective team performance. Whilst the specific details of recovery will ultimately be focused at the individual level, planning for effective recovery needs to take place at the team level to ensure equity in opportunity and provision. Recovery has been described as the psychosociophysiological process of eliminating fatigue and regaining vitality (Kenttä and Dieffenbach, 2008) and has been specifically defined by Kellmann and Kallus (2001: p.22) as:

> An inter- and intra-individual multilevel (e.g. psychological, physiological, social) process in time for the re-establishment of performance abilities. Recovery includes an action-orientated component, and those self-initiated activities (proactive recovery) can be systematically used to optimize situational conditions to build up and to refill personal resources and buffers.

This definition clearly highlights the importance of the psychological, physiological, and social aspects of recovery.

Lundqvist and Kenttä (2010) also highlighted the impact that the conscious decisions taken by the individual and the team can have on recovery, suggesting that these decisions can influence the rate and organization of the recovery process. As a result, performers strive to choose the most efficient recovery options, but often this is constrained by both opportunity and knowledge. As well as physical recovery, psychological and emotional recoveries are also crucial aspects of the complete recovery process. The process of recovery is not just about the elimination of stress, but is also characterized by an active personalized process that must take place in order to re-establish psychological and physiological strength (Kellmann et al., 2001). There has historically been a greater focus on the mood aspects of psychological recovery (Lundqvist and Kenttä, 2010), but more recently the emotional responses that arise from engagement in sports performance have also been suggested to be an important factor influencing the recovery process (Sonnentag and Fritz, 2007).

A number of different emotions are cited as being important in the recovery process, and as a result these emotions either serve to support or interfere with recovery (Sonnentag and Fritz, 2007). In simple terms, negative emotions (such as anger) are seen to interfere with recovery, whereas positive emotions (such as hope and pride) are seen to support the recovery process (for further details on emotions please see Chapter 8). Fredrickson and Branigan (2005) took this notion one step further in suggesting that positive emotions can also undo or reverse the detrimental effects of negative emotions.

As previously mentioned, mood also appears to be an important consideration when focusing on recovery. Raglin (1993) highlighted the existence of a relationship between the volume of training undertaken and the performer's mood state. This dose–response relationship appears to demonstrate that increases in training volume have a negative effect on the athlete's mood (Kellman et al., 2001). Conversely, increases in performer mood state have been directly correlated with a reduction in the amount of training (Berger et al., 1999; Martin et al., 2000).

Achieving a balance between training/competition stress and recovery is essential to achieving consistently high levels of performance. Underrecovery can result in poor psychological and physiological outcomes, including overtraining and burnout. Specifically, a prolonged imbalance between stress and recovery can lead to over-training. To avoid underrecovery, both physiological and psychological recovery should be a significant part of any integrated recovery plan (Hooper and Mackinnin, 1995). Underrecovery relates to insufficient time for the team and team members to recover fully. This lack of a full recovery has the knock-on effect of reducing the level of stress both the team and team members can cope with.

Recovery is an active process, but at the same time is specific to each player. It is important for coaches and managers to plan regular rest sessions and recovery days as part of the overall training and competition structure. Indeed, good managers and coaches will also pay close attention to their players' responses and throw in extra unplanned recovery sessions and rest days if required. Kellmann (2002b) suggested that activities including dancing, meeting friends, stretching, playing indoor games, reading books, going for walks, going on sightseeing trips, and easy runs are all good examples of recovery activities. However, Kellmann (2002b) also highlighted that the same activities might not have the same recovery effect for different players. As a result the more individualized that recovery can be (within the constraints of planning for the whole team), the better. Good coaches will at times leave players to decide what to do by themselves, and at other times provide some direction or options. The key focus here is the re-establishment of physiological and psychological resources.

Sleep has been identified as one of the most important contributors to recovery. This can help the player adjust to, and cope with, the physical, neurological, immunological, and emotional stressors that the players would have experienced during the day. Griffin and Tyrell (2004) reported that poor sleeping patterns and insufficient rest is associated with individuals who suffer with high levels of anxiety and depression. Griffin and Tyrell further highlighted a link between excessive dreaming, poor sleeping patterns and depression. Evidence suggests that, when players are stressed, they spend more time in dream sleep and not enough time in slow-wave sleep, where physical regeneration and recovery mainly takes place. The reason why dreaming can be unhelpful to recovery is that the brain is in a similar state to when it is awake. Essentially, dreaming can be hard work. To your brain, dreams are real, and as such can be hormonally and emotionally draining, resulting in feelings of fatigue in the morning.

Different types of recovery

While all team members will require some type of recovery programme to perform effectively both individually and collectively, the types of recovery interventions that are most useful can change from person to person and situation to situation. The important aspect of this recovery planning is to match the recovery intervention to the stress symptoms that have depleted the individual's ability to cope. Kenttä and Hassmen (1998) highlighted four main categories of recovery interventions: nutrition and hydration, sleep and rest, relaxation and emotional support, and stretching and active rest.

- *Nutrition and hydration* – a poor diet with insufficient calorie and fluid intake will decrease the capacity for the performer to tolerate physiological and psychological stress. It is also important that a 'normal' diet for many sports performers will elicit the same outcome. As a result, it is important that the food and fluid intake for each performer matches their personal requirements based on the task and individual differences.
- *Sleep and rest* – these are seen as the obvious types of recovery. Rest in its purest sense relates to no physical activity, and crucially obtaining sufficient sleep. Often players and the team management alike give too little consideration to achieving optimal sleep. Humans are generally habitual creatures. As such, we all have pre-ferred environments and routines that enable us to gain the maximum amount of quality sleep. Changes to these routes can impact upon the quality and duration of sleep and as a result significantly impact upon recovery. Teams who travel to away fixtures and stay in hotels need to consider the impacts on the ability of team members to recover effectively in these changing environments.
- *Relaxation and emotional support* – relaxation techniques have been suggested as effective proactive recovery strategies (Marion, 1995). These could include the use of saunas, steam rooms, and massages. Also 'time-out' periods from training are recommended to enhance recovery.
- *Stretching and active rest* – active rest refers to low-volume and low-intensity activities (such as low-intensity cycling or low-intensity weight training) that are used to enhance the recovery process between training sessions and games. By increasing blood flow as part of this low-intensity activity, the body can remove waste products quicker and thereby limit the negative effects on relevant muscle tissue. Stretching is also seen as a positive recovery strategy due to the increased blood flow that is generated through the muscles.

Realistically, a combination of these four different categories of recovery interventions will be utilized most of the time. The crucial factor here relates to identifying the depleted resources (e.g. physical, emotional, psychological, biochemical) and utilizing interventions that specifically target these areas. The coach, manager, and support staff also need to be flexible and responsive in the recovery processes that are put in place. As demands change, so the recovery interventions need to reflect these demands. Coaches who are in tune with the physical, emotional, and mental state of the team can quickly modify the focus and duration of training sessions, consider the inclusion of rest days, and manage the inclusion of team events to ensure optimal performance is achieved.

Team factors influencing recovery

In any team, the very nature of that team can have a draining effect on the group and the individual team members. In particular, team social activities, travel, communication structures, and personal individual differences can all have an impact. Travel in particular can have a number of specific effects, particularly where travel across long distances is involved. In many cases travel as an activity can be stressful, particularly as it involves a greater degree of pre-planning on behalf of the players. Also, travelling by coach, plane, or train forces players to be stuck in relatively static positions for relatively long durations. This in itself can evoke physical soreness and discomfort that requires 'recovery'. There is also potentially the stress associated with the adaptation to a new environment, which might include sharing a hotel room or apartment. This can have an impact at an individual level but also, due to the associated fatigue, tiredness and stress can also impact upon the quality of group communication and interactions. Other factors relating to sleep are also important. Changes to the normal sleeping environment can have a negative impact on the quality and duration of sleep. Sleeping on a harder or softer mattress with more or less ambient noise can all impact upon sleep. This will in turn impact upon the amount of stressors the individual can cope with in subsequent days. Travelling to different time zones which might upset the body clock can be problematic, as can different environmental conditions (such as heat and humidity). If a team fails to plan effectively for these aspects of recovery, the team will either require more time to recover following travelling, or will only be able to perform at a lower level, neither of which is desirable.

Overtraining

Successful training must involve the physical and psychological overload of the individual for adaptation to take place. However, it is important to avoid either excessive overload or inadequate recovery. Overtraining can be characterized by an ongoing performance plateau that does not improve with normal amounts of rest and recovery. Common symptoms associated with overtraining include depressed mood, general apathy, decreased self-esteem and performance, emotional instability, restlessness, irritability, poor sleep, weight loss, loss of appetite, increased resting heart rate and vulnerability to injuries, hormonal changes, and the absence of super-compensation (Kellmann, 2010). There is also an increased risk of infection, which also suggests that impairment to the immune system is a further possible outcome of overtraining (Kellmann, 2002a). Fry and colleagues (1991) suggested four main categories of symptoms associated with overtraining: (i) physiological symptoms; (ii) psychological symptoms; (iii) biochemical symptoms; and (iv) immunological symptoms. A specific list of symptoms is presented in Table 11.1.

It is important, however, to highlight the variability in the symptoms that individual performers present. The observed symptoms can change from player to player and from one episode to another. In the sport and exercise literature various terminology is used to describe this concept. Current terminology includes overtraining syndrome, overtrained, overstrained, overused, overworked, overstressed, overreaching, stagnation, staleness, staleness syndrome, burnout, and chronic fatigue syndrome (Kenttä and Hassmen, 1998).

TABLE 11.1 Symptoms of overtraining

Symptoms
Altered resting heart rate and blood pressure
Chronic fatigue
Decreased efficiency of movement and physical performance
Decreased lactate response
Decreased maximum work capacity
Frequent nausea/gastrointestinal upsets
Headaches
Impaired muscular strength
Inability to meet previously attained performance standards or criteria
Increased frequency of respiration
Insatiable thirst
Insomnia
Joint aches and pains
Lack of appetite
Lower percentage of body fat
Menstrual disruptions
Muscle soreness and tenderness
Prolonged recovery from exercise
Reappearance of previously corrected mistakes
Changes in personality
Decreased self-esteem and motivation to work out
Difficulty concentrating during work, school, or training
Emotional instability
Fear of competition
Feelings of sadness and depression
General apathy
'Giving up' when the going gets tough
Being easily distracted during tasks

Source: adapted from Fry *et al.* (1991)

Overtraining has been suggested to result from a number of training factors, including monotonous and repetitive training sessions, in excess of three hours' training per day, failure to build in sufficient easy-training days, poor periodization, and no rest days (Smith and Norris, 2002).

Foster and Lehmann (1997) divided the training process into four specific levels: undertraining, optimal training, overreaching, and overtraining. The ultimate aim is to have the team operating at an optimal training level, without progressing through to overtraining. Many scholarly articles that focus on overtraining make reference to the work of Kreider *et al.* (1998) for definitions of both overreaching and overtraining. Kreider *et al.* (1998) referred to overreaching as an accumulation of training and non-training stress that in the short term results in a decrease in performance capacity without associated physiological or psychological symptoms. In this case restoration of performance capacity may take from a few days to several weeks.

Overtraining was described by Kreider *et al.* (1998) as an accumulation of training and/or non-training stress resulting from long-term decrements in performance capacity with or without associated physiological and psychological symptoms, where the restoration of performance capacity can take from a few weeks up to several months. These descriptions suggest that the main difference between overreaching and overtraining is the recovery time required (Meeusen *et al.*, 2006). Overtraining can have a catastrophic impact on both individual and team performance. Thus it is important to understand the symptoms and, importantly, the different approaches to assessing the existence of overtraining.

Another concept closely linked to overtraining is that of staleness. This term was defined by the American Medical Association (1966) as 'a physiological state of overtraining which manifests as deteriorated athletic readiness' (p.126). As a result, staleness is often seen as an end result or outcome of overtraining.

Staleness is seen as a psychobiological phenomenon in which physiological changes have a profound effect on psychological aspects and vice versa (Polman and Houlahan, 2004).

In general terms, staleness is often seen as a precursor to burnout.

Burnout

Another concept closely associated with recovery and overtraining is that of burnout. Burnout consists of emotional, physical, and psychological components, and is a result of a chronic imbalance between perceived demands and perceived capabilities to respond. Typical symptoms include a lack of energy, exhaustion, sleeplessness, depression, tension, irritability, anger, headaches, disillusionment with the sport, a loss of confidence, and a withdrawal from participation (Polman and Houlahan, 2004).

Burnout can affect dedicated and idealistic players who are motivated toward high achievement and who work in unrewarding situations: in particular, those players who work far too hard; for too long; with too much intensity; and are extremely dedicated (Fender, 1989). The physical, mental, and emotional exhaustion that results from burnout can lead to players developing a negative view of themselves (self-concept), negative attitudes towards the team, its goals, and teammates, and a loss of energy and purpose (Schaufeli *et al.*, 1993).

Calder (1996) highlighted a number of warning signs relating to the onset of burnout. These included:

- *Direct communication* – players communicating that they have heavy legs, don't feel well, are experiencing soreness, and feel tired.
- *Body language* – negative facial expressions and lack of facial colour, or slumped posture, or withdrawn demeanour demonstrate increased levels of frustration.
- *Performance* – poor skill execution, slow acceleration, heavy feet, poor and/or slow decision making, excessive weariness that is prolonged.
- *Psychological signs* – emotional and mood swings and imbalances, low motivation and apathy, low concentration, more aggression and hostility, confusion, increasing anxiety, loss of self-confidence.
- *Lifestyle* – poor eating habits, poor diet, poor sleeping patterns, external stress.

Smith (1986) suggested a cognitive-affective model of burnout in sport. In this model Smith proposes that burnout is a process that involves psychological, physiological, and behavioural components, all of which develop through four specific stages. Smith also suggested that each of these highlighted stages was influenced by individual differences (such as motivation and personality differences). The four stages highlighted were:

- *Situational demands* – here high demands are placed on the performer and, where the demands outweigh the available resources, stress occurs.
- *Cognitive appraisal* – in this stage the individual performer interprets the situation. Typically this is related to the degree of threat or challenge that is perceived.
- *Physiological responses* – if the situation is seen as threatening, then over time the associated stress can initiate physiological responses such as increased tension and increased fatigue. Typically those experiencing burnout also experience depleted emotional resources and are more susceptible to illness and injury.
- *Behavioural responses* – the responses in the previous stage result in behavioural adaptations that can include decreased performance, interpersonal challenges, and, potentially, withdrawal from the team or environment.

In Kenttä and Hassmén's (1998) conceptual model of overtraining and recovery, overtraining and burnout are seen as the negative products of long-term imbalances between the total stressors and total recovery efforts, which exceed a performer's maximum stress tolerance. Maslach and Jackson (1984) viewed burnout as a psychological syndrome characterized by emotional exhaustion, a reduced sense of accomplishment, and depersonalization. Building on the work of Maslach and Jackson, Raedeke (1997) defined burnout as a psychological syndrome of emotional/physical exhaustion, reduced sense of accomplishment, and sport devaluation.

Measuring and assessing recovery, overtraining, and burnout

Whilst a range of physiological and biochemical indicators have been monitored in an attempt to recognize the onset of overtraining, the research evidence to support their effectiveness has been mixed. Indeed, these findings have often been contradictory (Kuipers and Keizer, 1988). Trying to differentiate normal adaptionary changes in markers from abnormal ones has proven to be very difficult and complex at both a physiological and biochemical level. Also, there is often a time lag in the availability of these results due to the tests employed (Kellmann, 2010) and the complex processes used to assess their outcomes. As a result, it has been suggested that psychological measures might offer a more instantaneous and reliable indicator of increased risk of overtraining (Kellmann, 2002a).

O'Connor (1998) suggested four specific advantages in using psychological markers to monitor overtraining, recovery, and burnout. First, psychological changes were suggested to be more reliable, for example, changes in mood coincide with changes in training load. Second, some mood states are highly sensitive to increases in training load, whilst others are more sensitive to overtraining. Third, variations in measures of mood often correlate with those of physiological marks. Finally, the adjustment of training loads based on mood responses to overtraining appears to have good potential for preventing overtraining.

A number of different tools have been developed to assess recovery, overtraining, and burnout. These include the Emotional Recovery Questionnaire and the Total Quality Recovery Scale for recovery; the Profile of Mood States, the Recovery-Stress Questionnaire for Athletes, and the CR10 scale for overtraining; and the Athlete Burnout Questionnaire for burnout.

Lundqvist and Kenttä (2010) developed the Emotional Recovery Questionnaire (EmRecQ) to assess the emotional recovery of sports performers. The EmRecQ consists of 22 items that assess five emotional states. Answers are rated on a five-point likert scale ranging from one (not at all), to five (extremely). The five subscales are happiness, security, harmony, love, and vitality. The EmRecQ is designed to assess recovery actions and global perceptions of recovery on a daily basis.

The Total Quality Recovery Scale (TQR, Kenttä and Hassmén, 2002) is a framework for the training and recovery process. The TQR scale is composed of two subscales. The first is TQR perceived, which focuses on the performer's perception of recovery (concentrating on psychophysiological cues such as soreness, heaviness, and mood states). The second subscale is TQR action, which quantifies and monitors the actions that the performer engages in to recover. To this end, the player accumulates 'points' based on the recovery activities that they engage in (points activities are outlined in the TQR manual). The use of the TQR is designed to make it possible to monitor and potentially accelerate the recovery process by developing a greater understanding of the actions required to achieve recovery.

Historically the main psychological tools for monitoring training, overtraining, and underrecovery have either been the Profile of Mood States (POMS; McNair et al., 1992) or the Borg CR10 scale of perceived exertion (Borg, 1998). The POMS is a 64-item questionnaire that assesses players on specific moods including tension-anxiety, depression-dejection, anger-hostility, fatigue-inertia, confusion-bewilderment, and vigour-activity. Each item is scored on a five-point likert scale ranging from zero (not at all) to four (extremely). These mood factors are then combined to form an overall assessment of the performer's mood state that is termed the 'total mood disturbance'. This results in a value between -24 and 177, with lower scores indicative of people with more stable mood profiles. A shorter (37-item) version of the questionnaire has also been developed and has been shown to be highly correlated with the longer version. The POMS has quite a long tradition of use in both applied and research settings and has demonstrated good reliability and validity.

The Borg (1998) CR10 scale is a category ratio scale with values ranging from one (nothing at all) to ten (extremely strong) that is used to gain ratings of pain and exertion. Put simply, the greater the pain and exertion ratings, the greater the risk of overtraining. This scale is designed to quantify how well the player feels they are recovering, and thus can be a useful tool to increase self-awareness.

More recently the Recovery-Stress Questionnaire for Athletes (RESTQ-Sport) has been developed (Kellmann and Kallus, 2001) to assess overtraining. The RESTQ-Sport was developed to allow a systematic measurement of the recovery and stress of athletes. The recovery-stress state indicates the extent to which someone is physically or mentally stressed as well as whether they are capable of using strategies for recovery. Whilst there has been extensive use of the RESTQ-Sport for individual sports, there is a limited number of studies exploring recovery in team environments. Coutts and Reaburn (2008) explored the stress and recovery of rugby league players and reported that the RESTQ-Sport appeared to be a useful tool to monitor stress and recovery for team sports players.

In an attempt to quantify burnout Raedeke and Smith (2001) validated the Athlete Burnout Questionnaire (ABQ). The questionnaire consists of 15 items that participants rate on a five-point likert scale ranging from one (almost never) to five (almost always). The questionnaire consists of three subscales: RA – reduced sense of accomplishment, E – emotional/physical exhaustion, D – devaluation. The data collected in this questionnaire seek to provide a greater degree of understanding and monitoring of the antecedents of burnout.

Strategies to enhance mental and emotional recovery

The aim of any successful team must be to enhance recovery to reduce the potential effects of underrecovery. This requires a focus on physical, psychological, and social factors.

Calder (2003) highlighted a number of strategies that could be utilized to enhance psychological recovery in sports performers. Specifically Calder highlighted debriefing, emotional recovery contingency planning, access to social support, mental toughness skills, and relaxation techniques as being important.

Strategies to prevent overtraining

Kellmann (2010) suggested that the single biggest risk factor for overtraining is insufficient recovery time between practices and/or games. Other factors such as nutrition, sleep deficit, sickness, and travel serve to increase the effects of insufficient recovery. Peterson (2003) suggested four steps to recognize the symptoms of over-training, and to develop preventative strategies:

- Know the symptoms of overtraining.
- Increase the level of player self-awareness.
- Model and teach the value of recovery.
- Keep training fun, and keep sport in perspective.

In the first step it is crucial that the coach and support team are aware of the symp-toms of overtraining. This forms the basis of any preventative strategy. Assuming this knowledge is in place, the next step seeks to increase the awareness level of the players. In this step the coach will make a habit of asking the players how they are feeling (and listen to their responses), encourage the players to keep a record of their training and associated feelings/mood, and systematically evaluate player performance within the team. The third step involves the coaches and management staff acting as role models in utilizing good recovery strategies in their own work/life. The final step focuses on, as much as possible, keeping training and preparation as fun as possible. This can be achieved by innovating, changing things round, and factoring in enjoyment as a key influence in some activities.

Strategies to reduce the potential of burnout

A number of strategies have been suggested that seek to minimize the risk of burnout occurring (Dale and Weinberg, 1989; Gould *et al.*, 1996; Henschen, 1998). These strategies include:

- *Schedule breaks* – during practices, and between competitions, give players an opportunity to regroup, relax a little, and perhaps even waste time. Applying this idea to an entire season, it is important to provide players with a transition period where they can escape the sports environment.
- *Allow players a degree of decision-making autonomy* – anything that you can do to improve an individual's perception of personal control will improve that person's confidence, productivity, and enjoyment.
- *Teach skills* – including fundamental communication, stress management, and coping skills.
- *Try not to just go through the motions* – variety – and even a degree of unpredictability in practice – can prevent staleness while making practice more challenging and thereby more productive. Challenge players, but be realistic.
- *Try to control outcomes whenever possible* – this has a lot to do with the importance of perceiving control. Players who do not have a sense of control feel helpless, and perhaps even manipulated and hopeless. The coach could, for example, improve the probability of success in a particular drill. Minimize post-competitive tension. Teach athletes to deal with the results of competition (both good and bad) in a more mature fashion.

- *Be aware of burnout and overtraining* – do what you can to create an environment that does not generate negative (i.e. counter-productive) attitudes. If you know someone who is in a bit of a slump, be aware of the fact that it could be burnout. In helping such individuals, be sensitive and compassionate; it is not entirely their fault that they are burning out.

The emotional cost of defeat from a commanding position

Northampton Rugby Club appeared to be on the brink of a remarkable success at half-time in their Heineken Cup (European rugby club championship) final against Leinster on 21 May 2011. At half-time the Northampton Saints appeared to be in control with a 22–6-point lead, with the Saints dominating and almost scoring at will through Phil Dowson, Ben Foden, and Dylan Hartley. However, in the second half Leinster stepped up a gear and staged a remarkable second-half comeback to beat the Saints 33–22. After the defeat the Saints' Director of Rugby Jim Mallinder confessed that he may never get over his side's Heineken Cup final loss to Leinster.

However, if the team were to be successful in the competition in subsequent seasons, Mallinder insisted that his squad must move on from the disappointment at the Millennium Stadium in Cardiff. Mallinder reflected that 'we will probably never quite get over it, it was tremendous for us to get through to the final. We had a real good run to qualify and then had a fantastic first half to go in there beyond our expectations at half-time'. This defeat was further compounded for the Saints by the loss the week before to Leicester in the semi-final of the English Premiership play-off. In this game Leicester came out on top 11–13 in a bad-tempered game where Leicester squeezed the life out of the Saints. In a season that had looked like containing so much promise ten days earlier, the Saints had fallen from Premiership play-off challengers and Heineken Cup finalists to also-rans and losing finalists. But more than this, it is the manner of the defeat in the Heineken Cup final that will leave the biggest scar. To lose having dominated the first half of the game so completely is difficult to take. History will tell whether this team were able to bounce back from these disappointments.

Summary

Recovery is an important aspect of any sports team. Whilst individuals have ultimate responsibility for their own recovery, the team needs to both focus on recovery at the team level and ensure there is a framework within which the individual can manage their recovery. It is important for the coach and manager to understand the impact that team-related factors can have on both the recovery and stress levels of the team and its members. The most effective coaches are able to monitor the team and modify team practice accordingly to maximize the beneficial nature of the recovery time and activities used to aid recovery. While there is always an important focus on the physical demands of training and performing, the most effective teams understand the mental and emotional costs that are also associated with training and competition. The better the planning for emotional and mental recovery, the better the recovery of the team and the associated performance possibilities in relation to the level and duration of subsequent performances.

REFERENCES

Adler, P. (1981). *Momentum: A theory of social action*. Beverly Hills, CA: Sage.

Akkerman, S., Van den Bossche, P., Admiraal, W., Gijselaers, W., Segers, M., and Simons, R.-J. (2007). Reconsidering group cognition: From conceptual confusion to a boundary area between cognitive and socio-cultural perspectives? *Educational Research Review*, 2(1), 39–63.

American Medical Association. (1966). *Standard nomenclature of athletic injuries*. Chicago, IL: American Medical Association.

Ames, C. (1992). Achievement goals, motivational climate, and motivational processes. In G. C. Roberts (Ed.), *Motivation in sport and exercise* (pp.161–76). Champaign, IL: Human Kinetics.

Andrew, D. P. S. (2009). The impact of leadership behaviour on satisfaction of college tennis players: A test of the leadership behaviour congruency hypothesis of the multidimensional model of leadership. *Journal of Sport Behavior*, 32, 261–77.

Apitzsch, E. (2006). Collective collapse in team sports: A theoretical approach. In F. Boen, B. De Cuyper, and J. Opdenacker (Eds), *Current research topics in exercise and sport psychology in Europe*, 35–46. Leuven: Lannoo Campus Publishers.

Ashkanasy, N. M., Zerbe, W. J., and Härtel, C. E. J. (2002). Managing emotions in a changing workplace. In N. M. Ashkanasy, W. J. Zerbe, and C. E. J. Härtel (Eds), *Managing emotions in the workplace* (pp.3–22). Armonk, NY: M. E. Sharpe, Inc.

Athanasios, L. (2005). Communication problems in professional sports: The case of Greece. *Corporate Communications: An International Journal*, 10, 252–56.

Avolio, B., Kahai, S., Dumdum, R., and Sivasubramaniam, N. (2001). Virtual teams: Implications for e-leadership and team development. In M. London (Ed.), *How people evaluate others in organizations: Person perception and interpersonal judgement in I/O psychology*. Mahwah, NJ: Erlbaum Publishers Inc.

Baker, K. A. (2002). Organizational communication. In E. L. Malone, K. M. Branch, and K. A. Baker (Eds), *Managing science as a public good: Overseeing publicly funded science*. Unpublished manuscript (pp.1–11).

Bales, R. F. (1966). Task roles and social roles in problem solving groups. In B. J. Biddle and E. J. Thomas (Eds), *Role theory: Concepts and research* (pp.254–62). New York: John Wiley.

Bales, R. F., and Slater, P. E. (1955). Role differentiation in small decision-making groups. In T. Parsons and R. F. Bales (Eds), *Family socialization and interaction process* (pp.259–306). Glencoe, IL: The Free Press.

Baltes, B. B. (2001). Psychological climate in the work-setting. In N. J. Smelser and P. B. Baltes (Eds), *International encyclopaedia of the social and behavioural sciences*, 18 (pp.12355–59). New York: Elsevier/Pergamon.

Baltes, B. B., Zhdanova, L. S., and Parker, C. P. (2009). Psychological climate: A comparison of organizational and individual level referents. *Human Relations*, 62(5), 669–700.

Bandura, A. (1977). Self efficacy: Toward a unifying theory of behavioural change. *Psychological Review*, 84, 191–215.

——(1997). *Self-efficacy: The exercise of control*. New York: W. H. Freeman and Co.

——(2001). Social cognitive theory: An angetic. *Annual Review of Psychology*, 54, 1–26.

——(2006). Guide for creating self-efficacy scales. In F. Pajeras and T. Urdan (Eds), *Self-efficacy beliefs of adolescents* (pp.307–37). Greenwich, CT: Information Age Publishing.

Banks, A. P., and Millward, L. J. (2007). Running shared mental model as a distributed cognitive process. *British Journal of Psychology*, 91, 513–31.

Bar-Eli, M., Avugos, S., and Raab, M. (2006). Twenty years of 'hot hand' research: Review and critique. *Psychology of Sport and Exercise*, 7, 525–53.

Barrow, J. (1977). The variables of leadership. A review and conceptual framework. *Academy of Management and Review*, 2, 231–51.

Barsade, S. G. (2002). The ripple effect: Emotional contagion and its influence on group behavior. *Administrative Science Quarterly*, 47, 644–75.

Barsade, S. G., and Gibson, D. E. (1998). Group emotion: A view from top and bottom. In D. Gruenfield, E. Mannix, and M. Neale (Eds), *Research on managing groups and teams* (pp.81–102). Stamford, CT: JAI Press.

Bar-Tal, D. (2000). *Shared beliefs in a society: Social psychological analysis*. Thousand Oaks, CA: Sage.

Bass, B. M. (1990). From transactional to transformational leadership: Learning to share the vision. *Organisational Dynamics*, 18, 19–31.

Bass, B. M., and Avolio, B. J. (1994). *Improving organizational effectiveness through transformational leadership*. Thousand Oaks, CA: Sage.

Bass, B. M., and Steidlmeier, P. (1999). Ethics, character and authentic transformational leadership behaviour. *Leadership Quarterly Special Issue: Charismatic and transformational leadership: Taking stock of the present and future (Part 1)*, 10, 181–217.

Bass, B. M., and Riggio, R. E. (2006). *Transformational leadership* (2nd edn). Mahwah, NJ: Lawrence Erlbaum.

Bassin, M. (1988). Teamwork at General Foods: New and improved. *Personnel Journal*, 67(5), 62–70.

Baumeister, R. F., and Leary, M. R. (1995). The need to belong: Desire for interpersonal attachments as a fundamental human motivation. *Psychological Bulletin*, 117, 497–529.

Beauchamp, M. R., and Bray, S. R. (2001). Role ambiguity and role conflict within interdependent teams. *Small Group Research*, 32, 133–57.

Beauchamp, M. R., Bray, S. R., Eys, M. A., and Carron, A. V. (2002). Role ambiguity, role efficacy, and role performance: Multidimensional and mediational relationships within interdependent sport teams. *Group Dynamics: Theory, Research and Practice*, 6, 229–42.

Beer, M. (1976). The technology of organization development. In M. Dunnette (Ed.), *Handbook of industrial and organizational psychology* (pp.937–94). Chicago, IL: Rand McNally.

——(1980). *Organizational change and development: A systems review*. Glenview, IL: Scott Foresman.

Behling, O., and Schriesheim, C. (1976). *Organizational behaviour: Theory, research and application*. Boston, MA: Allyn and Bacon.

Belbin, M. R. (1993). *Team roles at work*. Oxford: Butterworth-Heinemann.

Berger, B. G., Motl, R. W., Butki, B. D., Martin, D. T., Wilkinson, J. G., and Owen, D. R. (1999). Mood and cycling performance in response to three weeks of high-intensity, short-duration overtraining, and a two week taper. *The Sport Psychologist*, 13, 444–57.

Bers, S. A., and Rodin, J. (1984). Social comparison jealous: A developmental and motivational study. *Journal of Personality and Social Psychology*, 47, 766–79.

Beswick, B. (2001). *Focused for soccer*. Champaign, IL: Human Kinetics.

Biddle, B. J. (1979). *Role theory: Expectations, identities, and behaviors*. New York: Academic Press, Inc.

Blake, R. R., and Mouton, J. S. (1978). *The new managerial grid: Strategic new insights into a proven system for increasing organization productivity and individual effectiveness, plus a revealing examination of how your managerial style can affect your mental and physical health*. Houston, TX: Gulf Publishing Co.

Booth, R. J., Petrie, K. J., and Pennebaker, J. W. (1997). Changes in circulating lymphocyte numbers following emotional disclosure: Evidence of buffering? *Stress Medicine*, 13, 23–29.

Borg, G. (1998). *Borg's perceived exertion and pain rating scales*. Champaign, IL: Human Kinetics.

Brawley, L. R., and Paskevich, D. M. (1997). Conducting team building research in context of sport and exercise. *Journal of Applied Sport Psychology*, 9, 11–40.

Brawley, L. R., Carron, A. V., and Widmeyer, W. N. (1993). The influence of the group and its cohesiveness on perceptions of group goal-related variables. *Journal of Sport & Exercise Psychology*, 15, 245–60.

Bray, S. R. (1998). *Role efficacy within interdependent teams: Measurement development and tests of theory*. Unpublished doctoral thesis. University of Waterloo, Waterloo, Canada.

——(2004). Collective efficacy, group goals, and group performance of a muscular endurance task. *Small Group Research*, 35, 230–38.

Bray, S. R., and Brawley, L. R. (2002). Role efficacy, role clarity, and role performance effectiveness. *Small Group Research*, 33, 233–53.

Bray, S. R., Widmeyer, W. N., and Brawley, L. R. (1998). Collective efficacy and role efficacy in sports teams [abstract]. *Journal of Sport & Exercise Psychology*, 20, S62.

Brearley, M. (2001). *The art of captaincy*. Basingstoke: Pan Macmillan Ltd.

Brewer, B. W., Van Raalte, J. L., and Linder, D. W. (1993). Athletic identity: Hercules' muscles or Achilles' heel? *International Journal of Sport Psychology*, 24, 237–54.

Brown, G. (2006). Explaining. In O. Harge, *The handbook of communication skills* (3rd edn) (pp.195–228). Hove: Routledge.

Brown, R. (2000). *Group processes: Dynamics within and between groups* (2nd edn). Oxford: Blackwell.

Bull, S. J., Albinson, J. G., and Shambrook, C. J. (1996). *The mental game plan*. Eastbourne: Sports Dynamics.

Burke, K. L. (1993). Psychological momentum: Are we on a roll yet? In J. Taylor (Chair), *Keeping the mo' in momentum research: The past, the present and the future of momentum in sports*. Symposium conducted at the eighth annual conference of the Association for the Advancement of Applied Sport Psychology, Montreal, Canada.

Burke, K. L., Burke, M. M., and Joyner, A. B. (1999). Perceptions of momentum in college and high school basketball: An exploratory case study investigation. *Journal of Sport Behavior*, 22, 303–9.

Burke, K. L., Edwards, T. C., Weigand, D. A., and Weinberg, R. S. (1997). Momentum in sport: A real or illusionary phenomenon for spectators. *International Journal of Sport Psychology*, 28, 79–96.

Burke, K. L., Aoyagi, M. W., Joyner, A. B., and Burke, M. M. (2003). Spectators' perceptions of positive momentum while attending NCAA men's and women's basketball regular season contests: Exploring the antecedents-consequences model. *Athletic Insight*, 5, 10–18.

Burton, D. (1992). The Jekyll/Hyde nature of goals: Reconceptualizing goal setting in sport. In T. S. Horn (Ed.), *Advances in sport psychology* (pp.267–97). Champaign, IL: Human Kinetics.

Burton, D., Naylor, S., and Holliday, B. (2001). Goal setting in sport: Investigating the goal effectiveness paradigm. In R. Singer, H. Hausenblas, and C. Janelle (Eds), *Handbook of sport psychology* (2nd edn) (pp.497–528). New York: Wiley.

Calder, A. (1996). Training for endurance and speed. In D. Jenkins and P. Raeburn (Eds), *Australian Coaching Council, recovery and overtraining*. Canberra, Australia: Allen and Unwin.

——(2003). Recovery strategies for sports performance. *Olympic Coach*, 10, 3.

Cannon-Bowers, J. A., and Salas, E. (2001). Reflections on shared cognition. *Journal of Organizational Behavior*, 22, 195–202.

Cannon-Bowers, J. A., Salas, E., and Converse, S. A. (1993). Shared mental models in expert team decision making. In N. J. Castellan (Ed.), *Individual and group decision making: Current issues* (pp.221–46). Hillsdale, NJ: Erlbaum.

Carron, A. V. (2003). 'What I have come to believe (so far)'. Paper presented at the annual meeting of the North American Society for the Psychology of Sport and Physical Activity, Savannah, GA.

Carron, A. V., and Ball, J. R. (1978). Cause-effect characteristics of cohesiveness and participant motivation in intercollegiate hockey. *International Review of Sport Sociology*, 12, 49–60.

Carron, A. V., and Spink, K. (1993). Team-building in the exercise setting. *The Sport Psychologist*, 7, 8–18.

——(1995). The group size–cohesion relationship in minimal groups. *Small Group Research*, 26, 86–105.

Carron, A. V., and Dennis, P. W. (1998). The sport team as an effective group. In J. M. Williams (Ed.), *Applied sport psychology: Personal growth to peak performance* (pp.27–41). Mountain View, CA: Mayfield.

Carron, A. V., and Hausenblas, H. A. (1998). *Group dynamics in sport*. Morgantown, WV: Fitness Information Technology.

Carron, A. V., and Dennis, P. (2001). The sport team as an effective group. In J. M. Williams, *Applied sport psychology* (4th edn) (pp.120–34). Mountain View, CA: Mayfield Publishing.

Carron, A. V., Widmeyer, W. N., and Brawley, L. R. (1985). The development of an instrument to assess cohesion in sport teams: The group environment questionnaire. *Journal of Sport Psychology*, 7, 244–66.

Carron, A., Spink, K. S., and Prapavessis, H. (1997). Team building and cohesiveness in the sport and exercise setting: Use of indirect interventions. *Journal of Applied Sport Psychology*, 9, 61–72.

Carron, A. V., Brawley, L. R., and Widmeyer, W. N. (1998). Measurement of cohesion in sport and exercise. In J. L. Duda (Ed.), *Advances in sport and exercise psychology measurement* (pp.213–26). Morgantown, WV: Fitness Information Technology.

——(2002). *The group environment questionnaire: Test manual*. Morgantown, WV: Fitness Information Technology.

Carron, A. V., Bray, S. R., and Eys, M. A. (2002). Team cohesion and team success in sport. *Journal of Sports Sciences*, 20, 119–26.

Carron, A. V., Hausenblas, H. A., and Eys, M. A. (2005). *Group dynamics in sport* (3rd edn). Morgantown, WV: Fitness Information Technology.

Cartwright, D. (1968). The nature of group cohesiveness. In D. Cartwright and A. Zander (Eds), *Group dynamics: Research and theory* (3rd edn.). New York: Harper & Row.

Cartwright, D., and Zander, A. (1968). *Group dynamics: Research and theory*. New York: Harper & Row.

Chase, M. A., Feltz, D. L., and Lirgg, C. D. (2003). Sources of collective efficacy and individual efficacy of collegiate athletes. *International Journal of Sport and Exercise Psychology*, 1, 180–91.

Chelladurai, P. (1984). Leadership in sports. In J. M. Silva III and R. S. Weinberg (Eds), *Psychological foundations of sport* (pp.329–39). Champaign, IL: Human Kinetics.

——(1990). Leadership in sports: A review. *International Journal of Sport Psychology*, 21, 47–55.

——(2006). *Human resource management in sport and recreation* (2nd edn). Champaign, IL: Human Kinetics.

Chen, C-C. (2010). Leadership and teamwork paradigms: Two models for baseball coaches. *Social Behavior and Personality*, 38, 1367–76.

Chen, G., and Bliese, P. D. (2002). The role of different levels of leadership in predicting self and collective efficacy: Evidence for discontinuity. *Journal of Applied Psychology*, 87, 549–56.

Chi, L. (2004). Achievement goal theory. In T. Morris and J. Summers (Eds), *Sport Psychology: Theory, applications and issues* (2nd edn). Milton: John Wiley.

Chow, G. M., and Feltz, D. L. (2007). Exploring new directions in collective efficacy and sport. In M. Beauchamp and M. Eys (Eds), *Group dynamics advances in sport and exercise psychology: Contemporary themes* (pp.221–248). New York: Routledge.

——(2008). Exploring the relationships between collective efficacy, perceptions of success, and team attributions. *Journal of Sports Sciences*, 26, 1179–89.

Cogan, K. D., and Petrie, T. A. (1995). Sport consultation: An evaluation of a season-long intervention with female collegiate gymnasts. *The Sport Psychologist*, 9, 282–86.

Collins, D., Moore, P., Mitchell, D., and Alpress, F. (1999). Role conflict and confidentiality in multidisciplinary athlete support programmes. *British Journal of Sports Medicine*, 33, 208–11.

Cooke, N. J., Salas, E., Cannon-Bowers, J. A., and Stout, R. (2000). Measuring team knowledge. *Human Factors*, 42, 151–73.

Cooper, C. L., Dewe, P. J., and O'Driscoll, M. P. (2001). *Organizational stress: A review and critique of theory, research, and applications.* Thousand Oaks, CA: Sage.

Cope, C. J., Eys, M. A., Beauchamp, M. R., Schinke, R. J., and Bosselut, G. (2011). Informal roles on sport teams. *International Journal of Sport and Exercise Psychology*, 9, 19–30.

Cornelius, A. E., Silva, J. M., Conroy, D. E., and Petersen, G. (1997). The projected performance model: Relating cognitive and performance antecedents of psychological momentum. *Perceptual and Motor Skills*, 84, 475–85.

Courneya, K. S. (1995). Cohesion correlates with affect in structured exercise classes. *Perceptual and Motor Skills*, 81, 1021–22.

Coutts, A., and Reaburn, P. (2008). Monitoring changes in rugby league players' perceived stress and recovery during intensified training. *Perceptual and Motor Skills*, 106(3), 904–1006.

Covey, S. R. (2004). *The 7 habits of highly effective people: Powerful lessons in personal change.* London: Simon & Schuster.

Cox, R. (2002). *Sport Psychology: Concepts and applications* (5th edn). New York: McGraw-Hill.

Crace, R. K., and Hardy, C. J. (1997). Individual values and the team building process. *Journal of Applied Sport Psychology*, 9, 41–60.

Crust, L., and Lawrence, I. (2006). A review of leadership in sport: Implications for football management. *Athletic Insight*, 8(4), 28–48.

Crust, L., and Nesti, M. (2006). A review of psychological momentum in sports: Why qualitative research is needed. *Athletic Insight*, 8, 1–15.

Daft, R. (2000). *Management* (5th edn). Hinsdale, IL: Dryden Press.

Dale, J., and Weinberg, R.S. (1989). The relationship between coaches' leadership style and burnout. *The Sport Psychologist*, 3, 1–13.

DeChurch, L. A., and Mesmer-Magnus, J. R. (2010). Measuring shared team mental models: A meta-analysis. *Group Dynamics: Theory, Research, and Practice*, 14(1), 1–14.

DeChurch, L. A., Hamilton, K. L., and Haas, C. (2007). Effects of conflict management strategies on perceptions of intragroup conflict. *Group Dynamics: Theory, Research, and Practice*, 11(1) 66–78.

Deci, E. L. (1980). *The psychology of self-determination.* Lexington, MA: Health.

Deci, E. L., and Ryan, R. M. (1985). *Intrinsic motivation and self-determination in human behaviour.* New York: Plenum.

De Dreu, C. K. W. (2010). Social conflict: The emergence and consequences of struggle and negotiation. In S. T. Fiske, D. T. Gilbert, and G. Lindzey (Eds), *Handbook of social psychology* (5th edn) (pp.983–994). New York: Wiley.

De Dreu, C. K. W., and Weingart, L. R. (2003a). A contingency theory of task conflict and performance in groups and organizational teams. In M. A. West, D. Tjosvold, and K. G. Smith (Eds), *International handbook of teamwork and cooperative working* (pp.151–66). Chichester: Wiley.

——(2003b). Task versus relationship conflict, team performance, and team member satisfaction: A meta-analysis. *Journal of Applied Psychology*, 88(4), 741–49.

De Dreu, C. K. W., Harinck, F., and Van Vianen, A. E. (1999). Conflict and performance in groups and organizations. In C. Cooper and I. Robertson (Eds), *International review of industrial and organizational psychology* (pp.369–414). Chichester: Wiley.

Depree, M. (1989). *Leadership is an art.* New York: Doubleday.

Desjardins, G. (1996). The mission. In J. H. Salmela (Ed.), *Great job coach: Getting the edge from proven winners* (pp. 67–100). Ottawa, ON: Potentium.

Deutsch, M. (1973). *The resolution of conflict: Constructive and destructive processes*. New Haven, CT: Yale University Press.

Dillenbourg, P., and Traum, D. (2006). Sharing solutions: Persistence and grounding in multimodal collaborative problem solving. *Journal of the Learning Science*, 15(1), 121–51.

Donnelly, P., Carron, A. V., and Chelladurai, P. (1978). *Group cohesion and sport*. Ottawa, ON: CAHPER Sociology of Sport Monograph Series.

Dorsey-Palmateer, R., and Smith, G. (2004). Bowlers' hot hands. *The American Statistician*, 58, 38–45.

Duda, J. L., and Balaguer, I. (2007). Coach-created motivational climate. In S. Jowett and D. Lavallee (Eds), *Social psychology in sport*. Champaign, IL: Human Kinetics.

Dugo, J. M., and Beck, A. P. (1997). Significance and complexity of early phase in the development of the co-therapy relationship. *Group Dynamics: Theory, Research and Practice*, 1, 294–305.

Dunn, J. G. H., and Holt, N. L. (2004). A qualitative investigation of personal-disclosure mutual-sharing team building activity. *The Sport Psychologist*, 18, 363–80.

Dupuis, M., Bloom, G. A., and Loughead, T. M. (2006). Team captains' perceptions of athlete leadership. *Journal of Sport Behavior*, 29, 60–78.

Eccles, D. W., and Tenenbaum, G. (2004). Why an expert team is more than a team of experts: A social-cognitive conceptualisation of team co-ordination and communication in sport. *Journal of Sport & Exercise Psychology*, 26, 542–60.

Eisler, L., and Spink, K. S. (1998). Effects of scoring configuration and task cohesion on the perception of psychological momentum. *Journal of Sport & Exercise Psychology*, 20, 311–20.

Ekman, P. (1999). Basic emotions. In T. Dalgleish and M. Power (Eds), *Handbook of cognition and emotion* (pp.45–60). New York: John Wiley & Sons.

——(2006). Cross-cultural studies of facial expression. In P. Ekman (Ed.), *Darwin and facial expression: A century of research in review*. Cambridge, MA: Malor Books.

Eys, M., and Carron, A. V. (2001). Role ambiguity, task cohesion, and task self-efficacy. *Small Group Research*, 32, 356–73.

Eys, M. A., Beauchamp, M. R., and Bray, S. R. (2006). A review of team roles in sport. In S. Hanton and S. D. Mellalieu (Eds), *Literature reviews in sport psychology* (pp.227–255). Hauppauge, NY: Nova Science Publishers Inc.

Eys, M. A., Schinke, R. J., and Jeffery, S. M. (2007). Role perceptions in sport groups. In M. R. Beauchamp and M. A. Eys (Eds), *Group dynamics in exercise and sport psychology: Contemporary themes*. Abingdon: Routledge.

Eys, M. A., Carron, A. V., Bray, S. R., and Beauchamp, M. R. (2003). Role ambiguity in sport teams. *Journal of Sport & Exercise Psychology*, 25, 534–50.

Eys, M. A., Carron, A. V., Beauchamp, M. R., and Bray, S. R. (2005). Athletes' perceptions of the sources of role ambiguity. *Small Group Research*, 36, 383–403.

Eysenck, M. W. (2004). *Psychology: An international perspective*. Hove: Psychology Press.

Feltz, D. L., and Lirgg, C. D. (1998). Perceived team and player efficacy in hockey. *Journal of Applied Psychology*, 83, 557–64.

Fender, L. K. (1989). Athlete burnout: Potential for research and intervention strategies. *The Sport Psychologist*, 3, 63–71.

Fiedler, F. E. (1967). *A theory of leadership effectiveness*. New York: McGraw-Hill.

Filby, W., Maynard, I., and Graydon, J. (1999). The effect of multiple goal strategies on performance outcomes in training and competition. *Journal of Applied Sport Psychology*, 11, 230–46.

Fiore, S. M., Salas, E., and Cannon-Bowers, J. A. (2001). Group dynamics and shared mental model development. In M. London (Ed.), *How people evaluate others in organizations: Person perception an interpersonal judgement in I/O psychology* (pp.309–36). Mahwah, NJ: Erlbaum.

Fisher, B., and Thomas, B. (1996). *Real dream teams: Seven practices used by world-class leaders to achieve extraordinary results*. Delray Beach, FL: St Lucie.

Fiske, J. (1990). *Introduction to communication skills* (2nd edn). London: Routledge.

Fletcher, D. and Hanton, S. (2003). Sources of organisational stress in elite sports performers. *The Sport Psychologist*, 17, 175–95.

Foa, U. G., and Foa, E. B. (1974). *Societal structures of the mind.* Springfield, IL: Charles C. Thomas.

Foot, H. C., and McGreaddie, M. (2006). Humour and laughter. In O. Harge, *The handbook of communication skills* (3rd edn) (pp.293–323). Hove: Routledge.

Forgas, J. P. (1992). Affect in social judgements and decisions: A multi-process model. *Advances in Experimental Social Psychology*, 25, 227–75.

Foster, C., and Lehmann, M. (1997). Overtraining syndrome. In G. N. Guten (Ed.), *Running injuries* (pp.173–88). Philadelphia, PA: Saunders.

Frederick-Recascino, C. M., and Morris, T. (2004). Intrinsic and extrinsic motivation in sport and exercise. In T. Morris and J. Summers (Eds), *Sport psychology: Theory, applications and issues* (2nd Edn) (pp.121–146). Milton: John Wiley.

Fredrickson, B. L. (2005). Positive emotions. In C. R. Snyder and S. J. Lopez (Eds), *Handbook of positive psychology* (pp.120–34). New York: Oxford University Press.

Fredrickson, B. L., and Branigan, C. A. (2005). Positive emotions broaden the scope of attention and thought-action repertoires. *Cognition and Emotion*, 19, 313–32.

Friedkin, N. E. (2004). Social cohesion. *Annual Review of Sociology*, 30, 409–25.

Frijda, N. H., Kuipers, P., and ter Schure, E. (1989). Relations among emotion, appraisal, and emotional action readiness. *Journal of Personality and Social Psychology*, 57, 212–28.

Frontiera, J. (2006). *The relationship between leadership, efficacy beliefs, and performance among boys' high school basketball players.* Unpublished Master's thesis. University of West Virginia.

Fry, R. W., Morton, A. R., and Keast, D. (1991). Overtraining in athletes: An update. *Sports Medicine*, 12, 32–65.

Gallogly, V., and Levine, B. (1979). Co-therapy. In B. Levine (Ed.), *Group psychotherapy: Practice and development* (pp.296–305). Prospect Heights, IL: Waveland.

Gardner, D. E., Shields, D. L., Bredemeier, B. J., and Bostrom, A. (1996). The relationship between perceived coaching behaviours and team cohesion among baseball and softball players. *The Sport Psychologist*, 10, 367–81.

George, T. R., and Feltz, D. L. (1995). Motivation in sport from a collective efficacy perspective. *International Journal of Sport Psychology*, 26, 98–116.

Gibson, C. B. (1999). Do they do what they believe they can? Group efficacy and group effectiveness across tasks and cultures. *Academy of Management Journal*, 42, 138–52.

Gilovich, T., Vallone, R., and Tversky, A. (1985). The hot hand in basketball: On the misperception of random sequences. *Cognitive Psychology*, 17, 295–314.

Gladding, S. T. (2003). *Group work: A counselling speciality* (4th edn). Upper Saddle River, NJ: Merrill/Prentice Hall.

Glenn, S. D., and Horn, T. S. (1993). Psychological and personal predictors of leadership behaviour in female soccer athletes. *Journal of Applied Sport Psychology*, 5, 17–34.

Golden, W. L., and Dryden, W. (1986). Cognitive behavioural therapies: Commonalities, divergences and future development. In W. Dryden and W. L. Golden (Eds), *Cognitive-behavioural approaches to psychotherapy* (pp.356–78). London: Harper & Row.

Good, D. (2001). Language and communication. In C. Fraser, B. Burchell, D. Hay, and G. Duveen (Eds), *Introducing social psychology* (pp.76–94). Cambridge: Polity.

Goode, W. J. (1960). A theory of role strain. *American Sociological Review*, 25, 483–96.

Gould, D., Udry, E., Tuffey, S., and Loehr, J. (1996). Burnout in competitive junior tennis players: I. A quantitative psychological assessment. *The Sport Psychologist*, 10, 322–40.

Gould, D., Guinan, D., Greenleaf, C., Medbery, R., and Peterson, K. (1999). Factors affecting Olympic performance: Perceptions of athletes and coaches from more or less successful teams. *The Sport Psychologist*, 13, 371–94.

Graen, G. B., and Uhl-Bien, M. (1995). Relationship-based approach to leadership: Development of leader–member exchange (LMX) theory of leadership over 25 years: Applying a multi-level multi-domain perspective. *Leadership Quarterly*, 6, 219–47.

Granito, V. J., and Rainey, D. W. (1988). Differences in cohesion between high school and college football starters and nonstarters. *Perceptual and Motor Skills*, 66, 471–77.

Gray, R. (2004). *How people work: And how you can help them to give their best.* Edinburgh: Pearson Education.

Greenlees, I. A., Graydon, J. K., and Maynard, I. W. (2000). The impact of individual efficacy beliefs on group goal commitment. *Journal of Sports Sciences*, 18, 451–59.

Griffin, J., and Tyrell, I. (2004). *Dreaming reality: How dreams keep us sane, or can drive us mad.* Chalvington, Hailsham: HG Publishing.

Griffin, M. A., Neal, A., and Parker, S. K. (2007). A new model of work role performance: Positive behaviour in uncertain and interdependent contexts. *Academy of Management Journal*, 50, 327–47.

Gruber, J. J., and Gray, G. R. (1982). Responses to forces influencing cohesion as a function of player status and level of male varsity basketball competition. *Research Quarterly for Exercise and Sport*, 53, 27–36.

Gully, S. M., Incalcaterra, K. A., Joshi, A., and Beaubien, J. M. (2002). A meta-analysis of team-efficacy, potency, and performance; Interdependence and level of analysis as moderators of observed relationships. *Journal of Applied Psychology*, 87, 819–32.

Gump, B. B., and Kulik, J. A. (1997). Stress, affiliation, and emotional contagion. *Journal of Personality and Social Psychology*, 72, 305–19.

Hackman, J. R. (1987). The design of work teams. In J. Lorsch (Ed.), *Handbook of organizational behaviour* (pp.315–42). Palo Alto, CA: Consulting Psychologist Press.

Hanin, Y. L. (1992). Social psychology and sport: Communication processes in top performance teams. *Sport Science Review*, 1, 13–28.

——(1999). Individual zones of optimal functioning (IZOF) model. In Y. L. Hanin (Ed.), *Emotions in sport* (pp.65–89). Champaign, IL: Human Kinetics.

Harge, O. (2006). *The handbook of communication skills* (3rd edn). Hove: Routledge.

Harge, O., and Dickson, D. (2004). *Skilled interpersonal communication: Research, theory, and practice.* London: Routledge.

Harris, D. V., and Harris, B. L. (1984). *Sport psychology: Mental skills for physical people.* Champaign, IL: Leisure Press.

Hartel, C. E. J., Gough, H., and Hartel, G. F. (2008). Work-group emotional climate, emotion management skills, and service attitudes and performance. *Asia Pacific Journal of Human Resources*, 46, 21–37.

Harter, S. (1978). Effectance motivation reconsidered: Toward a developmental model. *Human Development*, 1, 34–64.

Harwood, C., and Beauchamp, M. R. (2007). Group functioning through optimal achievement goals. In M. R. Beauchamp and M. A. Eys (Eds), *Group dynamics in exercise and sport psychology: Contemporary themes*. Abingdon: Routledge.

Hatfield, E., Cacioppo, J., and Rapson, R. L. (1994). *Emotional contagion.* New York: Cambridge University Press.

Hawkins, K., and Power, C. (1999). Gender differences in questions asked during small decision-making group discussions. *Small Group Research*, 30, 235–56.

Henschen, K. P. (1986). Athletic staleness and burnout: Diagnosis, prevention and treatment. In J. M. Williams (Ed.), *Applied sport psychology: Personal growth to peak performance* (pp.327–42). Palo Alto, CA: Mayfield.

——(1998). Athletic staleness and burnout: Diagnosis, prevention, and treatment. In J. M. Williams (Ed.), *Applied sport psychology: Personal growth to peak performance* (3rd edn) (pp.398–408). Mountain View, CA: Mayfield Publishing Company.

Hersey, P., and Blanchard, K. (1982). *Management of organizational behaviour: Utilizing human resources.* Englewood Cliffs, NJ: Prentice-Hall.

Higham, A. (2000). *Momentum: The hidden force in tennis.* Leeds: Coachwise.

Higham, A., Harwood, C., and Cale, A. (2005). *Momentum in soccer.* Leeds: Coachwise.

Hirsch, S. K. (1993). *MBTi team building program.* Palo Alto, CA: Consulting Psychologists Press.

Hoigaard, R., Jones, G. W., and Peters, D. M. (2008). Preferred coach leadership behaviour in elite soccer in relation to success and failure. *International Journal of Sports Science and Coaching*, 3, 241–49.

Holman, D., Batt, R., and Holtgrewe, U. (2007). *The global call center report: International perspectives on management and employment* (electronic version). Ithaca, NY: Authors.

Holt, N. L., and Dunn, J. G. H. (2006). Guidelines for delivering personal-disclosure mutual-sharing team building interventions. *The Sport Psychologist*, 20, 348–67.

Hooper, S. L., and Mackinnin, L. T. (1995). Monitoring overtraining in athletes. *Sports Medicine*, 20, 321–27.

Hoption, C., Phelan, J., and Barling, J. (2007). Transformational leadership in sport. In M. R. Beauchamp and M. A. Eys (Eds), *Group dynamics in exercise and sport psychology: Contemporary themes*. Abingdon: Routledge.

Howe, P. D. (2004). *Sport, professionalism and pain: Ethnographies of injury and risk*. London: Routledge.

Isen, A. M. (2001). An influence of positive affect on decision-making in complex situations: Theoretical issues with practical implications. *Journal of Consumer Psychology*, 11, 75–85.

Isen, A. M., and Daubman, K. A. (1984). The influence of affect on categorisation. *Journal of Personality and Social Psychology*, 47, 1206–17.

Isen, A. M., Daubman, K. A., and Nowicki, G. P. (1987). Positive affect facilitates creative problem solving. *Journal of Personality and Social Psychology*. 52, 1122–31.

Iso-Ahola, S. E., and Mobily, K. (1980). Psychological momentum: A phenomenon and an empirical (unobtrusive) validation of its influence in a competitive sport tournament. *Psychology Reports*, 46, 391–401.

Jacob, C. S., and Carron, A. V. (1998). The association between status and cohesion in sport teams. *Journal of Sports Sciences*, 16, 187–98.

James, L. R., and James, L. A. (1989). Integrating work environment perceptions: Exploring into the measurement of meaning. *Journal of Applied Psychology*, 74, 739–51.

Janis, I. L. (1982). *Victims of group think*. Boston, MA: Houghton Mifflin.

Jehn, K. A. (1995). A multimethod examination of the benefits and detriments of intragroup conflict. *Administrative Sciences Quarterly*, 40, 256–82.

Jeong, H., and Chi, M. T. H. (2007). Knowledge convergence and collaborative learning. *Instructional Science*, 35, 287–315.

Johnson, D. J., Donohue, W. A., Atkin, C. K., and Johnson, S. (1994). Differences between formal and informal communication channels. *The Journal of Business Communication*, 31, 111–22.

Jones, G. (1993). The role of performance profiling in cognitive behavioural interventions in sport. *The Sport Psychologist*, 7, 160–72.

Jones, G., Gittins, M., and Hardy, L. (2009). Creating an environment where high performance is inevitable and sustainable: The high performance environment model. *Annual Review of High Performance Coaching and Consulting*, 139–48.

Jones, M. I., and Harwood, C. (2008). Psychological momentum within competitive soccer: Players' perspectives. *Journal of Applied Sport Psychology*, 20, 57–72.

Jordan, P. J., and Troth, A. C. (2004). Managing emotions during team problem solving: Emotional intelligence and conflict resolution. *Human Performance*, 17, 195–218.

Joyce, W. F., and Slocum, J. W. (1984). Collective climate: Dimensions and relationships of individual and aggregated climates in organizations. *Academy of Management Journal*, 27, 721–42.

Judge, T. A., Bono, J. E., Ilies, R., and Megan, M. W. (2002). Personality and leadership: A qualitative and quantitative review. *Journal of Applied Psychology*, 87, 765–80.

Kahn, R. L., Wolfe, D. M., Quinne, R. P., Snoek, J. D., and Rosenthal, R. A. (1964). *Organizational stress: Studies in role conflict and ambiguity*. New York: Wiley.

Kamphoff, C. S., Gill, D. L., and Huddleston, S. (2005). Jealousy in sport: Exploring jealousy's relationship to cohesion. *Journal of Applied Sport Psychology*, 17, 290–305.

Karau, S. J., and Williams, K. D. (1993). Social loafing: A meta-analytic review and theoretical integration. *Journal of Personality and Social Psychology*, 65, 681–706.

Karau, S. J., Markus, M. J., and Williams, K. D. (2000). On the elusive search for motivation gains in groups: Insights from the collective effort model. *Zeitschrift Für Sozialpsychologie*, 31, 179–90.

Kark, R., and Shamir, B. (2002). The dual effect of transformational leadership: Priming relational and collective selves and further effects on followers. In B. J. Avolio and F. J. Yammarion (Eds), *Transformational and charismatic leadership: The road ahead* (pp.67–91). Oxford: Elsevier Science.

Katz, D., and Kahn, R. L. (1978). *The social psychology of organizations* (2nd edn). New York: Wiley.

Kellmann, M. (2002a). Underrecovery and overtraining: Different concepts – similar impacts? In M. Kellmann (Ed.), *Enhancing recovery: Preventing underperformance in athletes* (pp. 3–24). Champaign, IL: Human Kinetics.

——(2002b). Current status and future directions of recovery research. In M. Kellmann (Ed.), *Enhancing recovery: Preventing underperformance in athletes* (pp.3–24). Champaign, IL: Human Kinetics.

——(2010). Overtraining and recovery. In S. J. Hanrahan and M. B. Anderson (Eds), *Routledge handbook of applied sport psychology* (pp.292–302). London: Routledge.

Kellmann, M., and Kallus, K. W. (2001). *The recovery-stress questionnaire for athletes; User manual*. Champaign, IL: Human Kinetics.

Kellmann, M., Altenburg, D., Lormes, W., and Steinacker, J. M. (2001). Assessing stress and recovery during preparation for the world championships in rowing. *The Sport Psychologist*, 15, 151–67.

Kelly, J. R., and Barsade, S. G. (2001). Mood and emotions in small groups and work teams. *Organizational Behavior and Human Decision Processes*, 86, 99–130.

Kenttä, G., and Hassmén, P. (1998). Overtraining and recovery. *Sports Medicine*, 26, 1–16.

——(2002). Underrecovery and overtraining: A conceptual model. *Sports Medicine* (Auckland, NZ), 26, 1–16.

Kenttä, G., and Dieffenbach, K. (2008). Athlete perceptions of the role of recovery in elite training: Three case studies. *Proceedings from the 23rd Annual Conference of the Association for the Advancement of Applied Sport Psychology*. St Louis, MO: Association for the Advancement of Applied Sport Psychology.

Kerick, S. E., Iso-Ahola, S. E., and Hatfield, B. D. (2000). Psychological momentum in target shooting: Cortical, cognitive-affective, and behavioural responses. *Journal of Sport & Exercise Psychology*, 22, 1–20.

King, L. A. (2001). The health benefits of writing about life goals. *Personality and Social Psychology Bulletin*, 27, 798–807.

King, L. A., and King, D. W. (1990). Role conflict and role ambiguity; A critical assessment of construct validity. *Psychological Bulletin*, 107, 48–64.

Kirkman, B. L., and Rosen, B. (1999). Beyond self management: The antecedents and consequences of team empowerment. *Academy of Management Journal*, 42, 58–74.

Klaassen, F. J. G. M., and Magnus, J. R. (2001). Are points in tennis independent and identically distributed? Evidence from a dynamic binary panel data model. *Journal of the American Statistical Association*, 96, 500–9.

Klein, K. J., Conn, A. B., Smith, D., and Sorra, J. S. (2001). Is everyone in agreement? An exploration of within-group agreement in employee perceptions of the work environment. *Journal of Applied Psychology*, 86, 3–16.

Klein, K. J., Bliese, P. D., Kozlowski, S. W. J., Dansereau, F., Gavin, M. B., Griffin, M. A., et al. (2000). Multilevel analytical techniques: Commonalities, differences and continuing questions. In K. J. Klein and S. W. J. Kozlowski (Eds), *Multilevel theory, research and methods in organizations* (pp.512–56). San Francisco, CA: Jossey-Bass.

Klimoski, R., and Mohammed, S. (1994). Team mental model: Construct or metaphor? *Journal of Management*, 20(2), 403–37.

Kline, W. B. (2003). *Interactive group counselling and therapy*. Upper Saddle River, NJ: Merrill/ Prentice Hall.

Koehler, J. J., and Conley, C. A. (2003). The 'hot hand' myth in professional basketball. *Journal of Sport & Exercise Psychology*, 25, 253–59.

Kouzes, J. M., and Posner, B. Z. (2007). *The leadership challenge* (4th edn). San Francisco, CA: Jossey-Bass.

Koys, D. J., and DeCotiis, T. A. (1991). Inductive measures of psychological climate. *Human Relations*, 44, 265–85.

Kozlowski, S. W. J., and Ilgen, D. R. (2006). Enhancing the effectiveness of work groups and teams. *Psychological Science in the Public Interest*, 7(3), 77–123.

Kozlowski, S. W. J., and Klein, K. J. (2000). A multilevel approach to theory and research in organizations. In K. J. Klein and S. W. J. Kozlowski (Eds), *Multilevel theory, research and methods in organizations* (pp.3–90). San Francisco, CA: Jossey-Bass.

Kozlowski, S. W. J., Gully, S. M., Nason, E. R., and Smith, E. M. (1999). Developing adaptive teams: A theory of compilation and performance across levels and time. In D. R. Ilgen and E.D. Pulakos (Eds), *The changing nature of work performance: Implications for staffing, personnel actions, and development* (pp.240–92). San Francisco, CA: Jossey-Bass.

Kozub, S. A., and McDonnell, J. F. (2000). Exploring the relationship between cohesion and collective efficacy in rugby teams. *Journal of Sport Behavior*, 23, 120–29.

Kozub, S. A., and Pease, D. G. (2001). Coach and player leadership in high school basketball. *Journal of Sport Pedagogy*, 7, 1–15.

Kramer, R. M., and Lewicki, R. J. (2010). Repairing and enhancing trust: Approaches to reducing organizational trust deficits. *The Academy of Management Annals*, 4(1), 245–77.

Kreider, R., Fry, A. C., and O'Toole, M. (1998). Overtraining in sport: Terms, definitions, and prevalence. In R. Kreider, A. C. Fry, and M. O'Toole (Eds), *Overtraining in sport* (pp.vii–ix). Champaign, IL: Human Kinetics.

Kremer, J. M., and Scully, D. M. (1994). *Psychology in sport*. New York: Taylor & Francis.

Kuipers, H., and Keizer, H. (1988). Overtraining in elite athletes. *Sports Medicine*, 6, 79–92.

Kyllo, L. B., and Landers, D. M. (1995). Goal setting in sport and exercise: A research synthesis to resolve the controversy. *Journal of Sport & Exercise Psychology*, 17, 117–37.

Laios, A. (1999). *The application of basic principles of sport management in coaching*. Thessaloniki: University Studio Press.

Laios, A., Theodorakis, N., and Gargalianos, D. (2003). Leadership and power: Two important factors for effective coaching. *International Sports Journal*, 7(1), 150–54.

Landers, D. M., Wilkinson, M. O., Hatfield, B. D., and Barber, H. (1982). Causality and the cohesion–performance relationship. *Journal of Sport Psychology*, 4, 170–83.

Larsen, R. J., and Diener, E. (1992). Promises and problems with the circumplex model of emotion. In M. S. Clark (Ed.), *Review of personality and social psychology. Vol. 13. Emotion* (pp.25–29). Newbury Park, CA: Sage.

Latimer, A. E., Rench, T. A., and Brachett, M. A. (2007). Emotional intelligence: A framework for examining emotions in sport and exercise groups. In M. R. Beauchamp and M. A. Eys (Eds), *Group dynamics in exercise and sport psychology; Contemporary themes* (pp.3–24). Abingdon: Routledge.

Lausic, D., Tennebaum, G., Eccles, D., Jeong, A., and Johnson, T. (2009). Intrateam communication and performance in doubles tennis. *Research Quarterly for Exercise and Sport*, 80, 281–90.

LaVoi, N. M. (2007). Expanding the interpersonal dimension: Closeness in the coach–athlete relationship. *International Journal of Sport Science and Coaching*, 2, 497–512.

Lazarus, R. S. (1991). Cognition and motivation in emotion. *The American Psychologist*, 46, 352–67.

——(1999). Hope: An emotion and a vital coping resource against despair. *Social Research*, 66, 653–78.

——(2000). How emotions influence performance in competitive sports. *The Sport Psychologist*, 14, 229–52.

Lee, M. J., and Partridge, T. R. (1983). Influence of team structure in determining leadership function in football. *Journal of Sport Behavior*, 6, 59–66.

Lewin, K. (1935). *A dynamic theory of personality*. New York: McGraw-Hill.

Locke, E. A. (1976). The nature and causes of job satisfaction. In M. D. Dunnette (Ed.), *Handbook of industrial and organizational psychology* (pp.1297–1349). Chicago, IL: Rand McNally.

Locke, E. A., Shaw, K. N., Saari, L. M., and Latham, G. P. (1981). Goal-setting and task performance. *Psychological Bulletin*, 90, 125–52.

Lord, R. G., De Vader, C. L., and Alliger, G. M. (1986). A meta-analysis of the relation between personality traits and leadership perceptions: An application of validity generalization procedures. *Journal of Applied Psychology*, 71, 402–10.

Loughead, T. M., and Hardy, J. (2005). A comparison of coach and peer leader behaviors in sport. *Psychology of Sport and Exercise*, 6, 303–12.

——(2006). Team cohesion: From theory to research to team building. In S. Hanton and S. Mellalieu (Eds), *Literature reviews in sport psychology* (pp.257–87). Hauppauge, NY: Nova Science Publishers.

Lowe, K. B., Kroeck, K. G., and Sivasubramaniam, N. (1996). Effectiveness correlates of transformational and transactional leadership: A meta-analytic review of the MLQ literature. *Leadership Quarterly*, 7, 385–425.

Lundqvist, C., and Kenttä, G. (2010). Positive emotions are not simply the absence of the negative ones: Development and validation of the emotional recovery questionnaire (EmRecQ). *The Sport Psychologist*, 24, 468–88.

Lynch, J. (2001). *Creative coaching*. Champaign, IL: Human Kinetics.

Mabry, E. A., and Barnes, R.E. (1980), *The dynamics of small group communication*. Englewood Cliffs, NJ: Prentice Hall.

Mace, F. C., Lalli, J. S., Shea, M. C., and Nevin, J. A. (1992). Behavioral momentum in college basketball. *Journal of Applied Behavior Analysis*, 25, 657–63.

McBride, A. B. (1990). Mental health effects of women's multiple roles. *American Psychologist*, 45, 381–84.

McGrath, J. E. (1984). *Groups: Interaction and performance*. Englewood Cliffs, NJ: Prentice Hall, Inc.

Mack, M. G., and Stephens, D. E. (2000). An empirical test of Taylor and Demick's multidimensional model of momentum in sport. *Journal of Sport Behaviour*, 23, 349–63.

MacMillan, J., Entin, E. E., and Serfaty, D. (2004). A framework for understanding the relationship between team structure and the communication necessary for effective team cognition. In E. Salas and S. M. Fiore (Eds), *Team cognition: Understanding the factors that drive process and performance* (pp.61–82). Washington, DC: American Psychological Association.

McNair, D., Lorr, M., and Droppleman, L. F. (1992). *Profile of mood states manual*. San Diego, CA: Educational and Industrial Testing Service.

MacPherson, A. C., and Howard, P. W. (2011). The team perspective: Promoting excellence in performance teams. In D. Collins, A. Button, and H. Richards (Eds), *Performance psychology: A practitioner's guide* (pp.121–138). Edinburgh: Churchill-Livingston, Elsevier.

Magyar, T. M., Feltz, D. L., and Simpson, I. P. (2004). Individual and crew level determinants of collective efficacy in rowing. *Journal of Sport & Exercise Psychology*, 26, 136–53.

Mankad, A., Gordon, S., and Wallman, K. (2009). Perceptions of emotional climate among injured athletes. *Journal of Clinical Sports Psychology*, 3, 1–14.

Marion, A. (1995). Overtraining and sport performance. *Coaches Report*, 2, 12–19.

Marks, M. A., Mathieu, J. E., and Zaccaro, S. J. (2001). A temporally based framework and taxonomy of team processes. *Academy of Management Review*, 26, 356–76.

Marks, S. R. (1977). Multiple roles and role strain: Some notes on human energy, time and commitment. *American Sociological Review*, 42, 921–36.

Martens, R. (1987). *Coaches guide to sport psychology*. Champaign, IL: Human Kinetics.

Martens, R., and Peterson, J. A. (1971). Group cohesiveness as a determinant of success and member satisfaction in team performance. *International Review of Sport Sociology*, 6, 49–61.

Martin, D. T., Anderson, M. B., and Gates, W. (2000). Using profile of mood states (POMS) to monitor high-intensity training in cyclists: Group versus case studies. *The Sport Psychologist*, 14, 138–56.

Martin, K. A., Moritz, S. E., and Hall, C. R. (1999). Imagery use in sport: A literature review and applied model. *The Sport Psychologist*, 13, 245–68.

Martin, L. J., Carron, A. V., and Burke, S. M. (2009). Team building interventions in sport: A meta-analysis. *Sport & Exercise Psychology Review*, 5(2), 3–18.

Martin, R. A. (2004). Sense of humor and physical health: Theoretical issues, recent findings and future directions. *Humor*, 17, 1–19.

Maslach, C., and Jackson, S. E. (1984). Burnout in organizational settings. In S. Oskamp (Ed.), *Applied social psychology annual: Applications in organizational settings*, Vol. 5 (pp.133–53). Beverly Hills, CA: Sage.

Matheson, H., Mathes, S., and Murray, M. (1997). The effect of winning and losing on female interactive and coactive team cohesion. *Journal of Sport Behavior*, 20, 284–98.

Matthews, G. (1992). Mood. In A. P. Smith and D. M. Jones (Eds), *Handbook of human performance. Vol. 3. State and trait* (pp.161–93). London: Harcourt Brace Jovanovich.

Maxwell, J. P. (2004). Anger rumination: An antecedent of athlete aggression? *Psychology of Sport and Exercise*, 5, 279–89.

Mayer, J. D. (1986). How mood influences cognition. In N. E. Sharkey (Ed.), *Advances in cognitive science* (pp.290–314). Chichester: Ellis Horwood.

Meeusen, R., Duclos, M., Gleeson, M., Rietjens, G., Steinacker, J., and Urhausen, A. (2006). Prevention, diagnosis and treatment of the overtraining syndrome. *European Journal of Sport Science*, 6(1), 1–14.

Melnick, M. J., and Loy, J. W. (1996). The effects of formal structure on leadership recruitment: Analysis of team captaincy among New Zealand provincial rugby teams. *International Review for the Sociology of Sport*, 31, 91–105.

Messner, M. A. (1992). *Power at play: Sports and the problem of masculinity*. Boston, MA: Beacon Press.

Miller, S., and Weinberg, R. (1991). Perceptions of psychological momentum and their relationship to performance. *The Sport Psychologist*, 5, 211–22.

Mohammed, S., and Dumville, B. C. (2001). Team mental models in a team knowledge framework: Expanding theory and measurement across disciplinary boundaries. *Journal of Organizational Behavior*, 22, 89–106.

Moore, P., and Collins, D. (1996). Role conflict in sports team management. In J. Annett and H. Steinberg (Eds), *How teams work in sport and exercise psychology* (pp.40–48). Leicester: British Psychological Society.

Moll, T., Jordet, G. and Pepping, G–J. (2010). Emotional contagion in soccer penalty shootouts: Celebration of individual success is associated with ultimate team success. *Journal of Sports Sciences*, 28(9), 983–92.

Moran, A. (2004). *Sport and exercise psychology: A critical introduction*. Hove: Routledge.

Moran, M. M., and Weiss, M. R. (2006). Peer leadership in sport: Links with friendship, peer acceptance, psychological characteristics, and athletic ability. *Journal of Applied Sport Psychology*, 18, 97–113.

Moritz, S. E., and Watson, C. B. (1998). Levels of analysis issues in group psychology: Using efficacy as an example of a multilevel model. *Group Dynamics: Theory, Research and Practice*, 2, 285–98.

Mosher, M. (1979). The team captain. *Volleyball Technical Journal*, 4, 7–8.

Mosier, K. L., and Chidester, T. R. (1991). Situation assessment and situation awareness in a team setting. In Y. Quéinnec and F. Daniellou (Eds), *Designing everyone: Proceedings of the 11th Congress of the International Ergonomics Association* (pp.798–800). London: Taylor & Francis.

Mullen, B., and Copper, C. (1994). The relation between group cohesiveness and performance: An integration. *Psychological Bulletin*, 115, 210–27.

Mullin, E. M. (2009). Effective on-field communication: An element of success. *Soccer Journal*, January–February, 26 & 60.

Murphy, S., Nodin, S., and Cumming, J. (2008). Imagery in sport, exercise and dance. In T. Horn (Ed.), *Advances in sport psychology* (3rd edn). Champaign, IL: Human Kinetics.

Murray, M. C., and Mann, B. L. (2006). Leadership effectiveness. In J. M. Williams (Ed.), *Applied sport psychology: Personal growth to peak performance*. New York: McGraw-Hill.

Murray, N. P. (2006). The differential effect of team cohesion and leadership behaviour in high school sports. *Individual Differences Research*, 4, 216–25.

Myers, N. D., Feltz, D. L., and Short, S. E. (2004). Collective efficacy and team performance: A longitudinal study of collegiate football teams. *Group Dynamics: Theory, Research and Practice*, 8, 126–38.

Newman, B. (1984). Expediency as benefactors: How team building saves time and gets the job done. *Training and Development Journal*, 38, 26–30.

Nicholls, J. G. (1989). *The competitive ethos and democratic education*. Cambridge, MA: Harvard University Press.

Norrick, N. R. (1993). *Conversational joking: Humor in everyday life*. Bloomington, IN: Indiana University Press.

Northouse, P. G. (2001). *Leadership: Theory and practice* (2nd edn). Thousand Oaks, CA: Sage.

O'Connor, P. J. (1998). Overtraining and staleness. In W. P. Morgan (Ed.), *Physical activity and mental health* (pp.145–60). Washington, DC: Taylor & Francis.

Okech, J. E. A., and Kline, W. B. (2005). A qualitative exploration of group co-leader relationships. *Journal for Specialists in Group Work*, 30(2), 173–90.

Olson, M., and Zanna, P. (1993). Attitudes and attitude change. *Annual Review of Psychology*, 44, 117–54.

O'Neill, D. F. (2008). Injury contagion in alpine ski racing: The effect of injury on teammates' performance. *Journal of Clinical Sport Psychology*, 2, 278–92.

Orasanu, J. M. (1990). *Shared mental models and crew performance* (Report No. CSLTR-46). Princeton, NJ: Princeton University Press.

——(1993). Decision making in the cockpit. In E. Wiener, B. Kanki, and R. Helmreich (Eds), *Cockpit resource management* (pp.137–72). San Diego, CA: Academic Press.

Orlick, T. (2000). *In pursuit of excellence: How to win in sport and life through mental training* (3rd edn). Champaign, IL: Human Kinetics.

Ostroff, C., Kinicki, A. J., and Tamkins, M. M. (2003). Organizational culture and climate. In W. C. Borman and D. R. Ilgen (Eds), *Handbook of psychology: Industrial and organizational psychology*, Vol. 12 (pp.565–93). New York: Wiley.

Pain, M. A., and Harwood, C. G. (2007). The performance environment of the England youth soccer teams. *Journal of Sports Sciences*, 25, 1307–24.

——(2008). The performance environment of the England youth soccer teams: A quantitative investigation. *Journal of Sports Sciences*, 26, 1157–69.

——(2009). Team building through mutual sharing and open discussion of team functioning. *The Sport Psychologist*, 23, 523–42.

Parker, S. K., Williams, H., and Turner, N. (2006). Modeling the antecedents of proactive behavior at work. *Journal of Applied Psychology*, 91, 636–52.

Parkinson, B. (1994). Emotion. In A. M. Coleman (Ed.), *Companion encyclopaedia of psychology*, Vol. 2. London: Routledge.

Parkinson, B., Totterdell, P., Briner, R. B., and Reynolds, S. (1996). *Changing moods. The psychology of mood and mood regulation*. Harlow: Longman.

Partington, J., and Shangi, G. (1992). Developing an understanding of team psychology. *International Journal of Sport Psychology*, 23, 28–47.

Paskevich, D. M., Brawley, L. R., Dorsch, K. D., and Widmeyer, W. N. (1999). Relationship between collective efficacy and cohesion: Conceptual and measurement issues. *Group Dynamics*, 3, 210–22.

Pearson, Q. M. (2008). Role overload, job satisfaction, leisure satisfaction, and psychological health among employed women. *Journal of Counseling & Development*, 86, 57–63.

Pease, D. G., and Kozub, S. A. (1994). Perceived coaching behaviours and team cohesion in high school girls basketball teams. *Journal of Sport and Exercise Psychology*, 16, S93.

Pennebaker, J. W. (1989). Confession, inhibition, and disease. *Advances in Experimental Social Psychology*, 27, 211–44.

Pennebaker, J. W., Zech, E., and Rimé, B. (2001). Disclosing and sharing emotion: Psychological, social, and health consequences. In M. S. Stroebe, R. O. Hansson, W. Stroebe, and H. Schut (Eds), *Handbook of bereavement research: Consequences, coping and care* (pp. 517–44). Washington, DC: American Psychological Association.

Peptitpas, A. J. (2000). Managing stress on and off the field: The littlefoot approach to learned resourcefulness. In M. B. Anderson (Ed.), *Doing sport psychology* (pp.33–43). Champaign, IL: Human Kinetics.

Perreault, S., Vallerand, R. J., Montgomery, D., and Provencher, P. (1998). Coming from behind: On the effect of psychological momentum on sport performance. *Journal of Sport & Exercise Psychology*, 20, 421–36.

Peterson, K. (2003). Athlete overtraining and underrecovery. Recognising the symptoms and strategies for coaches. *Olympic Coach*, 18(3), 16–17.

Polman, R., and Houlahan, K. (2004). A cumulative stress and training continuum model: A multidisciplinary approach to unexplained underperformance syndrome. *Research in Sports Medicine*, 12, 301–16.

Poole, M.S., and McPhee, R. D. (1985). Methodology in interpersonal communication research. In M. L. Knapp and G. R. Miller (Eds), *Handbook of interpersonal communication*. (pp.100–70). Beverly Hills, CA: Sage.

Posthuma, B. W. (2002). *Small groups in counseling and therapy* (4th edn). Boston, MA: Allyn and Bacon.

Prapavessis, H., and Carron, A. V. (1996). The effect of group cohesion on competitive state anxiety. *Journal of Sport & Exercise Psychology*, 18, 64–74.

Prapavessis, H., Carron, A., and Spink, K. (1996). Team building in sport. *International Journal of Sport Psychology*, 27, 269–285.

Pruitt, D. G., and Runbin, J. Z. (1986). *Social conflict: Escalation, stalemate, and settlement*. New York: Random House.

Quinn, R. E., and Rohrbaugh, J. (1983). A spatial model of effectiveness criteria: Towards a competing values approach to organizational analysis. *Management Science*, 29 (3), 363–77.

Raedeke, T. D. (1997). Is athlete burnout more than just stress? A sport commitment perspective. *Journal of Sport & Exercise Psychology*, 19, 396–417.

Raedeke, T. D., and Smith, A. L. (2001). Development and preliminary validation of an athlete burnout measure. *Journal of Sport & Exercise Psychology*, 23, 281–306.

Raglin, J. S. (1993). Overtraining and staleness: Psychometric monitoring of endurance athletes. In R. B. Singer, M. Murphey, and L. K. Tennant (Eds), *Handbook of research on sport psychology* (pp.840–50), New York: Macmillan.

Rail, G. (1987). Perceived role characteristics and executive satisfaction in voluntary sport associations. *Journal of Sport Psychology*, 9, 376–84.

Ramzaninezhad, R., Keshtan, M. H., Shahamat, M. D., and Kordshooli, S. S. (2009). The relationship between collective efficacy, group cohesion and team performance in professional volleyball teams. *Brazilian Journal of Biomotricity*, 3, 31–39.

Reeve, J. (2005). *Understanding motivation and emotion* (4th edn). Hoboken, NJ: Wiley.

Remington, N. A., Fabrigar, L. R., and Visser, P. S. (2000). Re-examining the circumplex model of affect. *Journal of Personality and Social Psychology*, 79(2), 286–300.

Resick, P. A., and Schnicke, M. K. (1996). *Cognitive processing therapy for rape victims: A treatment manual*. Newbury Park, CA: Sage.

Richert, A. J. (2006). Narrative psychology and psychotherapy integration. *Journal of Psychotherapy Integration*, 16, 84–110.

Rieke, M., Hammermeister, J., and Chase, M. (2008). Servant leadership in sport: A new paradigm for effective coach behaviour. *International Journal of Sports Science & Coaching*, 3, 227–39.

Rilling, C., and Jordan, D. (2007). Important co-leader skills and traits on extended outdoor trips as perceived by leaders. *Leisure Studies*, 26(2), 193–212.

Ristow, A. M., Amos, T. L., and Staude, G. E. (1999). Transformational leadership and organizational effectiveness in the administration of cricket in South Africa. *South African Journal of Business Management*, 30, 523–39.

Ronglan, L. T. (2007). Building and communicating collective efficacy: A season-long in-depth study of an elite sport team. *The Sport Psychologist*, 21, 78–93.

Roseman, I., Spindel, M. S., and Jose, P. E. (1990). Appraisals of emotion-eliciting events: Testing a theory of discrete emotions. *Journal of Personality and Social Psychology*, 59, 899–915.

Rousseau, D. M. (1988). The construction of climate in organizational research. In C. L. Cooper and I. Robertson (Eds), *International review of industrial and organizational psychology* (pp.139–58). Indianapolis, IN: Wiley,.

——(1995). *Psychological contracts in organizations: Understanding written and unwritten agreements.* Thousand Oaks, CA: Sage.

Rowold, J. (2006). Transformational and transactional leadership in martial arts. *Journal of Applied Sport Psychology*, 18, 312–25.

Russell, J. A. (1980). A circumplex model of affect. *Journal of Personality and Social Psychology*, 39, 1161–78.

Ryska, T. A., Yin, Z., Cooley, D., and Ginn, R. (1999). Developing team cohesion: A comparison of cognitive-behavioral strategies of US and Australian sport coaches. *The Journal of Psychology*, 133, 523–39.

Salas, E., Cannon-Bowers, J. A., and Johnston, J. H. (1997). How can you turn a team of experts into an expert team? Emerging training strategies. In C. Zsambok and G. Klein (Eds), *Naturalistic decision making: Where are we now?* (pp.359–70). Hillsdale, NJ: Erlbaum.

Salovey, P., and Birnbaum, D. (1989). Influence of mood on health-relevant cognitions. *Journal of Personality and Social Psychology*, 57, 539–51.

Schaufeli, W. B., Maslach, C., and Marek, T. (1993). *Professional burnout: Recent developments in theory and research.* Washington, DC: Taylor & Francis.

Scherer, K. R., and Wallbott, H. G. (1994). Evidence for universality and cultural variation of differential emotion response patterning. *Journal of Personality and Social Psychology*, 66 (7), 310–28.

Schneider, B., and Rentsch, J. R. (1988). Managing climates and cultures: A future perspective. In J. Hage (Ed.), *Futures of organizations* (pp.181–200). Lexington, MA: Lexington.

Schulte, M., Ostroff, C., and Kinicki, A. J. (2006). Organizational climate systems and psychological climate perceptions: A cross-level study of climate–satisfaction relationships. *Journal of Occupational and Organizational Psychology*, 79, 645–71.

Scollon, R., and Scollon, S. W. (2001). *Intercultural communication: A discourse approach* (2nd edn). Oxford, Blackwell.

Settles, I. H., Seller, R. M., and Damas, A. (2002). One role or two? The function of psychological separation in role conflict. *Journal of Applied Psychology*, 87, 574–82.

Shannon, C., and Weaver, W. (1949). *The mathematical theory of communication.* Illinois: University of Illinois Press.

Shaw, D., Gorely, T., and Corban, R. (2005). *Instant notes: Sport and exercise psychology.* Abingdon: Garland Science/BIOS Scientific Publishers.

Shaw, J. M., Dzewaltski, D., and McElroy, M. (1992). Self-efficacy and causal attributions as mediators of perception of psychological momentum. *Journal of Sport & Exercise Psychology*, 14, 134–47.

Shearer, D. A., Holmes, P., and Mellalieu, D. (2009). Collective efficacy in sport: The future from a social neuroscience perspective. *International Review of Sport and Exercise Psychology*, 2, 38–53.

Sherman, C. A., Fuller, R., and Speed, H. D. (2000). Gender comparisions of preferred coaching behaviours in Australian sports. *Journal of Sports Behaviour*, 23, 389–406.

Shoenfelt, E. L. (2003). *A structured approach to increasing role clarity with intercollegiate volleyball players* [abstract]. Association for the Advancement of Applied Sport Psychology 2003 Conference Proceedings, 90.

——(2010). 'Value added' teambuilding: A process to ensure understanding, acceptance, and commitment to team values. *Journal of Sport Psychology in Action*, 1 (3), 150–60.

Short, S. E., Sullivan, P., and Feltz, D. L. (2005). Development and preliminary validation of the collective efficacy questionnaire for sports. *Measurement in Physical Education and Exercise Science*, 9, 181–202.

Silva, J. M., Hardy, C. J., and Crace, R. (1988). Analysis of psychological momentum on male and female tennis players revisited. *Journal of Sport and Exercise Psychology*, 10, 346–54.

Slater, M. R., and Sewell, D. F. (1994). An examination of the cohesion–performance relationship in university hockey teams. *Journal of Sport Sciences*, 12, 423–31.

Smith, D. J., and Norris, S. R. (2002). Training load and monitoring an athlete's tolerance for endurance training. In M. Kellmann (Ed.), *Enhancing recovery: Preventing under-performance in athletes* (pp.3–24). Champaign, IL: Human Kinetics.

Smith, G. (2003). Horse shoe pitchers' hot hands. *Psychonomic Bulletin and Review*, 10, 753–58.

Smith, R. E. (1986). Toward a cognitive-affective model of athletic burnout. *Journal of Sport Psychology*, 8, 36–50.

Smith, S. L., Fry, M. D., Ethington, C. A., and Li, Y. (2005). The effect of female athletes' perceptions of their coaches' behaviors on their perceptions of the motivational climate. *Journal of Applied Sport Psychology*, 17, 170–77.

Snyder, C. R., Lassegard, M., and Ford, C. E. (1986). Distancing after group success and failure: Basking in reflected glory and cutting off reflected failure. *Journal of Personality and Social Psychology*, 51, 382–88.

Sonnentag, S., and Fritz, C. (2007). The recovery experience questionnaire: Development and validation of a measure for assessing recuperation and unwinding from work. *Journal of Occupational Health Psychology*, 12, 204–21.

Spink, K. S., and Carron, A. V. (1994). Group cohesion effects in exercise classes. *Small Group Research*, 25, 26–42.

Stahl, G. (2006). *Group cognition: Computer support for building collaborative knowledge*. Cambridge, MA: MIT Press.

Stangor, C. (2004). *Social groups in action and interaction*. Hove: Taylor & Francis.

Stevens, D. E. (2002). Building an effective team. In J. M. Silva and D. E. Stevens (Eds), *Psychological foundations of sport* (pp.306–27). Boston, MA: Allyn and Bacon.

Stevens, M. J., and Campion, M. A. (1994). The knowledge, skill and ability requirements for teamwork: Implications for human resource management. *Journal of Management*, 20, 503–30.

Strack, F., Martin, L. L., and Stepper, S. (1988). Inhibiting and facilitating conditions of facial expressions: A non-obtrusive test of the facial feedback hypothesis. *Journal of Personality and Social Psychology*, 54, 768–76.

Sullivan, P. A. (1993). Communication skills training for interactive sports. *The Sport Psychologist*, 7, 79–91.

Sullivan, P. A., and Feltz, D. L. (2003). The preliminary development of the Scale for Effective Communication in Team Sports (SECTS). *Journal of Applied Social Psychology*, 33, 1693–715.

Super, D. E. (1990). A life-span, life-space approach to career development. In D. Brown, L. Brooks, and Associates (Eds), *Career choice and development: Applying contemporary theories and practice* (2nd edn) (pp.197–261). San Francisco, CA: Jossey-Bass.

Tasa, K., Taggar, S., and Seijts, G. H. (2007). The development of collective efficacy in teams: A multilevel and longitudinal perspective. *Journal of Applied Psychology*, 92, 17–27.

Taylor, J., and Demick, A. (1994). A multidimensional model of momentum in sports. *Journal of Applied Sport Psychology*, 6, 51–70.

Tellegen, A. (1985). Structure of mood and personality and their relevance to assessing anxiety, with an emphasis on self-report. In A. H. Tuma and J. D. Maser (Eds), *Anxiety and the anxiety disorders* (pp.681–706). Hillsdale, NJ: Erlbaum.

Terry, P. C., Carron, A. V., Pink, M. J., Lane, A. M., Jones, G. J. W., and Hall, M. P. (2000). Perceptions of group cohesion and mood in sports teams. *Group Dynamics: Theory, Research and Practice*, 4, 244–53.

Tharrett, S., and Peterson, J. A. (2008). Common communication errors in a team environment. *Fitness Management*, November.

Thayer, R. E. (1996). *The origin of everyday moods: Managing energy, tension, and stress*, New York: Oxford University Press.

Thompson, N. (2003). *Communication and language: A handbook of theory and practice*. Basingstoke: Palgrave MacMillan.

Tickle-Degnan, L., and Puccinelli, N. M. (1999). The nonverbal expression of negative thoughts: Peer and supervisor responses to occupational therapy students' emotional attributes. *The Occupational Therapy Journal of Research*, 19, 18–39.

Totterdell, P. (2000). Catching moods and hitting runs: Mood linkage and subjective performance in professional sport teams. *Journal of Applied Psychology*, 85, 848–59.

Totterdell, P., and Leach, D. (2001). Negative mood regulation expectancies and sports performance: An investigation involving professional cricketers. *Psychology of Sport and Exercise*, 2, 249–65.

Tran, V. (1998). The role of the emotional climate in learning organisations. *The Learning Organisation*, 5, 79–103.

Turman, P. D. (2003). Coaches and cohesion: The impact of coaching techniques on team cohesion in the small group sport setting. *Journal of Sport Behavior*, 26, 86–102.

Vallerand, R. J. (1983). On emotion in sport: Theoretical and social psychological perspectives. *Journal of Sport Psychology*, 5, 197–215.

Vallerand, R. J., and Blanchard, C. M. (2000). The study of emotion in sport and exercise: Historical, definitional, and conceptual perspectives. In Y. L. Hanin (Ed.), *Emotions in sport* (pp.3–37). Champaign, IL: Human Kinetics.

Vallerand, R. J., Colavecchio, P. G., and Pelletier, L. G. (1988). Psychological momentum and performance inferences: A preliminary test of the antecedents-consequences psychological momentum model. *Journal of Sport & Exercise Psychology*, 10, 92–108.

Van den Bossche, P., Gijselears, W., Segers, M., Woltjer, G., and Kirschner, P. (2011). Team learning: Building shared mental models. *Instructional Science*, 39(3), 283–301.

Vargas-Tonsing, T. M., Warners, A. L., and Feltz, D. L. (2003). The predictability of coaching efficacy on team efficacy and player efficacy in volleyball. *Journal of Sport Behavior*, 26, 396–407.

Vealey, R. S. (2005). *Coaching for the inner edge*. Morgantown, WV: Fitness Information Technologies.

Vergin, R. (2000). Winning streaks in sports and the misperception of momentum. *Journal of Sport Behaviour*, 23, 181–97.

Voight, M., and Callaghan, J. (2002). A team building intervention program: Application and evaluation with two university soccer teams. *Journal of Sport Behavior*, 24(4), 420–31.

Vroom, J. H. (1964). *Work and motivation*. New York: Wiley.

Vroom, V. H., and Jago, A. G. (2007). The role of the situation in leadership. *American Psychologist*, 62, 17–24.

Walumbwa, F. O., Wang, P., Lawler, J. J., and Shi, K. (2004). The role of collective efficacy in the relations between transformational leadership and work outcomes. *Journal of Occupational and Organizational Psychology*, 77, 515–30.

Watson, D., Wiese, D., Vaidya, J., and Tellegen, A. (1999). The two general activation systems of affect: Structural findings, evolutionary considerations, and psychobiological evidence. *Journal of Personality and Social Psychology*, 76, 820–838.

Weick, K. E. (1993). The collapse of sensemaking in organisations: The Mann Gulch disaster. *Administrative Science Quarterly*, 38, 628–53.

Weinberg, R. S. (2002). Goal-setting in sport and exercise. In J. Van Raalte and B. W. Brewer (Eds), *Exploring sport and exercise psychology* (2nd edn) (pp.25–48). Washington, DC: American Psychological Association Press.

——(2010). Making goals effective: A primer for coaches. *Journal of Sport Psychology in Action*, 1(2), 57–65.

Weinberg, R. S., and Gould, D. (2007). *Foundations of sport and exercise psychology* (4th edn). Champaign, IL: Human Kinetics.

Weinberg, R. S., Butt, J., and Knight, B. (2001). High school coaches' perceptions of the process of goal-setting. *The Sport Psychologist*, 15(1), 20–47.

Weiss, H. M., and Cropanzano, R. (1996). Affective events theory: A theoretical discussion of the structure, causes and consequences of affective experiences at work. *Research in Organizational Behavior*, 18, 1–74.

Weiss, R., and Ferrer-Caja, E. (2002). Motivational orientation in sport. In T. S. Horn (Ed.), *Advances in sport psychology* (2nd edn) (pp.101–83). Champaign, IL: Human Kinetics.

West, M. A., and Unsworth, K. L. (1998). Developing a team vision. In G. M. Parker (Ed.), *Handbook of best practices for teams*, Vol. 2 (pp.295–310). Amhesrt, MA: HRD Press.

Westre, K. R., and Weiss, M. R. (1991). The relationship between perceived coaching behaviours and group cohesion in high school football teams. *The Sport Psychologist*, 5, 41–54.

Widmeyer, W. N., and Ducharme, K. (1997). Team building through goal setting. *Journal of Applied Sport Psychology*, 9, 97–113.

Widmeyer, W. N., and Williams, J. N. (1991). Predicting cohesion in an interacting sport. *Small Group Research*, 22, 548–70.

Widmeyer, W. N., Brawley, W. N., and Carron, A. V. (1985). The development of an instrument to assess cohesion in sports teams. The Group Environment Questionnaire. *Journal of Sport Psychology*, 7, 244–66.

Widmeyer, W. N., Carron, A. V., and Brawley, W. N. (1993). Group cohesion in sport and exercise. In R. N. Singer, M. Murphey, and L. Tenant (Eds), *Handbook of research in sport psychology* (pp.672–92). New York: Macmillan.

Wildman, J. C. (2006). The athlete leader role: Interaction of gender, sport type, and coaching style. Unpublished PhD thesis. University of North Texas.

Williams, H. M., Parker, S. K., and Turner, N. (2010). Proactively performing teams: The role of work design, transformational leadership, and team composition. *Journal of Occupational and Organizational Psychology*, 83, 301–24.

Williams, J. M., and Hacker, C. M. (1982). Causal relationships among cohesion, satisfaction, and performance in women's intercollegiate field hockey teams. *Journal of Sport & Exercise Psychology*, 4, 324–37.

Williams, P. (1997). *The magic of teamwork: Proven principles for building a winning team.* Nashville, TN: Thomas Nelson.

Windsor, P. M., Barker, J., and McCarthy, P. (2011). Doing sport psychology: Personal-disclosure mutual-sharing in professional soccer. *The Sport Psychologist*, 25, 94–114.

Wittenbaum, G. M., Vaughan, S. I., and Stasser, G. (1998). Coordination in task-performing groups. In R. S. Tindale and L. Heath (Eds), *Theory and research on small groups: Social psychological applications to social issues*, Vol. 4 (pp.177–204). New York: Plenum.

Woodcock, M., and Francis, D. (1994). *Team building.* Aldershot: Ashgate.

Woodman, T., and Hardy, L. (2001). A case study of organisational stress in elite sport. *Journal of Applied Sport Psychology*, 13, 207–38.

Young, K., White, P., and McTeer, W. (1994). Body talk: Male athletes reflect on sport, injury and pain. *Sociology of Sport Journal*, 11, 175–94.

Yukelson, D. (1997). Principles of effective team building interventions in sport: A direct services approach to Penn State University. *Journal of Applied Sport Psychology*, 9, 73–96.

——(2006). Communicating effectively. In J. M. Williams (Ed.), *Applied sport psychology: Personal growth to peak performance* (5th edn) (pp.174–91). Boston, MA: McGraw Hill.

Yukelson, D., Weinberg, R., and Jackson, A. (1984). A multidimensional group cohesion instrument for intercollegiate basketball teams. *Journal of Sport Psychology*, 6, 103–17.

Yukelson, D., Weinberg, R., Richardson, P., and Jackson, A. (1983). Interpersonal attraction and leadership within collegiate sport teams. *Journal of Sport Behavior*, 6, 28–36.

Yukl, G. (1989). *Leadership in organizations* (2nd edn). Englewood Cliffs, NJ: Prentice Hall.

Yusof, A., and Muraleedharan, V. (2007). Group cohesion of Malaysian National Junior Athletes. *Journal of the International Council for Health, Physical Education, Recreation, Sport and Dance*, 43, 12–14.

Zaccaro, S. J., Blair, V., Peterson, C., and Zazanis, M. (1995). Collective efficacy. In J. Maddux (Ed.), *Self-efficacy, adaptation, and adjustment* (pp.305–28). New York: Plenum.

Zacharatos, A., Baring, J., and Kelloway, E. K. (2000). Development and effects of transformational leadership in adolescents. *The Leadership Quarterly*, 11, 211–26.

Zander, A. (1985). *The purposes of groups and organizations*. San Francisco, CA: Jossey-Bass.

INDEX

t = table, f = figure